WITHDRAWN

TANKS, FIGHTERS & SHIPS

TITLES OF RELATED INTEREST

Art et al. REORGANIZING AMERICA'S DEFENSE: LEADERSHIP IN WAR & PEACE

Bush NATIONAL SECURITY STRATEGY OF THE UNITED STATES

Deibel & Gaddis CONTAINING THE SOVIET UNION: A CRITIQUE OF U.S. POLICY

Hartley THE ECONOMICS OF DEFENCE POLICY

Hartmann & Wendzel DEFENDING AMERICA'S SECURITY

Pfaltzgraff NATIONAL SECURITY: ETHICS, STRATEGY, AND POLITICS

Record BEYOND MILITARY REFORM: AMERICAN DEFENSE DILEMMAS

Schelling & Halperin STRATEGY AND ARMS CONTROL

Yoder THE CONDUCT OF AMERICAN FOREIGN POLICY SINCE WORLD WAR II

RELATED JOURNALS*

Armed Forces Journal International

Defense Analysis

Middle East Strategic Studies Quarterly

Survival

*Sample copies available upon request

TANKS, FIGHTERS & SHIPS

U.S. CONVENTIONAL FORCE PLANNING SINCE WWII

MAURICE A. MALLIN

BRASSEY'S (US), INC.

WASHINGTON • NEW YORK • LONDON • OXFORD
BEIJING • FRANKFURT • SÃO PAULO • SYDNEY • TOKYO • TORONTO

U.S.A. (Editorial)	Brassey's (US), Inc. 8000 Westpark Drive, First Floor, McLean, Virginia 22102, U.S.A.
(Orders)	Attn: Order Dept., Macmillan Publishing Co., Front & Brown Streets, Riverside, N.J. 08075
U.K. (Editorial) (Orders)	Brassey's (UK) Ltd. 24 Gray's Inn Road, London WC1X 8HR, England Brassey's (UK) Ltd. Headington Hill Hall, Oxford OX3 OBW, England
PEOPLE'S REPUBLIC OF CHINA	Pergamon Press, Room 4037, Qianmen Hotel, Beijing, People's Republic of China
FEDERAL REPUBLIC OF GERMANY	Pergamon Press GmbH, Hammerweg 6, D-6242 Kronberg, Federal Republic of Germany
BRAZIL	Pergamon Editora Ltda, Rua Eça de Queiros, 346, CEP 04011, Paraiso, São Paulo, Brazil
AUSTRALIA	Pergamon-Brassey's Defence Publishers Ltd., P.O. Box 544, Potts Point, N.S.W. 2011, Australia
JAPAN	Pergamon Press, 5th Floor, Matsuoka Central Building, 1-7-1 Nishishinjuku, Shinjuku-ku, Tokyo 160, Japan
CANADA	Pergamon Press Canada, Suite No. 271, 253 College Street, Toronto, Ontario, Canada M5T 1R5

Copyright © 1990 Brassey's (US), Inc.

Brassey's (US), Inc., books are available at special
discounts for bulk purchases for sales promotions,
premiums, fund-raising, or educational use through the
Special Sales Director, Macmillan Publishing Company,
866 Third Avenue, New York, NY 10022.

**Library of Congress Cataloging in
Publication Data**

Mallin, Maurice A.
  Tanks, fighters & ships: U.S. conventional
force planning since WWII / Maurice A.
Mallin.
    p. cm.
  ISBN 0-08-036745-3
  1. United States—Military policy. 2. United
States—History, Military—20th century.
3. United States—Armed Forces—History—
20th century. 4. Warfare, Conventional. I.
Title. II. Title: Tanks, fighters, and ships.
UA23.M275 1990
355'.033573—dc20   89-25307
                                          CIP

**British Library Cataloguing in Publication
Data**

Mallin, Maurice A.
  Tanks, fighters & ships: U.S. conventional
force planning since WWII.
  1. United States. Military resources:
Conventional weapons
  I. Title
  355.8'2

  ISBN 0-08-036745-3

Printed in the United States of America

To My Parents

The son always strives to please the father

CONTENTS

FOREWORD

Today, prompted by a volatile international environment, persistent budget and trade deficits, and evolving public attitudes toward defense, the United States faces the prospect of major adjustments in defense strategy and programs. *Tanks, Fighters & Ships* traces the major trends in U.S. defense programs since World War II and is extremely relevant to the current situation. By showing the relationship between changes in national strategy and service doctrine and specific weapons programs, this volume reminds us that we have seen a series of major changes in the direction of our defense programs over the past forty-five years and that the current pressures for change are not entirely unique. In addition, it suggests some of the factors likely to influence the current reexamination of defense programs and priorities.

Each era has its own unique problems, of course. Today we are witnessing political and social transformations in the Soviet Union and Eastern Europe that can qualify as revolutionary. At the same time, the Western Alliance is facing unprecedented strains, brought on in part by differing perceptions of the new opportunities for changing relations with the East. Nevertheless, there is much to be learned from studying history, and this particular study includes a number of useful insights.

The study suggests that two factors have alternatively dominated the development of U.S. defense programs over the period examined: the threat and the budget. Perceptions of the threat dominated defense planning following the Soviet consolidation of power in Eastern Europe and the Korean War, again during much of the 1960s, and during the recent Reagan administration buildup. The budget, meanwhile, drove defense programs during the immediate postwar period, during much of the Eisenhower administration, and during the detente era of the 1970s. It seems clear that we are again entering a period in which budget considerations will be dominant.

The budget and the threat tend to be two sides of the same coin. During periods when budget considerations dominated planning, the threat was usually minimized by governmental decision makers. Yet seemingly intractable budget constraints have been cast aside when the sense of threat was strong enough. The classic example occurred following the outbreak of the Korean War, when the U.S. defense budget leapt from $13 billion to about $50 billion in less than six months.

Perceptions of the threat and of fiscal constraints shape overall defense programs and budgets, but there are other factors that also profoundly affect the internal shape and distribution of defense programs. Most important of these is bureaucratic politics or the constant battle between the military services to shape priorities and budgets. As the author demonstrates, the debate often is couched in terms of quite sophisticated doctrinal constructs such as the maritime strategy, flexible response, or massive retaliation. These constructs significantly affect the allocation of budgetary resources among the services. When Secretary of Defense Robert McNamara promulgated flexible response in the 1960s, for example, the army contributed heavily to the doctrine's development and its relative share of the budget increased to reflect this. Service doctrine has often developed as an argument for budgetary allocations, and the share of the budget has been an important symbol and barometer of bureaucratic power.

It is implicit in this history that personalities also play a significant role in shaping defense programs—often with a deleterious effect on the planning process. For example, Eisenhower's concerns about the military-industrial complex and the costs of maintaining a robust nonnuclear deterrent obviously influenced the general's decisions about military programs. But Eisenhower's reluctance to maintain robust nonnuclear forces led to an overdependence on nuclear forces. This situation compelled Kennedy to expend significant resources in building up conventional forces. McNamara also had a profound personal influence on defense programs. By introducing systems analysis, he revolutionized the way in which defense programs were formulated and justified. Yet the McNamara years were marked by an absence of serious strategic thinking in the Pentagon, as systems analysis became a substitute for strategy.

This history reveals few efforts to undertake long-range strategic planning efforts and even fewer such efforts that succeeded in translating long-range goals into specific plans and forces. Most defense planning exercises have a five-year horizon at best. NSC–68, the result of a major governmental planning exercise that occurred in 1950, remains a landmark effort because it is virtually unique. No planning exercise since NSC–68 has had as direct an impact on force planning and procurement. Such an exercise was attempted by the Reagan administration in 1987, but coming at the end of Reagan's second term in office and following (rather than preceding) a major defense buildup, the impact of this effort was modest at best. During the intervening years, there were major reviews that did in fact impact upon force procurement and planning, as discussed in this volume. But none had the impact of NSC–68.

More difficult than formulating a long-range strategy is carrying one out. We see in this study how the major thrust of defense programs has periodically changed quite radically. Yet major weapons systems tend to have long lead times, and thus a decision that is made in the context of one era may result in a weapon system that is not available until the environment has changed quite dramatically. Seldom is there a match between the policies that are advocated by a given administration and the military capabilities that are available to it. The B-1 bomber is probably the classic example. It was conceived over twenty years ago but only recently entered service, and there are considerable questions about its utility in today's environment. Most aircraft and naval vessels take years to develop and build and, once acquired, often spend decades in the force. These systems significantly affect the way U.S. forces are configured over the long term, creating difficulties for new administrations that seek to fundamentally change force structure.

Another theme in this volume is that efforts to develop appropriate global postures commensurate with U.S. global commitments and within fiscal resource constraints have generally not been successful. Even when defense budgets seemed generous, as during the Korean War and Vietnam War eras, much of the budget was devoted to military operations, making it difficult for the United States to maintain a worldwide posture. Much effort was devoted to devising a formula for meeting U.S. commitments to NATO while also maintaining capabilities to deter and fight wars elsewhere. Thus, the United States had two-and-one-half war and one-and-one-half war strategies which were really no more than rationalizations for overstretching already-thin resources. For example, during the Vietnam War era, carriers committed to NATO operated in Southeast Asia, and planning assumed they would move to the European theater within thirty days, if the need for mobilization arose. The viability of this plan was questioned; yet at the time, the United States had little alternative.

After reading this comprehensive history, one is left with two nagging questions. Can we do better in formulating and executing consistent long-range strategies, and can the massive U.S. defense establishment really be managed? The latter is a daunting task. The Defense Department moves, in response to leadership, like a large dreadnought operating at flank speed: it responds slowly. Nevertheless, this history shows that defense programs do respond to new policy directions and new external stimuli, albeit slowly and imperfectly. If one compares the forces that we have today with those we had twenty years ago, the changes are readily apparent. New weapons, new doctrine, and new command arrangements have evolved in response to new challenges and new opportunities.

In the next twenty years, change is likely to be even more rapid and the task of adapting to change more demanding. Even in the next few years a principal challenge for a new administration is to set new directions that respond to change without overresponding. A principal challenge for the Department of Defense will be to respond to new directions rapidly enough to keep pace with change. This will require strong leadership and strong management in the Pentagon.

LEON SLOSS
Leon Sloss and Associates
May 1989

PREFACE

This book surveys the evolution of U.S. military planning since World War II. The reader should be aware that the emphasis of this book is on the nonnuclear side of the planning equation. It is recognized, of course, that since the development of the atomic bomb, policies and doctrines guiding the employment of nuclear and conventional weapons have necessarily been deeply intertwined. Separating the two is therefore somewhat artificial. Nonetheless, here the conventional component of planning and the conventional, or general purpose, forces the United States has procured to carry out its national military plans are focused upon. Nuclear weapons and the policies guiding their employment are considered primarily in terms of how such weapons affected, and were affected by, developments in the conventional realm. As such, they are primarily discussed when conventional and nuclear plans or strategies are so intertwined that one component cannot realistically be discussed alone.

This approach was chosen for a number of reasons. It is the author's view that the analytical literature tends to devote a disproportionate amount of time and energy to the nuclear component of military policy, at the expense of rigorous examination of its conventional component. Nuclear weapons–related issues sometimes appear more clear cut than those relating to conventional forces; there are less ambiguities and fewer indices of relative strength and weakness with which to grapple. There also seems to be an underlying view that because nuclear weapons are generally more destructive than conventional forces, dealing with them requires a greater amount of attention. Finally, there is a novelty to nuclear weapons, which are less than fifty years old. Their very destructiveness makes them "attractive" to analysts in the sense that not only are the implications of having them or using them intriguing, but much of the reading public is terrified by, and at the same time very curious about, them. The implications of nuclear weapons, moreover, still do not seem to be adequately understood by those powers that have them or by those that would like to have them. Their political usefulness has tended to outweigh their military usefulness in preventing or resolving crises. Conventional forces, however, have been with us since a stone was first thrown in anger, and it sometimes seems like little is left to be said about them.

Yet even in the 1950s, when nuclear weapons were the central component of U.S. military policy, no more than 15 percent of the total U.S. defense budget was dedicated to their procurement and upkeep. This compares to at about 40 percent (on the average) of the defense budget dedicated to the acquisition and upkeep of U.S. nonnuclear forces. At present, nuclear weapons–related allocations approximate 12 percent of the total defense budget.

Moreover, the fact of the matter is that nuclear weapons have not been used in any conflict since the bombing of Hiroshima and Nagasaki—this in a generation where wars of all sizes are commonplace. The intent here is not in any way to understate the importance of studying nuclear weapons–related issues. One would think, however, that the fact that nonnuclear, or conventional, forces have been used so extensively would be a great impetus to study and understand the strategies that have influenced their use and the foundations and wisdom of the policy-making process that led to the various strategies and doctrines. Yet relative to nuclear weapons, there is a real dearth of study in this area.

This book is meant to contribute to filling this particular void. It is based on the assumption that the best way to understand the particulars of the conventional policy-making and force-acquisition processes as they now occur, and as they may occur in the future, is first to come to appreciate the forces which contributed to those processes in the past.

Analysis begins at the end of World War II. The events of that war and the environment that emerged from the ashes of that conflict largely set the context for military decision making for both the United States and the Soviet Union to the present day. It was after World War II that the United States emerged as the preeminent world power and that the United States and the Soviet Union became global adversaries. It would, of course, be useful to go back further, perhaps to the conclusion of the First World War; but one must begin somewhere, and the end of World War II seems the most logical starting point, given its immense impact on today's environment.

Two caveats should be made. One, the marine corps is not discussed as extensively in this book as are the army, the navy, and the air force. In large part, this stems from the fact that, unique among the services, the size of the marine corps is legally bound. The National Security Act of 1947 mandated that the marines consist of at least three active divisions and three tactical air wings. To be sure, how the marines have been equipped and trained has often varied, and there have been debates, often vigorous, over how these divisions and tactical air wings should be configured. But these debates have generally not been as intense as the debates that have occurred among (and often within) the three other services. More-over, there has been a general consensus that the United States must maintain a capability to respond quickly to global crises, and the marines have proven well suited to that role. At times, there have been various navy, army, or air force leaders who saw the corps as a competitor for scarce resources or who argued that their service could carry out the marines' functions; but the marine corps has generally been insulated from the bureaucratic and organizational pressures that tend to arise when new budgets are formed.

Two, in looking at the force employment guidance for each of the services, it is sometimes necessary to switch abruptly from discussions of doctrine to strategy or to mission statements, or to other forms of guidance. This is because the services are generally not consistent with respect to how they develop their own guidance. The army develops new doctrines, the navy tends to couch its guidance in terms of strategy, and the air force tends to build on long-standing conceptions of missions and tasks rather than develop new plans to guide the employment of air assets. This disparity in approach is reflected in the following pages. It may, at times, seem unsettling to switch from discussing one element of policy to another, but this should be seen as a reflection of the disparate approaches to planning associated with each of the three major services.

ACKNOWLEDGMENTS

I would first and foremost like to acknowledge and thank Ed Scholz of Orion Research, Inc., for his support, encouragement, and always constructive criticism, not only while this book was being written but throughout my professional career. Ed Scholz and the entire staff at Orion—and Charles Goodnight, in particular—provided both intellectual and technical support in the preparation of this book and a challenging atmosphere in which to grow professionally.

It is also important to acknowledge Leon Sloss for taking time to write the foreword and for extensively commenting (particularly on later chapters) on earlier drafts of this book. I notice that his influence on my writing—and on my thinking—grows almost daily, and that is certainly something for which I am grateful. I also want to thank Clark Clifford, George Elsey, and William Kaufmann for their valuable insights into the planning process corresponding to periods of their involvement. I also wish to thank Captain George Thibault (ret.); Colonel William Shepherd at the Army's Office of Deputy Chief of Staff, Doctrine, at HQ TRADOC, Fort Monroe, Virginia; Tom Hone, a faculty member at the Defense Systems Management College at Ft. Belvoir, Virginia; Jeffrey Record at the Hudson Institute; Lee Hunt at the Naval Studies Board; Dr. Paul Hammond at the University of Pittsburgh, whose incisive comments led me to rethink major arguments with respect to the roots of the policy of containment; Dr. Robert Gromoll, currently at the Arms Control and Disarmament Agency; Colonel Harry Summers (ret.); Steven Shaker of Strategic Future Visions, Inc.; Fred Laykam of the Washington Defense Research Group; Peter Wilson; and Michael Deault for commenting on earlier drafts (or parts thereof) of this book. I also want to thank Don McKeon and Vicki Chamlee of Brassey's for their assistance and encouragement in preparing this book for publication. Of course, any errors of fact or analysis are entirely my own. I also wish to acknowledge the Center for National Security Studies at Los Alamos National Laboratory for providing the initial support for this research.

Finally, a note on the use of research material. The staffs at the Army's Center for Military History, the Office of Air Force History, and the Navy Historical Center at the Navy Yard were particularly helpful in making available materials from their respective services. As for declassified documents, most were made available to me by the staff at the National Security Archives in Washington, D.C. In the text, all such materials are indicated by an *(NSA)* at the end of the citation in the footnote. I would particularly like to thank Laurence Chang of the NSA for his assistance in this regard.

Finally, I wish to note four documents which were particularly useful in helping me understand changes in national security and service planning in the postwar era. They are John Lewis Gaddis, *Strategies of Containment* (New York: Oxford University Press, 1982); Major Robert Doughty, *The Evolution of US Army Tactical Doctrine, 1946–76*, Leavenworth Papers no. 1 (Fort Leavenworth, Kansas: Combat Studies Institute, August 1979); James Lacy, *Within Bounds: The Navy in Postwar American Security Policy*, CNA 83-1178 (Alexandria, Virginia: Center for Naval Analyses, 1983); and Robert Futrell, *Ideas, Concepts, Doctrine: A History of Basic Thinking in the United States Air Force, 1907–1964* (Maxwell Air Force Base, Alabama: Air University Press, 1974). These documents provided the foundation upon which my research into service planning was based.

1
Planning for Defense

CONVENTIONAL POSTWAR PLANNING: THE CONTENT AND CONTEXT

Tanks, Fighters & Ships is a historical analysis of the evolution of U.S. conventional military planning since World War II. Particularly emphasized are the relationship between U.S. national security and military policy, on the one hand, and the geopolitical, parochial, and budgetary factors that contribute to that relationship, on the other. Also emphasized is the relationship between policy making and force-employment planning at the national level and at the service level. The basic questions at the heart of this book are

- How have U.S. national security and military decision makers sought to contain the Soviet Union and ensure the integrity of Western Europe and other U.S. allies?
- How did geopolitical, technological, budgetary, and parochial factors influence doctrinal decisions? What other factors may have affected such decisions, and to what extent?[1]
- How did the services conceive the battlefield throughout the postwar era, and how did these conceptions affect force planning and strategy?
- How did such factors affect choices of weapons and support elements procured to support various doctrines?

Three levels of policy and strategy formulation are also examined. They are U.S. national security policy; U.S. military policy and its basis in U.S. national security policy; and service planning for force employment. Service planning, as discussed below, may be based on strategies, doctrines, mission statements, or any number of possible forms of guidance. As a shorthand, therefore, the term *service planning* is used to describe preparations for the battlefield at the service level. The aim is to determine the factors that influence

1

evolutions in national security and military policies as well as the factors that influence weapons acquisition to support those policies.[2]

U.S. military policy and the service planning that supports it are considered in the context of U.S. national security policy. This is because policy changes tend to be "top-down." Although not always, evolutions in national security policy generally lead to changes in military strategy and supporting service planning. Service planning thus generally reflects changed priorities at the higher levels.

Evolutions in these components are due to a number of factors. The most preeminent seem to be an administration's perception of the threat, technological innovation, the size of the military budget, and interservice parochialism. These factors are isolated throughout this book, but other factors, such as technological or personality-based factors, are discussed as appropriate.

NATIONAL SECURITY POLICY

An examination of U.S. national security policy properly begins with some consideration of the global security environment within which such policies are formulated. The central concern here is how policy makers have *perceived* that environment. Since the Second World War, every president has viewed the policies of the Soviet Union as posing the most serious threat to U.S. national security. Consequently, U.S. national security policy has been remarkably consistent in its basic objective: to contain a perceived Soviet and/or Communist expansionist tendency. At times, various administrations have sought a more aggressive policy aimed at rolling back Soviet gains (i.e., early Reagan), or to deemphasize containment's centrality in U.S. foreign policy (i.e., Carter in his first two years). But containment has triumphed over such vacillations and to this day remains the basis of security policy.

Each U.S. president charged with implementing containment has perceived it to be his foremost priority.[3] The objective of containment—as put by the eminent historian John Lewis Gaddis in his seminal book *Strategies of Containment*—is "to prevent the Soviet Union from using the power and position it won as a result of [the Second World War] to reshape the postwar international order."[4] Because containment is primarily intended to prevent Soviet global expansionism, and not to be a means of facilitating an aggressive U.S. policy, each president has perceived his containment policy to be defensively oriented. This has often created a problem for U.S. decision makers, however, because containment's defensive nature tends to relinquish the global political and military initiative to the Soviets.[5] That is, the United States has constantly had to react to

Soviet initiatives, thereby allowing the Soviets to set the global agenda. This often hinders U.S. efforts to obtain the resources required to meet its own objectives.

Different administrations have dealt with this problem in varying ways. These variations often include tactical offensives to support the overall defensive policy. In this vein, even the Vietnam War was justified by U.S. decision makers as an operation being conducted for the purpose of *maintaining* the status quo, and denying the Communists the opportunity to further expand their influence. Other operations, such as the Bay of Pigs invasion of 1961 or the Grenada invasion of 1983, were justified because they would *restore* the status quo. Rarely, if ever, have operations been justified because U.S. decision makers wanted to *change* the status quo.

Containment is not a strictly military policy. It has economic and political components, ideally synchronized with and complementing the military policy in furthering the national security aims of the administration. Of course, this ideal is not often realized, but administrations nonetheless do usually make some effort to present a cohesive global policy. Here, we focus on the military component, although the other elements are discussed as appropriate.

NATIONAL MILITARY POLICY AND STRATEGY

The role an administration envisions for the military in supporting its national security policy will largely determine the broad contours of the nation's military strategy. However, varying administrations have differed sharply over *how* containment should proceed. Generally, these differences are over the appropriateness of either of two approaches, which Gaddis has termed *symmetrical* and *asymmetrical* responses. Gaddis has developed and applied this conceptual framework and has described it thus:

> Symmetrical response simply means reacting to threats to the balance of power at the same location, time, and level of the original provocation.
>
> Asymmetrical response involves shifting the location or nature of one's reaction onto terrain better suited to the application of one's strength against adversary weakness.[6]

These two facets represent competing perceptions of how best to apply containment and have generally been the basis of a new administration's national security policy, as new presidents reorient their national security priorities away from those of their predecessors. If the predecessor followed a symmetrical strategy, he is usually accused by the new administration of busting the budget, overcommitting the United States to secondary and peripheral interests, and over-emphasizing the military component of foreign policy. If he adhered to an asymmetrical strategy, he is said to have based his defense policies on the budget (rather than on a coherent conception of the threat), ignored potentially vital U.S. interests, and invited worldwide aggression by allowing U.S. defenses to erode.[7]

Symmetrical-response regimes tend to be costly. They require the development and deployment of forces for effectively meeting and containing conflict "across the spectrum of violence"—i.e., at any level that violence occurs. This requires a large standing army trained and equipped to fight ground wars as well as a robust air force and navy. For the United States, maintaining such forces has historically been problematic. In wartime, the United States has traditionally tried to exploit technological superiority in order to preserve its manpower, and this orientation is reflected in the U.S. peacetime deterrent posture as well. In the European theater, for instance, the United States has counted on its technological edge over the Soviet Union to compensate for the Soviets' numerical superiority in manpower and weapons systems.

Asymmetrical-response regimes allow the United States to exploit its strengths, the most preeminent of which are its technological superiority, its ability to maintain control of the seas, and its ability to deliver air power over great distances. Asymmetrical-response regimes have tended to rely heavily on nuclear weapons and are thus usually less costly than symmetrical-response regimes. However, asymmetrical-response regimes have not fared much better than their symmetrical counterparts at preventing aggression. Their effectiveness is closely tied to the credibility of the threat to employ nuclear weapons, and as the Soviets built up their nuclear arsenal, this threat has rung increasingly hollow.

In this book, a variation of the Gaddis framework is applied. Rather than focusing upon asymmetrical and symmetrical responses, the focus here is on two factors that tend to be most influential on U.S. national security decision making: the decision maker's perception of the threat before the United States and his assessment of what the nation is willing, or able, to afford in meeting the threat. In no case, it should be emphasized, did an administration proceed to formulate its defense policy without consideration of both of these components. But there has been a vacillation in the emphasis accorded to one or the other factor. It is this vacillation, and its attendant implications for force planning and acquisition, that serves as the basis of this book. Asymmetrical and symmetrical responses are seen as factors derived from these considerations rather than as the basis of decision making itself.

SERVICE PLANNING

This level addresses the plans that the military services, either acting unilaterally or in conjunction with their sister or allied services, develop for the purpose of carrying out their responsibilities in the national policy. The analyst Carl Builder has defined service plans as the

> components of the defense strategy—but more likely . . . proposed alternatives to, or reinterpretations of, the defense strategy—which the services then use for setting their own institutional agendas, rationalizing their requirements, and arguing for a larger or protected slice of the budget.[8]

This level of military policy refers to the conceptualization of the battle arena that military decision makers bring to their planning. Here, we refer to the service's guidance that it provides for the employment of its forces, either acting alone or in conjunction with its sister or allied services. This guidance can be in the form of doctrine, strategy, or mission. The guidance should be related to the service's conception of the threat it faces and guide force procurement for meeting that threat. Of course, reality does not always work quite so smoothly. Indeed, force procurement, organizational and bureaucratic politics, budgetary pressures, and technological innovation often drive strategic and doctrinal development, as discussed within this text.

Sometimes military doctrines are rooted in sound geopolitical perceptions of interests, threats, and resources available to carry out a desired policy. Often, however, parochial and budgetary factors play important if not *decisive* roles in determining military and weapons-systems acquisition policies. They are therefore accorded equal weight in this analysis as geopolitical factors. Thus, this book recognizes the multifaceted nature of military policy formulation and avoids determinations of single causal factors, except when such determinations can be made with some certainty.

In looking at developments in service planning, this level of analysis considers service strategies and doctrines, and their operational and tactical conceptions of the battlefield. The operational level of war is that level of engagement "below the level of military strategy and above the tactics of battles and engagements—in practice, the planning and conduct of campaigns."[9] Thus, the operational level resides between the strategic and tactical.

The operational level is especially relevant to army doctrine, which is more battlefield oriented than naval or air strategies. One will thus note that discussions of navy and air force military planning tend toward the strategic aspects, while similar discussions of army planning tend toward the tactical and operational aspects. Each service's conception of its own role in the battle serves as the unifying theme in these discussions and, perhaps, more precisely describes this level of analysis than the terms *service planning* or *service doctrine*. The latter terms, however, are used as a shorthand.

WEAPONS-SYSTEM ACQUISITION TRENDS

Finally, these levels of policy are considered in light of weapons-system acquisition trends. This level of analysis is concerned with the weapons systems procured to support all levels of policy. For example, in the early 1960s, President John F. Kennedy implemented a symmetrical strategy calling for forces able to respond to Communist aggression in any theater. This was reflected in military policy, which sought a capability to respond flexibly to any threat against U.S. interests. Force procurement in the Kennedy administration was thereafter judged for flexibility. In 1961, for example, Defense Secretary Robert McNamara stepped up the procurement of U.S. strategic airlift capabilities, so "highly ready" forces could be moved "promptly wherever . . . needed."[10]

One negative aspect of the weapons procurement process, however, is that it does not lend itself to the persistent vacillations in security policy that new administrations impose on the defense bureaucracy. There is usually a considerable lead time between weapons-system conception, development, and procurement. The B-1 bomber, for example, was developed just prior to Richard Nixon's assumption of the presidency, and while a prototype was built in the late 1970s, mass production of the bomber (the B-1B) did not begin until the late 1980s. As a result, the weapons desired to carry out a policy may not, in fact, be available, and decisions about their procurement may have to be made by a new administration rather than the one that first sought to develop the weapons. The next administration may have an entirely new approach to national security that it is trying to institutionalize and may have no desire to procure the system. (Jimmy Carter's decision to cancel the B-1 bomber illustrates this problem.) Budgetary constraints may also prevent an administration from procuring desired systems, forcing it to plan its policies around the forces that already exist. It would therefore not be particularly useful to look for a perfect congruence between desired and actual capabilities. What can be examined, however, are *trends* in systems acquisition and the extent to which such trends are commensurate with the military posture they are to support.

This book also touches upon the weapons systems acquired by successive administrations and the extent to which those acquisitions supported the administration's national security and military policies. As the United States considers its policies for the future, and to the extent that there are enduring policy goals that outlast the particular directional pulls of new administrations, acquisition trends become all the more salient. Consideration of the overall trends of weapons-system development and the context within which such weapons are planned is as important as their particular application at any given time.

Consideration not only of the content of U.S. military posture but also the *context* within which such policies are formulated and acted upon is integral to this book. In the final analysis, this book is a historical examination of military policy and strategy. Strategy has been defined in numerous ways. Jeffrey Record provides the definition most applicable to this book: "the tailoring of goals to resources within a specific internal and external political, military, and economic framework."[11]

An appreciation of the context within which national security decisions have been made is vital to wise decision making in the future. Since developments in the future evolve from present policy decisions, understanding how doctrine and forces have developed in the past should provide a sound basis for consideration of such aspects for the future. And, to the extent that future trends diverge from the past, this analysis should prove useful in cultivating an appreciation of those divergences.

FRAMEWORK OF ANALYSIS

In examining the evolution of U.S. conventional military policy, this book follows a chronological framework of analysis. Essentially, six "eras" are considered. Their demarcation is usually seen with a change in administration. That this is not always the case reflects in part the degree that external global events affect policy formulation.[12] Thus military planning in the postwar period proceeded as follows:

First era, 1945–1948: Containment
Second era, 1949–1952: New Realities and Responsibilities
Third era, 1953–1958: The Absence of the Conventional
Fourth era, 1959–1969: Limited War in Theory and Practice

Fifth era, 1969–1979: Global Military Retrenchment
Sixth era, 1979–Present: Military Buildup and Assertion

While security and military policies have evolved over time, a number of aspects of those policies have remained constant. These include the perception, shared by most U.S. decision makers, that the Soviet Union is expansionist and must be contained,[13] the principally defensive orientation of U.S. policy, the preeminent importance placed on the NATO alliance and on global alliance systems in general to the effective realization of U.S. objectives, and the importance put on maintaining forward-deployed forces around the world. These factors tend to emerge as the central considerations around which new military postures are formulated.

It is worth noting that the persistent emphasis on Western Europe has not been to the exclusion of planning for the periphery, i.e., for the Third World or elsewhere. Indeed, U.S. decision makers, perhaps spurred by the Vietnam War, have gradually but increasingly recognized that a major conventional war may be fought at least somewhat outside of the European theater. Nonetheless, planning for a war in Europe has been and remains the basis of U.S. planning.

Here, aspects of planning for war in both Europe and outside the European theater are discussed, but the U.S. emphasis of planning for a European war is reflected in this book. The three major tasks such planning encompasses are repelling the Warsaw Pact's ground offensive into Central Europe; protecting the sea lines of communication (SLOC) between the continental United States and Western Europe, across which literally hundreds of ships would carry U.S. personnel and materiel; and holding Europe's northern and southern flanks—situated around Norway and Denmark, and Greece and Turkey, respectively—to block a Soviet end-run around NATO's central front.[14] These three tasks should be kept in mind during subsequent discussions of U.S. military planning in the European theater.

ORGANIZATION

Briefly, this book is organized as follows. Chapters 2 through 10 review the six historical eras of military planning as noted above. Generally, one chapter is devoted to each era. However, certain issues are worthy of greater discussion, and separate chapters are devoted to their consideration. Thus, chapter 4 looks at the origins of the NATO alliance, chapter 6 briefly discusses some changes in national security policy that occurred toward the end of the Eisenhower administration, and chapter 8 focuses on the Vietnam War. Chapter 11 presents conclusions drawn from this book, and following chapter 11 are various appendices relating to force procurement and defense budgeting.

NOTES

1. This assumes that the three key influences on U.S. national security and military decision making are geopolitical, budgetary, and parochial in nature. Other factors, ranging from technological innovation to the personalities of the actors involved, have played some role, and such influences will be discussed. But the value judgment implicit in the analysis should be clear at the outset.

   Parochialism is herein used to encompass the bureaucratic, organizational, and other such factors that contribute to policy making. Budgetary factors are considered as worthy of distinction.

2. The assumption here is that U.S. security policy will be evolutionary and that the next thirty years will not see radical changes. Radical change—for example, that brought about by global nuclear war—is not seen as particularly likely.

   This is not to say that changes of a sweeping nature will not occur. As an increasing number of countries acquire nuclear capabilities, for example, the possibility of regional nuclear wars becomes a serious consideration.

3. The only real exception to this rule would be Carter in his first two years. Carter seemed to follow a regionalist, rather than a global strategic, foreign policy. By 1979, however, attention returned to the Soviets. See chapters 9 and 10.

4. John Lewis Gaddis, *Strategies of Containment* (New York: Oxford University Press, 1982), p. 4.

5. Containment is directed toward communism in general and the Soviet Union in particular, but not all uses of U.S. force have a geopolitical component. The use of force should be considered in a broader context. This is the case even though the primary and overwhelming justification for the use of force has, in nearly every case since the second World War, been related to containment. Conflicts occur on local and regional levels and are

dealt with on those levels, but they are always at least partially viewed in terms of their geopolitical implications. It would be wrong, therefore, to disregard the Communist or Soviet impetus when examining the use of force and its doctrinal and structural development. But local and regional factors must be considered as well.

6. John Lewis Gaddis, "Containment: Its Past and Future," *International Security* 5, no. 4 (Spring 1981): 80.

7. The Bush administration will prove unique in that it represents the first time since World War II that a sitting president has been succeeded by a candidate from his own party (with the exception, of course, of Lyndon Johnson, who assumed the presidency after John F. Kennedy's assassination). Therefore, one does not see this process occurring. However, the observation would have remained true had Michael Dukakis won the presidency in 1988.

8. Carl Builder, *The Army in the Strategic Planning Process: Who Shall Bell the Cat?* (Bethesda, Maryland: U.S. Army Concepts Analysis Agency, 1986), p. 90.

9. John Romjue, *From Active Defense to AirLand Battle: The Development of Army Doctrine 1973–1982* (Fort Monroe, Virginia: TRADOC Historical Monograph Series, February 1985), p. 69.

10. Robert McNamara, *The Essence of Security* (New York: Harper & Row, 1968), p. 84.

11. Jeffrey Record, *Revising U.S. Military Strategy: Tailoring Means to Ends* (McLean, Virginia: Pergamon-Brassey's, 1984), p. 1.

12. Other factors necessarily play a part when an administration reformulates its national security policies. Global events may have been largely responsible for Truman's decision to expand the defense budget in FY1950, but Carter's mid-term turnabout seems to have been influenced by domestic as well as geopolitical considerations.

13. Again, the principal exception was Carter, but he ultimately accepted this view.

14. See, e.g., *U.S. Defense Policy*, 3rd ed. (Washington, D.C.: Congressional Quarterly, 1983), p. 127.

2
Era I: Containment and Aerial Bombardment

THE ROOTS OF A POLICY

As World War II drew to a close, the subject of U.S. relations with its wartime ally from the East, the Union of Soviet Socialist Republics (the USSR), was much on the minds of U.S. officials. Prior to the war, relations with the Soviets had been anything but smooth; however, the Soviets had been reliable and competent allies in defeating the Axis powers. It was also becoming clear that both the United States and the Soviet Union were destined to be major actors on the postwar stage and that the Russians could not simply be ignored.

Hopeful that accommodation and cooperation could be the basis of postwar U.S.-Soviet relations, President Franklin D. Roosevelt put forth a vision of "four policemen" safeguarding the world from hostile activities. It didn't matter if such hostilities originated from an outside party or from one of the four. "When there [are] four people sitting in a poker game and three of them [are] against the fourth, it is a little hard on the fourth," Roosevelt reasoned. In particular, Roosevelt included China in his plan because China, he believed, would act as a counterbalance to the Soviet Union.[1]

However, Roosevelt's vision of "four policemen" safeguarding the world was not soon to be realized. At first Harry S Truman, Roosevelt's successor, was optimistic that some sort of peaceful world order could be established based on cooperation among the emerging great powers. After the Potsdam Conference of July 1945, where Truman met the Soviet Premier Joseph Stalin face to face and arrangements for the postwar environment were hammered out, Truman proclaimed that Stalin was someone the United States could do business with. But Soviet behavior increasingly undermined this optimism. At Yalta, the Soviets had promised free elections in Poland but instead took steps to tighten their grip over that nation and the other states of Eastern Europe. They recanted on other agreements (of varying significance) as well.[2] On February 9, 1946, Stalin made

11

a major speech in which he blamed World War II on capitalism and declared that a peaceful international order was "impossible under the present capitalistic economy." To guarantee his country "against any eventuality," Stalin announced a five-year rearmament plan that called for tripling iron, steel, and coal production and nearly doubling the production of oil.[3] To support Stalin's armament plans, it soon became clear to U.S. decision makers that the Soviets had to practically eliminate the production of consumer goods. Many in the administration interpreted Stalin's program as a direct threat to the United States.

The administration asked George Kennan, a Moscow-based diplomat, to explain the increasingly anti-Western rhetoric in Soviet policy declarations and speeches. Kennan's lengthy response of February 1946, now referred to as the "long telegram," turned out to be somewhat vague with respect to proper U.S. policy toward the Soviet Union. But the telegram was most illuminating in its discussion of the ideological and historical factors that motivated the Soviets' international behavior and was influential in shaping the Truman administration's perceptions of and attitudes toward the Communist giant. "At [the] bottom of Kremlin's neurotic view of world affairs," Kennan explained, "is traditional and instinctive Russian sense of insecurity." Moreover, the Communist leaders believe that the Soviet Union "still lives in [the midst of] antagonistic 'capitalist encirclement' with which in the long run there can be no permanent coexistence." Kennan continued,

> Soviet leaders are driven [by] necessities of their own past and present position to put forward a dogma which [views the] outside world as evil, hostile, and menacing, but . . . destined to be wracked with growing internal convulsions until it . . . yields to new and better [socialist] world. This thesis provides justification for that increase of military and police power of Russian state, for that isolation of Russian population from outside world, and for that fluid and constant pressure to extend limits of Russian police power which are together the natural and instinctive urges of Russian rulers.[4]

Kennan argued that the Soviet regime *required* a hostile outside power to legitimize its authority within the Soviet Union and that the United States had assumed the necessary role. But Kennan's views offered no practical solution to the emerging threat.[5] He essentially argued that a policy of negotiation, conciliation, and resolve—coupled with sufficient U.S. force and the readiness to use it—would ultimately lead the Soviets to adopt a nonconfrontational policy.[6]

If the Soviets were the problem, the long telegram only provided half the answer. It was useful to have some idea of what motivated the Soviet leadership, but policies were required if the United States was to influence Soviet behavior. Kennan left the crucial question unanswered: What should those policies comprise? In the summer of 1946, Truman requested Clark Clifford (at that time his special council) to supervise a sweeping study aimed at answering that question. George Elsey, an administrative assistant to the president, was the principal author of the report titled "American Relations with the Soviet Union," which is often referred to as the Clifford-Elsey Report.

In examining the roots of containment, it would be misguided to underestimate the importance of the long telegram or Kennan's subsequent elaboration of his views in *Foreign Affairs* (discussed below).[7] To be sure, in his article, Kennan did take a more practical perspective. The Clifford-Elsey Report, however, was as influential on Truman's policies as the long telegram and was written after intensive consultations with the secretaries of war, state, and navy, as well as all other military leaders at the time. Clifford recalls that the report "was the view of the top people; you saw the germs of the policy that became so important."[8] Ken Hechler, Truman's White House research director, points out that "the document helped lay the foundation for Truman's major foreign policy decisions. The Truman Doctrine, Marshall Plan, North Atlantic Treaty Organization [NATO] and containment of aggressive communism were rooted in the analysis developed in the Elsey report."[9]

The report accepted Kennan's description of the Soviets as motivated by ideology and historical insecurity. But the report was much more resolute with respect to what was to be done. The report flatly rejected negotiation as a workable basis for resolving U.S.-Soviet disputes, arguing that

> compromises and concessions are considered, by the Soviets, to be evidences of weakness and they are encouraged by our "retreats" to make new and greater demands. . . . The United States . . . should entertain no proposal for disarmament or limitation of armament as long as the possibility of Soviet aggression exists.[10]

Rather, the Clifford-Elsey Report argued that the key to avoiding conflict was in maintaining sizable forces-in-being and making clear that if provoked, the U.S. was willing to use its forces. It asserted:

> The language of military power is the only language which disciples of power politics understand. The United States must use that language

in order that Soviet leaders will realize that our government is determined to uphold the interests of its citizens and the rights of small nations.[11]

The influence of the Clifford-Elsey Report is seen in the numerous activities that were taken in consonance with its recommendations. For example, the United States instituted its still active policy of sending the Sixth and Seventh fleets to trouble spots in the Mediterranean and the Pacific Far East, respectively, and resisted Soviet efforts to play an active role in the Japanese occupation.[12] But the most resolute demonstration of the new policy came in March 1947, just six months after the Clifford-Elsey Report was presented to the president. The Soviets had been making demands on the Turkish government for base rights and boundary concessions, while simultaneously supporting a communist insurgency movement against the Greek government. In early 1947, Great Britain informed the Truman administration that it could no longer afford to extend financial and military support to those governments. The United States quickly moved to fill the void. In seeking congressional support for economic aid for those nations, President Truman proclaimed that

it must be the policy of the United States to support free peoples who are resisting attempted subjugation by armed minorities or by outside pressures. I believe that we must assist free peoples to work out their own destinies in their own way. I believe that our help should be primarily economic and financial aid, which is essential to economic stability and orderly processes.[13]

As the above declaration (the Truman Doctrine) demonstrates, the president originally sought to emphasize the economics of containment. The Marshall Plan, which quickly followed Truman's pronouncement, demonstrates this. The Marshall Plan to rebuild the economies of Western Europe was primarily an economic program, intended to strengthen the capabilities of the Western Europeans to counter directly Soviet political overtures. However, in short time, the plan's military elements came to be emphasized, and even the Truman Doctrine was soon imbued with a much more militaristic orientation,[14] consistent with the recommendations of the Clifford-Elsey Report.

The pronouncement of the Truman Doctrine was followed by Kennan's July 1947 *Foreign Affairs* article, written under the pseudonym "Mr. X." Kennan wrote that "the main element of any policy toward the Soviet Union must be that of a long term, patient but firm and vigilant containment of Russian expansionist tendencies. . . . "[15]

Kennan continued to hold out the prospect that, over time, containment could be a means of modifying Soviet activities through the positive reinforcement of nonbelligerent Soviet behavior—a view given increasingly less credence within the administration. The new Secretary of State Dean Acheson, for example, was more concerned with what he termed the building of "situations of strength." This involved taking any necessary steps—such as formalizing an alliance with the Europeans—that could enhance the strength of the United States over the Soviet Union, even if such steps made conciliation and negotiation less tenable. Over time, Acheson's views were given greater weight in the White House and Kennan's were gradually given less. As the next chapter shows, moreover, by 1950 Kennan's views would be largely discounted altogether.

Even given such disagreements over how containment was to be implemented, some consensus on the policy of containment was developing in the Truman administration. As this was taking place, however, the president was imposing stringent budgetary restrictions on the defense establishment and rapidly demobilizing the U.S. armed forces—a step that ran counter to the Clifford-Elsey Report, to the president's own rhetoric, and to the recommendations of Truman's advisers. In a paper prepared by the Joint Strategic Survey Committee of the Joint Chiefs of Staff, demobilization was not seen as a viable option:

> The advent of the [atomic weapon] does not at this time justify elimination of the conventional armaments. . . . The ground forces will still have to be equipped to attack, occupy and defend territory. The air forces will still have the same roles which they had in (World War II). . . . The Navy will still have to control the sea, transport and land amphibious forces and furnish air defense and air attacks where shore-based facilities cannot be made available.[16]

But Truman was not about to finance a peacetime military buildup, which he viewed as likely to have an inflationary effect on the economy and certain to be unpopular among a war-weary citizenry. His defense budgets from FY1947 through FY1950 were each less than $14 billion, representing radical reductions from World War II budgets, which topped $82 billion at their height.[17] Truman's early budgets were figured according to the "remainder method": to balance the budget, Truman would take total revenues and subtract interest, foreign aid, and domestic obligations, and authorize the remainder for defense.[18]

Defense allocations were thus increasingly determined by budgetary considerations. They were not rooted in a strategic vision of the threat before the United States. Indeed, Truman's budgets barely supported his own doctrine, and choices had to be made between vital and peripheral interests. Such budgets emasculated the services and intensified the usual scrapping among them for scarce dollars. As discussed below, interservice rivalries became acute and hot tempered, particularly between the air force and the navy.

INITIAL SERVICE MANEUVERING

Leaders of the army, air force, and navy all assessed the lessons of World War II and judged their own service's contribution toward the war's resolution as preeminent. And indeed, each service had been successful in its war effort. Army occupation forces were still in Germany and Japan, symbolizing the great U.S. power that had been brought to bear by the land forces. While the significant contribution of the army air forces was acknowledged, army leaders remained confident that the war proved "ultimate" victory in any future conflict would be won on the ground.

Integrating the carrier into its wartime operations, the navy had fought on two fronts successfully. The navy leadership thus extolled the virtue of a balanced fleet, praising the contribution of the aircraft carrier in bringing the war to an end. Indeed, the aircraft carrier was replacing the battleship as the basis of naval planning. Fleet Admiral Ernest King, for example, noted that the aircraft carrier had become an "integral and primary component of the fleet" capable of carrying out a number of missions, including support, reconnaissance, and the defeat of "hostile land-based planes over positions held in force by the enemy."[19]

The leadership of the U.S. Army Air Forces (USAAF), later to become the U.S. Air Force, felt that the war had proven the supremacy of strategic aerial bombardment. The USAAF was certain, moreover, that the atomic bomb had forever changed the military equation in its favor. Thanks to the atomic bomb, the aerial bombing theories of Italian General Giulio Douhet and General William "Billy" Mitchell, two early apostles of strategic bombardment, seemed practicable. No longer would protracted ground campaigns (or, therefore, a large army) be the keystone to winning the next war. Future wars would be decided by strategic bombing campaigns against an opposing country's industrial potential and population. Such attacks would destroy the enemy's will to fight, leading to an inevitable surrender. As early as October 1945, Carl Spaatz (later commanding general, AAF) argued that "we have one real defense: A planned and ready air offensive."[20] Through the next decade, the air force hierarchy echoed repeatedly Spaatz's sentiment.

The leaders from each of the services proceeded to plan for the postwar environment on the basis of their World War II experience. The army was mired in occupation missions and did not complete its demobilization until June of 1947. But the navy and the air force largely completed their demobilization by 1946,[21] allowing them to turn their attention to future force requirements and the attendant budgetary battles. As each tried to establish its preeminence, disagreements over roles and missions developed with alarming regularity.

The air force, while not completely neglecting its tactical and support missions, geared its force development predominantly toward the strategic air mission. Although the Tactical Air Command (TAC) had been established on March 21, 1946, the Air Force's Strategic Air Command (SAC) emerged as its most preeminent.

Contrary to the air force view, the army held that the next war would not necessarily be atomic and maintained that a traditional land-based army would be the key to victory in a future war. However, if war were to come swiftly, the army would have run into trouble in making its case. On V-J Day, the army had 8,020,000 personnel; by January 1, 1946, this figure was cut to almost half, and by July of the same year, the army was down to 1,889,690 men.[22] Army planners did not agree that strategic bombing would be the key to victory in future wars, but demobilization made it impossible for the service to plan future wars around its own role. Thus at this time, the army put up little organized opposition to the air force's aerial bombardment strategy.

Not so the navy. In the summer of 1945 James Forrestal succeeded Frank Knox as secretary of the navy and initiated sweeping changes in navy planning based on an expanded role for the aircraft carrier. Forrestal was becoming increasingly concerned over the Soviet threat and questioned the utility of a large battleship-based navy in the face of a land-oriented adversary. Maritime superiority itself, he realized, would serve little purpose against a country that possessed relatively insignificant naval forces and did virtually all of its fighting on land. Forrestal's concept of the new carrier-oriented navy was described in the 1946 unification hearings:

> The carrier Task Forces of this war have been the spearhead of our attack, both against the Japanese empire and against the submarine packs in the Atlantic. These carrier Task Forces are a unique creation of the United States—and are one of the most powerful forces in existence in the world today. They have a remarkable mobility and

an enormous reach. In my judgment, these great carrier Task Forces, backed up by the surface power of the fleet and by the amphibious striking forces of the Marine Corps, constitute an all purpose weapon which . . . can give this nation and the world a swift and effective means of dealing with arrogance wherever it might raise its head . . . (the Navy envisions) great carrier striking forces which . . . will be capable of delivering atomic bomb attacks.[23]

Such talk was simply anathema to air force planners, who interpreted the navy's vision of atomic-carrier task forces as an effort to encroach upon air force roles and missions. The air force argued the case for "constant readiness" through air power. As one writer put it, "The Douhet doctrine of strategic bombing was repeatedly hammered into the sympathetic ears of Congress until it almost completely preempted the thinking of Congress about military strategy."[24]

THE NATIONAL SECURITY ACT OF 1947

As the services grappled with the dilemma of their World War II forces quickly becoming obsolete and dramatically reduced budgets, the Truman administration made a wide-reaching attempt to reorganize the armed services. One lesson of World War II was that the effectiveness of military operations could be significantly enhanced if land, sea, and air forces could be unified under a single theater command. The 1947 National Security Act sought to institutionalize the unification and control mechanisms necessary to ensure effective joint operations in future conflicts. To this day, the 1947 reorganization remains the most fundamental and far-reaching of all the postwar reorganization efforts. This act established dramatic changes in the defense structure. Subsequent efforts have sought to modify, strengthen, and build upon, but not overturn, the 1947 act.

The roots of the 1947 act can be traced to congressional hearings on unification held in April 1944. At that time, there was a War Department and a separate Department of the Navy, both of which favored unification in principle but disagreed pointedly over how such unification should proceed. In a joint letter to the president dated May 31, 1946, Navy Secretary James Forrestal and War Secretary Robert Patterson detailed the most significant differences between them. The most pressing was over organization. The army wanted one unified department with three separate branches. The navy agreed to the concept of a single secretary with limited authority over all the armed forces with respect to specific matters but wanted to maintain its independence as a separate department with full cabinet rank. The army also wanted the new air force to assume responsibility for all missions at the time performed by the navy's land-based aircraft, such as reconnaissance, and to limit the amphibious warfare functions of the marine corps.[25] The navy disagreed with both of these propositions.

The differences between the departments were gradually narrowed, and on January 16, 1947, the two secretaries wrote a new letter to the president, this time detailing their compromise positions and agreements. Because the president was so strongly in favor of a unified department, the creation of a civilian defense secretary (although with limited authority) was agreed to; however, each of the services was to have its own cabinet-level secretary. The navy was given operational control over its land-based reconnaissance and patrol aircraft, and the marines were given principal responsibility for amphibious warfare. Other disagreements with respect to roles and missions were to be resolved separately, in an executive order of the president to be released simultaneously with the new legislation.

The January 16 letter paved the way for the National Security Act of 1947, which Congress approved on June 26, 1947. That act created the National Security Council and delineated the members of that council, created a Central Intelligence Agency, and ordered specific military reorganization measures. For example, the act

- created the post of secretary of defense and mandated that the secretary should have a civilian staff answerable directly to him;
- created a separate Department of the Air Force, which was in essence an outgrowth of the army air forces, and elevated each department to cabinet-level status;
- mandated that the marine corps would consist of at least three active divisions and three air wings;
- renamed the War Department the Department of the Army; and
- provided a statutory charter for each of the services, as well as the Joint Chiefs of Staff, and provided for a staff answerable directly to the Joint Chiefs.[26]

The act empowered the Joint Chiefs of Staff to establish, as they deemed appropriate, unified theater commands, and a number of such commands were created. Through the creation of the position of secretary of defense and other measures, the act took important steps to ensure that civilian control would be maintained over the military establishment. However, the act did not resolve the disputes over roles and missions that were simmering between the services. This was to be accomplished through the Executive Order that Truman committed to sending up to Congress on passage of the National Security Act. He did so, but Executive Order 9877 proved highly contentious among the services. As a result, debates over roles and missions continued throughout 1947 and into 1948. An earnest (although unsuccessful) attempt to resolve them was not made until 1948, as embodied in the "Key West" agreement of that year, discussed below.

On March 5, 1949, President Truman recommended to Congress a number of amendments aimed at strengthening the 1947 National Security Act. The amendments sought to control service disputes by strengthening the role of the secretary of defense. The position of chairman of the Joint Chiefs of Staff was created to preside over the service chiefs, and the size of the Joint Staff was increased from 100 to 210 officers. The military services lost their executive status and were henceforth subordinate units within the Department of Defense, and the service secretaries lost their cabinet-level positions. But these amendments were not to become law for another two years, and while they were important in addressing some of the flaws of the 1947 act, they did little to control service disputes over force procurement and functions.

CONTINUED SERVICE DISPUTES OVER FUNCTIONS

An important aspect of the 1947 reorganization act was its creation of an independent air force. In this period of budgetary restraint, this fledgling service was to take on the central role in U.S. national security policy in the immediate postwar era. The air force proved best equipped to offer an approach to containment that was commensurate with national policy and capabilities. Its aerial bombing strategy was the least costly and least manpower-intensive of all the approaches offered by the services and thus appealed to Truman. The country would not support a conventional buildup; the army was skeletonized and much of the navy was mothballed. Though the air force's preparedness levels were down, the air arm argued vigorously for "constant preparedness" and a strategic atomic capability based on a 70-group air force and 400,000 personnel. Capitalizing on occasional congressional calls for preemptive strategies, the air force often stressed the need to "get in the first blow" and seize the initiative. As if in response to the public's demand for demobilization, the air force program emphasized U.S. technology rather than manpower. Air force officials also argued that by establishing a ring of overseas bases around the Soviet Union, they could ensure that war would be kept far from U.S. shores. As Edward Kolodziej notes,

> The Air Force reshaped and reformulated Douhet's gospel to fit an American audience but the message was basically the same: An overwhelmingly *superior* strategic bombing capacity would deter aggression and if deterrence failed, it would destroy the enemy's military forces, his homeland, and his will to fight. Air power, not sea power, was to be America's first line of defense—and offense. Strategic bombing was heralded as the quick, relatively inexpensive, and ultimately decisive means to victory in any future war.[27]

The navy, on the verge of exclusion from the strategic planning process, had to protect its own functional ability and ensure for itself some piece of the budgetary pie. In June 1946, Chief of Naval Operations (CNO) Chester Nimitz initiated Project Girder, an extensive navy research and development (R&D) program focusing on antisubmarine warfare (ASW).[28] In May 1947, the navy published USF-1, *Principles and Instructions of Naval Warfare*, which formally elaborated the navy's conception of its role in deterrence and defense. Borrowing air force rhetoric, the fleet manual called the "destruction of the enemy's will to resist . . . the fundamental objective of the armed forces in war" and stressed that air attacks should be aimed against the enemy's population and war-supporting industry.[29] However, reflecting the ascendency of the carrier proponents within the navy, air attacks would come from aircraft aboard navy carriers. Deputy CNO Admiral Arthur Radford argued that navy air units were

> a key weapon of [the navy's] fighting strength. [Navy air units would provide] the most mobile Air Force in the world . . . they would support . . . the economic and political interests of the nation in almost all parts of the world, and . . . in the event of war would bear the brunt of air fighting against shore based aircraft while . . . national mobilization [was] in process.[30]

Thus, Radford was implying that projecting power and engaging battles against shore-based aircraft would be the basis of future navy missions. This represented a shift from the navy's usual emphasis on control of the seas. Unlike the air force, however, the navy's postwar planning was not immediately based on atomic weapons.

The navy leadership was skeptical of the reliable availability of atomic weapons and thus found atomic strikes dubious concepts around which to plan a strategy. In the 1949 manual, it was noted that "atomic energy, together with publicity regarding guided missiles and high speed aircraft, has led to much uninformed comment that all other weapons or forms of warfare are obsolete. . . . [These developments] have not at this time displaced more orthodox arms and armaments."[31]

In fact, the fleet manual went into considerable detail about nonnuclear naval operations. Three were detailed in depth:

1. The *strike*, which involved "operations of intercepting, or proceeding to, and of attacking [a specific] enemy target with the objective of destroying or neutralizing the target";
2. the *raid*, which was a strike conducted when outnumbered, therefore requiring the rapid withdrawal in the aftermath; and
3. the *sweep*, which was a large-scale operation that projected "a task force of appropriate strength into areas otherwise under enemy control" for the purpose of attacking planned targets, or targets of opportunity.[32]

All of these operations could be conducted by naval aviation, but were not necessarily atomic. Navy officials reasoned that if atomic weapons were to be employed at all, their use should be in a much more limited and selective fashion than advocated by the air force. The navy planners also argued that their versatile carrier-based aircraft were better suited for atomic missions than the medium and heavy bombers procured and operated by the air force. In a 1947 planning document promulgated by the navy's Strategic Planning Division, this was explained in detail:

> [The carrier fleets] are organized as powerful striking weapons of great mobility and are prepared to meet any challenge. . . . They are capable of projecting power ashore into enemy coastal areas in support of forces ashore and by their mobility, they can apply their power swiftly and exploit opportunities that would otherwise be lost were it necessary to first establish land based air.[33]

The last sentence was clearly directed at the air force, for whom a supporting role mostly centered around air defense was envisaged.[34]

Even given its initial reservations, however, the navy's shift toward atomic weapons was already under way and was probably completed in July 1947, at the time of the Bikini Atoll tests. Although the reliability of these tests has been questioned, they provided ammunition for the navy's arguments with respect to the carrier's capability to withstand atomic attacks. This is reflected in the navy's FY1949 budget request, in which the navy sought funds for the development of an improved carrier, dubbed the CVA-58 *supercarrier*. This massive ship was to have enhanced conventional and nuclear capabilities (although in front of Congress it was usually referred to as the "atomic carrier"). It featured an extended flight deck, which meant that it could accommodate large numbers of the navy's next-generation heavy jet fighters and multi-engine attack planes.

In planning conducted in November 1947 for the Joint Chiefs of Staff (JCS), the navy projected that by 1955 it would require four four-carrier task groups, each with a CVA-58 class carrier at its nucleus. All carriers in each group were to be equipped with long-range, multi-engine bombers. Naval planners also projected a need for a nuclear-capable aircraft (the North American AJ-1, multi-engine, prop-jet attack plane) and the ADR-42, a multi-engine jet designed to operate primarily from CVA-58 type ships.[35]

The air force interpreted the navy's planning as a thinly disguised effort to encroach upon its strategic bombing mission. The air force hierarchy had seen the carrier demonstrate its potential for strategic missions against land-based forces in World War II and were not about to relinquish its growing preeminence in the planning process. Air force planners argued that a plentiful supply of atomic weapons would soon be available and that planning limited and selective strikes was unnecessary. Limited threats, it was constantly argued, were deterred by the threat of an all-out atomic response. The air force, whose own doctrine was codified in a 1943 manual called *The Command and Employment of Air Power*,[36] argued that the navy's self-perception as the first line of defense was "sadly outdated" and that even if the need for limited atomic responses actually arose, the air force B-29 bomber was more than adequate to carry out the task.

In ensuing battles over the budget, the air force emphasized the role of strategic bombing in Western Europe. The Soviets were doing little to demobilize their forces remaining in Eastern Europe, and Europe had clearly emerged as the basis of U.S. planning. The massive Soviet army in Eastern Europe discouraged a large ground campaign there, the air force leaders argued. Instead, they advocated defeating a future Soviet campaign into Western Europe indirectly, through sustained atomic bombing of the Soviet's war-supporting industry.

Neither the navy nor the army had the resources to present a viable alternative to this plan. The army maintained that the next war would be decided on the ground; therefore, the air force should be procuring capabilities necessary for providing close air support and interdiction. But the army simply lacked the resources to defeat Soviet forces straight on, even if heavily supported by air force assets. As for the navy, the air force noted that the supercarrier was still on the drawing board (and promised to be expensive), while the air force had its forces in position and ready to go.

Thus, as 1947 drew to a close, the air force had established itself as the dominant (and affordable) arm of the armed services.[37] Events of 1948, however, were to reopen the debates over strategic roles and priorities all over again, and the debates were to prove more contentious than ever.

THE EVENTS OF 1948 AND THEIR AFTERMATH

On February 24, 1948, an armed and violent Communist coup occurred in Czechoslovakia. The takeover was quick and total. As Walter Millis pointed out:

> The Czechoslovak Republic, which from its foundation at the end of the First World War had been a model of successful democratic governance in Central Europe, was subverted at a stroke into a satellite Communist dictatorship. . . . This was the first forcible Communist conquest of a strongly based free government, and in the eyes of most Western publics it put an altogether new light upon the power, ferocity and scope of Communist aggression.[38]

Also at this time, East-West tensions were rising over the status of occupied Berlin. Amid rumors of a blockade, the Soviets threatened to negotiate a separate peace treaty with East Germany. The Soviets were apparently seeking to drive a fissure between the United States and its European allies. A military challenge would reveal the extent of the U.S. commitment there. If the United States backed down, the embryonic alliance—not yet formalized by the NATO treaty—could crumble. For the first time, it appeared that war with the Communists could be imminent.

Despite these international crises, however, the interservice rivalries over roles and missions continued. Forrestal, now secretary of defense, called a meeting of the JCS and the service secretaries from March 11 to March 14 at the Key West Naval Base, Florida. Forrestal sought to establish specific roles for the services, engender a more cooperative spirit among them, and establish a foundation for the rebuilding of U.S. forces.

The two most contentious debates at the conference, predictably, were over whether the navy or the air force would be responsible for strategic air campaigns and the simmering army–air force disputes over control of fixed-wing and rotary-wing (helicopter) aircraft. The army protested the air force's deemphasis of TAC in its planning and was concerned about the air force's ability to provide close air support and perform interdiction. The army thus wanted to develop a fixed-wing capability that it would directly control. The air force, in turn, at first rejected the very notion of air power organic to the army as an affront to the "indivisibility of air power" (a principal tenet of its doctrine) and as an encroachment on its responsibilities.

A consensus over these issues and others related to proper functions, roles, and missions slowly emerged from the Key West meeting. As Morton and David Halperin conclude:

> The Key West agreement represented a compromise of sorts. The Navy gained many of its goals: retention of the Navy-based Marine Corps; the authority to provide close air support for marine land operations; and the authority to carry out those air operations, including ground-launched missions, which are required for sea battles. The Army and the Air Force, convinced that the services should avoid excessive duplication, were willing to give the Navy control over almost all sea operations. And the Army and Air Force agreed to cooperate with each other as a team on joint missions. Specifically, this meant that the Air Force pledged to provide the Army with airlift and close air support.[39]

It was also decided that the navy would be given access to the atomic bomb and would proceed with the development of the supercarrier and high-altitude aircraft "to carry heavy missiles therefrom."[40] This decision was important because it gave extra impetus to the navy's Polaris missile program. For the moment, the army–air force dispute was settled; it was decreed that the air force would provide close air support and interdiction for the army. The army was permitted to retain its own aviation units, consisting for the most part of light aircraft for artillery spotting and liaison work.[41]

Although there have been a number of supplements and amendments to the Key West agreement, it still serves as the basis of how the services distinguish their missions.[42] The Key West agreement appeared to institutionalize the ascendancy of strategic bombing and the air force's primary role in carrying it out. But the apparent reconciliation engendered by the meetings proved in many ways superficial; and while the Key West agreement may have been useful in ascribing general notions of roles and missions, it did little to end the quibbling among the services over these issues.

On April 21, Forrestal circulated among the services a functions statement delineating the agreement. The next day, CNO Admiral Denfield sent Forrestal a "clarifying note." While the navy recognized the air force's right to the strategic bombing role, the note said, the "Navy shall attack any targets inland or otherwise, necessary to the accomplishment of its mission . . . the capabilities of naval aviation will be utilized to the maximum in the air offensive against vital strategic targets." The navy also pointed out that joint war plans would exploit the capabilities of the carrier to deliver atomic bombing attacks "in the near future."[43]

The analyst Paul Hammond notes that before Forrestal even had a chance to publish the agreement for internal circulation, air force Generals Spaatz and Norstad informed him that they accepted the agreement as an interpretation of the National Security Act but disagreed with it in principle, nullifying any actual authority that may have been embodied in the agreement.[44]

As for the army–air force dispute, its resolution also proved short-lived. The air force continued to deemphasize TAC in its planning and, in December, eliminated TAC's independent status and subordinated it to the Continental Air Command (CAC). In June 1949, the Army Field Forces informed the air force that the air-support arrangements established in the guiding 1946 joint field manual 31-35, *Air-Ground Operations*, were no longer satisfactory.[45] The army persisted in its attempts to develop organic aviation.

Over time, numerous efforts were made to resolve the army–air force dispute and the many other disagreements that continued to emerge between the services.[46] But none have proved particularly successful, probably because it is in the services' collective interest that none are. After all, greater ambiguity of roles and missions provides service representatives with more leeway in arguing the case for the service they represent. It was not until 1950, when service budgets began to increase in the aftermath of NSC–68 (discussed in the next chapter) and the North Korean invasion of South Korea in June, that TAC re-emerged as an important arm of the air force. And even in the war, these disputes resurfaced and led to problems in establishing effective control and coordination of army and air force aviation assets.

The Key West agreement was to facilitate effective joint war planning. But such planning never effectively materialized. The army now joined the navy in vigorously protesting the persistent emphasis on the air force in U.S. war plans. One such plan, Operation Broiler, was typical. Broiler argued that "the success or failure of this plan depends upon the early effectiveness of the air offensive, particularly the strategic air offensive with atomic weapons." The air campaign was launched from the battery of overseas air bases that the United States was rapidly establishing around the perimeter of the USSR at locations such as the United Kingdom, Cairo-Suez, Syria, Morocco, Karachi, India, and the Ryukyu Islands. Conventional ground forces were to be employed in the wake of the atomic offensive in a somewhat ambiguous post-air campaign role, involving the removal of the remaining Soviet forces from occupied territories. The allied role in the plan was also principally supportive, involving the application of air and naval assets for such missions as destroying Soviet military installations and ports and destroying the "industrial potential and war-making capacity of Far Eastern USSR by air action against oil installations, factories, transportation, industrial and political centers and military installations."[47] Such plans typically proved schismatic, and the army and the navy simply began to draw up their own plans, emphasizing their own roles in the process.

As this was taking place, however, the Soviets blockaded the roads and waterways leading into the city of Berlin on June 24, 1948. In response, the United States initiated a massive airlift of food and materiel into Berlin. The air force greatly contributed to the airlift.[48] Some of SAC's bombers were even flown to Europe and put on alert. SAC's able response to the Berlin Blockade cemented its preeminent role in the planning process. At the time, SAC possessed 35 nuclear-capable B-29 bombers, and additional B-29s were being modified for atomic missions. The B-36 would soon be in service, and squadrons of air-refueling KB-29s were becoming operable.[49] However, as SAC's preeminence became evident in the share of the budget allocated to the air force, navy (and army) procurement tactics changed. The battle over Truman's $13.7-billion FY1950 budget further polarized the air force from both the army and the navy. As 1948 drew to a close, the army and navy began to emphasize conventional operations and the nominal utility of the strategic air campaign in limited conflicts.

THE ARMY STANDS FIRM

The year 1949 saw the reemergence of the army in the contingency planning process. Aside from the question of whether the United States could mount a military response to the Berlin Blockade, had it chosen to do so, the army's strategic rethinking was triggered by a number of events that occurred in that year. The Soviets consolidated their gains in Eastern Europe and actively supported or endorsed guerrilla activities in the Philippines, French Indochina, and Malaya. The Chinese Communists completed their revolution, and perhaps most important, the Soviets exploded an atomic device.[50] The army leadership questioned the wisdom of the air force's doctrine in light of the above crises. Threats to conduct air campaigns against the Soviet heartland did not deter the crises from occurring and were not really helpful in doing something about each crisis afterward. And if the Soviets now had their own atomic bomb, which at least in theory they could use against the United States, did it really make sense to rely so heavily on the atomic threat?[51]

In May 1949, General Omar Bradley, the army chief of staff, put forth his conception of the next war. He envisioned a three-part battle wherein the use of weapons delivered by air would play a limited role in the overall engagement, confined to delaying and disrupting the Soviet attack. U.S. military forces would then seize strategic bases from which the Soviets' homeland might be bombed or from which the Soviets could launch attacks on the United States. And rather than perform "mop-up" duties, the army would engage the adversary in an extensive and decisive ground campaign.[52]

Typical of army thinking at the time, Bradley's concept envisaged a principal role for the ground forces and a relatively minor role for air-delivered atomic weapons. In August 1949, barely two months after the events in Berlin, the army published a revision of its capstone operations manual, FM 100-5. At the time, the role of atomic weapons in U.S. policy was highly controversial. In this manual, the army simply ignored the issue altogether, giving it merely one paragraph. The manual concluded that the threatening effects of "radiological weapons" could be countered by "increased dispersion" but had no more to say about the topic.[53]

The new manual was much more concerned with the techniques for war on the nonatomic battlefield, particularly in Europe. As one analyst has put it, "Although the Army did not rule out the possibility of operations elsewhere, its doctrine was increasingly oriented toward a European type battlefield reminiscent of World War II."[54] The doctrine described the purpose of the offensive as "the destruction of the effectiveness of the enemy's armed forces and of his will to fight."[55] To accomplish this, the manual emphatically endorsed traditional army methods of warfare based more on the sheer concentration of overwhelming firepower than on maneuver tactics. Specifically, the destruction of enemy forces was to be accomplished by a combination of main and secondary attacks. In the main attacks, which involved the bulk of available forces, "the greatest possible offensive power is concentrated to bring about a decision." The aim of the supporting secondary attacks was to "render maximum assistance to the main attack."[56]

Two forms of offensive tactics, envelopment and penetration, were discussed. To be sure, the manual did not exclude maneuver and even went so far as to endorse an essentially maneuver-oriented tactic as the preferred method of operations. The envelopment, the manual stated, "seeks to surround that portion of the enemy's forces both in front of and on the objective [i.e., the terrain being fought over]."[57] But penetration operations, where "the main attack is directed to a penetration of a hostile front," was discussed much more prominently. In these operations, the main attack centered around the application of firepower and involved "three separate impulses"—"the initial breakthrough of the hostile position, a widening of the gap thus created by enveloping one or both interior hostile flanks, and the seizure of the objective. Exploitation which follows the seizure of the objective would include the destruction of the hostile forces enveloped."[58]

As for defensive operations, the manual stated that "the general object of defensive combat is to gain time pending the development of more favorable conditions for undertaking the offensive."[59] Defensive operations were primarily intended for maintaining control of the battle area at any cost. In practice, this meant that covering forces placed forward of the main battle area would delay and disorganize the enemy's advance, preventing the enemy from locating the actual center of the battle area.[60]

The main battle area to be defended consisted of a "zone of resistance" in which a series of occupied defense areas were organized for forward defense. The manual envisioned defense in depth rather than a linear concentration of forces. Large armored reserves would back up the armored and infantry-heavy units in the main battle position, participate in counterattacks, or occupy rear positions. If (and when) the attacking enemy penetrated the covering forces, it would encounter a defense made up of "islands of resistance" that would "canalize the attacker's forces and disorganize the cohesiveness of his attack."[61]

The biggest problem with implementing the army's doctrine was that both the offensive and defensive tactics the manual endorsed required massive forces, particularly if the tactics were to be successful in Europe. But the mobilization of the early 1950s had not yet begun, and the army was still a skeleton of its World War II size. The West Europeans were expected to contribute some manpower and materiel to the effort, but they were still recuperating from a major war and were not willing or able to begin a massive buildup of their armed forces. The army, therefore, had to reconcile the ambitious goals of its doctrine with limited manpower and material resources available for the task.

To help resolve this dilemma, the army prioritized the development of the tank and the helicopter. Tank development proceeded relatively smoothly. In 1946 the Stillwell Board was constituted by the army to review the lessons of World War II and to make specific recommendations as to how the army could proceed in force procurement. The Stillwell Board (named after its chairman, Joseph Stillwell) hailed the performance of the tank, especially noting the performance of armored divisions both in a primary attack role and in backing up infantry.[62] The board recommended that the army develop an array of tanks and antitank weapons and concluded that "the best antitank weapon is a better tank."[63] The tank was obviously a tool for the ground campaign and of little interest to the air force. The decision to accelerate its development was strictly an army matter, and there was little resistance to its increased procurement.

This was not the case with the helicopter. The helicopter continued to be a subject of dispute between the army and the air force, the latter doing all it could to forestall its development. In the years immediately following the war, the army envisaged an extremely limited support role for the helicopter—for example, in assisting ship-to-shore operations. As the mobile-area defense concept matured, however, a more significant role for the helicopter emerged. The army initially intended to procure its helicopters through the air force. The air arm practically refused to build them; in an era of fiscal austerity, the air force's priority was procuring SAC bombers such as the B-36. When army Lieutenant General James Gavin discussed the matter with the air force director of requirements, he was told "the helicopter is aerodynamically unsound. . . . No matter what the Army says, I know that it does not need any."[64] Thus, development fell to the marines, who saw the helicopter as a means of adapting amphibious warfare to the atomic era.[65] Finally, the helicopter would be produced for extensive use in military operations.

THE NAVY PLANS AND THE ADMIRALS' REVOLT

At this time, the navy once again started to emphasize its nonnuclear capabilities in its planning. A navy study completed in June 1948, at the time of the Berlin Blockade, typified the evolution in navy thinking. The study noted the carrier's contribution to the air offensive but

- did not specifically offer the carrier-based forces as an alternate to SAC and expressed reservations about the strategic air mission itself.

- said that control of the seas and the initiation of ground offensives must be considered along with, or in place of, strategic bombing.
- argued that attacks on cities were not as important as attacks on Soviet southern-based oil fields and principal naval and antisubmarine warfare (ASW) bases.
- identified ASW as the first mission of the carrier task forces. In pursuit of ASW capabilities, carrier forces would destroy and blockade "enemy submarine bases by atomic, radiological, conventional bombing or mine attacks."
- identified other carrier-based missions as support for amphibious forces, air cover for support forces, and convoys in sea lanes of communications.[66]

Thus, the navy returned to its traditional planning priorities. Strategic air campaigns were now blatantly criticized as a departure from proven war-fighting methods. War plans emphasizing control of the seas along with power projection were advocated.

Whereas the navy had previously put forth its case for the CVA-58 in terms of its contribution to the strategic air campaign, it was now advocated for its flexibility in carrying out conventional missions. Navy CNO Chester Nimitz, in public elaborations of the navy's new approach, assumed that a Soviet attack would commence with an air campaign against the United States, followed by ground attacks against U.S. occupation forces still in Europe. His response involved

- initial U.S. defense operations devoted to the air defense of the continental United States (CONUS);
- protection of sea lanes of communication in Europe;
- reinforcement or evacuation of U.S. occupation troops in Europe;
- an offensive follow-up exploiting U.S. technological superiority, with weapons deployed in extensive quantities; and
- a leading role for the navy in ASW, air defense, offensive bombing operations, and amphibious assaults.

Nimitz envisaged the use of carrier aircraft and shipboard missiles to blunt enemy air attacks at sea during the initial defensive phases of battle. Globally deployed fleets could serve as mobile air bases, and the navy's and marine corps's amphibious-assault capabilities would provide the spearhead for the final component of his strategy: invasion and occupation of the enemy homeland.[67] This final part, stressing an army offensive, was a direct repudiation of the air force, which viewed such operations as largely obsolete.

On April 23, 1949, Defense Secretary Louis Johnson canceled the CVA-58 (USS *United States*) carrier. Though Johnson's decision was primarily economic, he justified it as avoiding a duplication of air force capabilities. This seemed to ignore all the navy's arguments and efforts to reorient its forces for traditional missions. As if to rub salt into the wound, three months later, on July 5, Johnson set a tentative carrier level of only four ships (later adjusted to six), down from FY1950's initial allocation of eight.

These actions brought the disputes between the navy and the air force to new levels. In public hearings over unification and strategy held in the summer of 1949, navy officials vehemently expressed their consternation over trends in U.S. force planning. The cancellation of the CVA-58 led to the resignation of Navy Secretary John Sullivan and to the creation of an attack group led by Admiral Arleigh Burke.

The "revolt of the admirals," as the incident has become known, was unprecedented. Never before had interservice rivalries been publicly aired to this extent. In the hearings, a number of admirals and other high-ranking naval officials vented their frustration over the administration's "single-weapon strategy." They were especially critical of the air force's new B-36 bomber, which they argued was redundant in capability to their supercarrier. They questioned the utility of strategic bombing against lower intensity threats, such as the Soviet pressures in Greece and Turkey in 1947, and pointed to the carrier's contribution in defusing those crises through a naval "show of force" in the region.

The admirals argued that naval air power could be widely deployed, was inherently mobile, and was able to strike far inland. It could subtly distinguish between targets (what the air force's heavy bombers were, implicitly, unable to do) and thus limit the war's geographical area and duration. The supercarrier was now advocated because of its flexibility. The supercarrier, it was argued, could perform the navy's traditional missions such as providing a peacetime presence and, if required, could deliver the atomic bomb.

The generally shrill tenor of the navy's presentation worked against it. The navy appeared (correctly) to be "sour graping," and some of the navy's more caustic criticisms of the B-36 proved to be simply untrue. In the aftermath of the spectacle, a number of naval officers were forced to resign.[68] The budget for national defense remained below $14 billion, and navy allocations were slashed by $33 million.[69] Its total operating aircraft was cut to 7,783, or 3,000 below FY1949 levels. The navy pushed for an additional $300 million amendment for naval air aviation but this was turned down. The navy leaders were in a quandary. They remained skeptical about the strategic air mission, but they were getting nowhere in their efforts to acquire the forces necessary for conventional operations.

The naval budgetary dilemma was resolved essentially through a plan to procure tactical aviation to augment the forces required for sea control. In August 1949, the air warfare division of the office of the Division CNO (Air), OP-55, released a study spelling out specific roles for naval air assets based upon the delineation of functions in the 1947 National Security Act and in the Key West agreement. The navy's prime mission was identified as "control of vital sea areas and protection of vital sea lines of communication."[70] The study concluded that the Soviet antisubmarine threat had been exaggerated and said that present naval capabilities could control it through a "timely and aggressive anti-submarine campaign employing carrier air strikes, aerial minelaying, and anti-submarine subs as the spearheads, backed by the more conventional measures, such as barrier patrols, convoy escorts, and ASW hunter-killer carrier groups." The OP-55 study argued that Soviet tactical air forces were the most serious threat to the navy's ability to control the sea lanes in the eastern Atlantic and the Mediterranean over the next ten years. The report recommended that the navy focus on the development of general purpose fighter aircraft with "both offensive and defensive capabilities and on day-attack and close air-support attack airplanes." The study pressed for the CVA-58 but noted that smaller, more versatile carriers could be substituted if necessary.[71]

The navy's new plan was initially rejected as too costly, and the air force argued that it could carry out the tactical missions the navy envisaged. In fact, the air force had been gradually decreasing its total stockpile of tactical aircraft since December 1948, when the service placed TAC under CAC's control. Thus, the air force would have had to rely on its heavy bombers for such missions. Not surprisingly, navy leaders were extremely skeptical that SAC would readily allocate its bombers for such purposes.

But events outside the air force's control (in particular, the invasion of South Korea by the North) led to increased funding for naval tactical aviation and numerous other systems not strictly geared toward the aerial bombardment mission. Indeed, events in late 1949 and 1950 led to a fundamental reassessment of U.S. national security policy and to a comprehensive effort to rebuild U.S. general purpose forces. That era is discussed in the next chapter.

NOTES

1. Quotation is reprinted in John Lewis Gaddis, *Strategies of Containment* (New York: Oxford University Press, 1982), p. 9.

2. For example, the Soviets had agreed on September 11, 1945, to the participation of France and China in discussions at an upcoming meeting in London; on October 26, 1945, Soviet Foreign Minister Molotov recanted on this. Walter Millis, ed., *The Forrestal Diaries* (New York: Viking Press, 1951), p. 103.

3. Quoted in Millis, *Forrestal Diaries*, p. 134. In a conversation with Forrestal, Justice William O. Douglas called Stalin's speech "the declaration of World War III" (Millis, *Forrestal Diaries*, p. 134).

4. George Kennan, "Telegram to the Secretary of State," February 22, 1946, in *Foreign Relations of the United States*, vol. VI (Washington, D.C.: U.S. Department of State, 1969), p. 700.

5. George Kennan (Mr. X), "The Sources of Soviet Conduct," *Foreign Affairs* XXV (July 1947): 566–682.

6. Kennan, *Telegram*, p. 707.

7. Margaret Truman writes that "this report . . . has been considered one of the primary documents of the cold war, and the assumption seems to have been made by numerous historians that it profoundly shaped the thinking of the Truman Administration. I can say without qualification that such an assertion is nonsense." Margaret Truman, *Harry S. Truman* (New York: William Morrow and Co., 1973), p. 309. This may be an overstatement, however.

8. Interview with the author, April 11, 1989.

9. Ken Hechler, *Working With Truman: A Personal Memoir of the White House Years* (New York: G.P. Putnam's Sons, 1982), p. 45. Robert Underhill writes that "the report represented the first attempt to articulate a policy line toward the Soviet Union at a time when the cooperative wartime alliance was falling apart and the United States was searching for a new foreign policy." Robert Underhill, *The Truman Persuasions* (Ames, Iowa: Iowa State University Press, 1981), p. 193. Arthur Krock, then chief Washington correspondent for the *New York Times*, has written that the report charted with "startling prescience . . . the shape and thrust of Truman's subsequent great programs. Arthur Krock, *Memoirs: Sixty Years on the Firing Line* (New York: Funk and Wagnalls, 1968), p. 224.

10. *American Relations with the Soviet Union* (the Clifford-Elsey Report), transmitted to the president on September 24, 1946, reprinted in full in Krock, *Memoirs*, Appendix A, pp. 419–482, 477.

11. Krock, *Memoirs*, p. 477.

12. The United States, however, was not entirely successful. The Soviets seized some northern Japanese islands shortly after the war and continue to occupy them to this day.

13. Document 577, "The Truman Doctrine," March 12, 1947, in Henry Steele Commanger, ed., *Documents of American History* (New York: Appleton-Century-Crofts, Inc., 1949), p. 721.

14. The Truman Doctrine may have led to increased Soviet mischief rather than a diminishment. One writer has noted that "in response to Harry S. Truman's declaration of a crusade against communism and the depiction of the world as an unconstrained struggle between free people and those who sought to s ubjugate them, the Soviets moved over to the offensive. . . . Soviet policy became assertively confrontational, the process of installing pro-Soviet regimes in the states of Eastern Europe was hastened, and the constraints on the communist parties of Western Europe were lifted." Michael MccGwire, *Military Objectives in Soviet Foreign Policy* (Washington, D.C.: The Brookings Institution, 1987), p. 317.

15. Mister X, *Sources*, p. 575.

16. JCS, Joint Strategic Survey Committee, *Overall Effect of Atomic Bomb on Warfare and Military Organization*, 30 Oct. 1945 (NSA).

17. These and all subsequent budget-related figures throughout this text are from Office of the Assistant Secretary of Defense (Comptroller), *National Defense Budget Estimates for FY 1988/1989*, May 1987, or (as indicated) the subsequent edition.

18. Samuel Huntington, "The Interim Years: World War II to January, 1950," in Raymond O'Conner, ed., *American Defense Policy in Perspective* (New York: John Wiley and Sons, 1965), p. 303.

19. Quoted in David Alan Rosenberg, "American Postwar Air Doctrine and Organization: The Navy Experience," in Alfred Hurley and Robert Ehrhart, eds., *Air Power and Warfare* (Washington, D.C.: Office of Air Force History, 1979), p. 247.

20. Quoted in John Greenwood, "The Emergence of the Postwar Strategic Air Force, 1945–1953," in Hurley and Ehrhart, *Air Power*, p. 219.

21. On V-J day, the army air force had 218 combat groups, compared to 109 in early 1946. In approximately the same period, navy personnel fell from 3,400,000 men to 1,600,000.

22. Figures in Samuel Huntington, "The Interim Years: World War II to January, 1950," in Raymond O'Conner, ed., *American*

Defense Policy in Perspective (New York: John Wiley and Sons, 1965), p. 299.

23. Quoted in B.U. Davis, *Admirals, Politics, and Defense Policy* (Princeton: Princeton University Press, 1962), p. 466.

24. Edward Kolodziej, *The Uncommon Defense and Congress* (Columbus: Ohio State University, 1966), p. 39.

25. Millis, *Forrestal Diaries*, pp. 165–166.

26. John Norton Moore and Robert F. Turner, *The Legal Structure of Defense Organization*, memorandum prepared for the President's Blue Ribbon Commission on Defense Management, January 15, 1986 (Washington, D.C.: GPO, 1986), p. 17.

27. Kolodziej, *Uncommon Defense*, p. 39.

28. This program was also initiated because of the navy's concerns about a Soviet submarine fleet, spurred by the Soviet capture of a number of German U-boats in World War II. Rosenberg, "Navy Experience," p. 250.

29. U.S. Navy, Chief of Naval Operations, *Principles and Applications of Naval Warfare*, United States Fleet Publication no. 1 (1947) p. 3-4.

30. Kolodziej, *Uncommon Defense*, p. 66. Kolodziej points out that the navy's actual force procurement at this time hardly supported its rhetoric: for FY1948 the navy requested 579 planes, "well below the 2115 aircraft needed annually to replace those lost to attrition or obsolescence."

31. Fleet Publication no. 1 (1947), p. 11-3.

32. Fleet Publication no. 1 (1947), pp. 4-3 through 4-4.

33. Strategic Planning Division, *Study of Fundamentals For The Development of Naval Requirements*, 4 March 1947, in Naval Historical Center, Archives, Records of the Strategic Planning Division, Box 194, p. 6.

34. Rosenberg, "Navy Experience," p. 251.

35. Rosenberg, "Navy Experience," p. 253.

36. World War II operational planning document FM 100-20, *Command and Employment of Air Power* (War Department, 21 July 1943).

37. Even the air force, however, fell prey to the budgetary ax. The 70 groups it requested was cut by the War Department to 58, 12 at skeletonized levels. See Kolodziej, *Uncommon Defense*, p. 60.

38. Millis, *Forrestal Diaries*, p. 383.

39. Morton Halperin and David Halperin, "The Key West Key," *Foreign Policy* 53 (Winter 1983–84): 117.

40. Millis, *Forrestal Diaries*, pp. 392–393.

41. Richard G. Davis, *The 31 Initiatives* (Washington, D.C.: United States Office of Air Force History, United States Air Force, 1987), p. 9. In a 1952 agreement, the army was specifically limited to fixed-wing aircraft no greater than 5,000 pounds in weight.

42. For a good review of the various supplements and amendments, see *Defense Organization: The Need for Change*, Staff Report to the Committee on Armed Services, U.S. Senate, October 16, 1985 (Washington, D.C.: U.S. Government Printing Office, 1985), pp. 436–438.

43. Greenwood, "Emergence," p. 233.

44. Paul Hammond, *Organizing For Defense* (Princeton: Princeton University Press, 1961), p. 238.

45. Robert F. Futrell, *Ideas, Concepts, Doctrine: A History of Basic Thinking in the United States Air Force, 1907–1964* (Maxwell AFB, Alabama: Air University Press, 1974), p. 155. See also, Davis, *31 Initiatives*, p. 9.

46. Detailed in Davis, *31 Initiatives*, as well as Moore and Turner, *Defense Organization*.

47. Joint Strategic Plans Group of the JCS, *"Broiler:" A Joint Outline War Plan Based On the Assumptions, Strategic Concept, Basic Undertakings, and Initial Operations* (November 8, 1947), p. 3, 48. (NSA).

48. Western powers ruled out a military response to the Berlin Blockade; they were unprepared and unwilling to risk total war with the Soviet Union. A remarkably extensive airlift was undertaken instead. The Soviets, no more anxious for war than the West, did not challenge it. To feed the 2.5 million West Berliners, Western planes landing at three-minute intervals eventually flew over 13,000 tons of food into Berlin daily. This was 60 percent more than the 8,000 tons that had previously been sent in by ground. One analyst has noted that "by the spring of 1949, West Berliners were eating more than at the beginning of the blockade—and considerably more than the East Berliners!" John Spanier, *American Foreign Policy since World War II* (New York: Praeger Publishers, 1974), p. 62. In May, the Soviets ended the blockade.

49. Greenwood, "Emergence," p. 234.

50. And most unexpectedly. At that time, American experts projected a Soviet capability in 1954.

51. As discussed, the air force was able to use its forces effectively in the Berlin airlift.

52. General Omar N. Bradley, "Creating A Sound Military Force," *Military Review* (May 1949): 3–6.

53. Department of the Army, Field Manual (FM) 100-5, *Regulations* (Washington, D.C.: August 1949), (hereafter referred to as FM 100-5 [1949]), p. 60.

54. Major Robert Doughty, *The Evolution of US Army Tactical Doctrine, 1946–1976*, Leavenworth Papers no. 1 (Fort Leavenworth, Kansas: Combat Studies Institute, 1979), p. 2.

55. FM 100-5 (1949), p. 80.

56. FM 100-5 (1949), p. 81.

57. FM 100-5 (1949), p. 82.

58. FM 100-5 (1949), p. 85–86.

59. FM 100-5 (1949), p. 120.

60. Defensive operations are discussed in chapter 9, FM 100-5 (1949). See also Doughty, *Evolution*, p. 6.

61. Ibid.

62. "The uniformly better performance of infantry, in any operation, when closely supported by tanks is probably the biggest tactical lesson of the European campaign." *Types of Divisions, Post-war Army*, General Board, U.S. Forces, European theater, p. 8. Accordingly, tanks were added to the infantry division, and by the late 1940s, the infantry division contained a tank battalion, plus one tank company per regiment. Doughty, *Evolution*, p. 5.

63. General Joseph Stillwell, *Report on War Department Equipment Board*, U.S. Army Command and General Staff College, January 19, 1956. Quoted in Doughty, *Evolution*, p. 4.

64. General James Gavin, *War and Peace in the Space Age* (New York: Harper and Brothers, 1958), pp. 109–111.

65. Gavin, *War and Peace*.

66. The navy's General Board study, *National Security and Navy Contributions Thereto for the Next Ten Years*, released 25 June 1948, described in Rosenberg, "Navy Experience," pp. 255–257. The report advised against the "sole reliance on the complete success of violent and irretrievable departures from established concepts and techniques of war."

67. C.E. Nimitz, "Employment of Naval Forces—Who Commands The Sea—Controls Trade," *CNO Monthly Newsletter*, June 1948, p. 6.

68. General David C. Jones, chairman of the Joint Chiefs of Staff under President Carter, points out that as a result of the revolt of the admirals and other publicly aired disagreements (which will be discussed), the services now broker their differences in private, presenting a façade of unity where in fact no such unity exists. "Now, we don't have the Navy saying there's a better way to spend $25 billion than buying one hundred B-1 bombers or the Air Force saying, rather than pulling the battleships out of mothballs, that money would be better spent on airlift or on munitions." Quoted in Hedrik Smith, *The Power Game* (New York: Random House, 1988), p. 202.

69. The army's budget was cut by $123 million, while the air force's budget request was raised by $800 million. The $800-million air force supplement sealed the fate of a program being considered very seriously by the Truman administration, Universal Military Training (UMT) for the American people. UMT was intended primarily as a deterrent to make clear to Western Europe and the Soviets that the United States was prepared to go to war when needed. The idea never gained support among the citizenry and, with the advent of a dominant SAC, lost all support.

70. Quoted in Rosenberg, "Navy Experience," p. 261. Rosenberg points out that "the Navy's willingness to accept this definition did not indicate that it had capitulated to external pressures, but rather that the identification of naval air missions suitable to the postwar environment had given the service the confidence to pursue its own path without fear of restriction and encroachment."

Granted the navy was probably worn from its recent experiences and welcomed the chance to develop strategy and force levels away from bureaucratic and parochial pressures, but given the decidely deleterious and exhausting results of the unification hearings and that budget allocations for the navy were steadily decreasing, it would seem that some capitulation on the navy's part occurred.

71. Air Warfare Division (OP-55), *Study on Future Development of Carrier Aviation With Respect to Both Aircraft and Aircraft Carriers*, August 22, 1949, p. 4, quoted and discussed in Rosenberg, "Navy Experience," pp. 262–263.

3
Era II: NSC-68 and the Korean War

NSC-68

In the early summer of 1948, President Truman asked the Joint Chiefs of Staff to submit a defense budget based solely on their perceptions of U.S. national security requirements. The JCS essentially added up all the services' "wish lists" and came up with a request of about $30 billion. Truman found this totally unacceptable. In August, he had Defense Secretary James Forrestal establish an advisory board composed of the highest budgetary officials from each service to pare down the JCS budget. In December the McNarney Board (named after its chairman, Joseph T. McNarney) submitted a $23.6-billion budget. Forrestal whittled the still unacceptable figure down to $16.9 billion. The president remained unmovable from his $14.4-billion ceiling, calling into question the purpose of the exercise and forcing Forrestal to defend the budget as a "peace budget." If a conflict broke out and military mobilization was required, the air force would buy time for the army and navy to mobilize, and additional funds would be allocated for defense at that time.

By 1950, it was clear that Truman's budgets could not adequately support the growing number of overseas bases and U.S. global commitments. By this time, the United States had established an extensive number of global alliances, including the North Atlantic Treaty Organization (NATO) in Western Europe. But the means to support such alliances were constricted as defense manpower levels steadily decreased, from 1.61 million (total) in FY1949 to 1.46 million a year later.[1] As Congress funded the air campaign, the navy and the army absorbed about 80 percent of those cutbacks. In short, as one writer has concluded, "strategic and budgetary policies were neither allies or friends. They were essentially strangers to each other. . . . In a number of important senses, too, the President's military budget was even unrelated to the strategic picture which the administration drew for popular consumption."[2]

By July 1949 even the views of George Kennan were beginning to evolve. Originally, Kennan perceived containment to be a largely political and economic policy. But he had come to accept the importance of the military component. Kennan argued that by its excessive reliance on SAC, the United States had limited itself to only two responses to Soviet aggression: atomic bombing and doing nothing. He urged a buildup of ground forces, including at least two mechanized and mobile army divisions trained and ready to fight "brush" wars when needed.[3]

Still, Kennan was increasingly being shut out of the policy-making process, and in early 1950, Secretary of State Dean Acheson appointed Paul Nitze, Kennan's successor at the State Department's policy planning staff, to chair a small committee of State and Defense Department representatives reviewing U.S. defense policy. Under Nitze's guidance, this group produced National Security Council document NSC–68, which enunciated a dramatic change from the containment strategy put forth by Kennan in his *Foreign Affairs* article.[4]

Essentially the break from Kennan was in NSC–68's greater emphasis on the military component of containment. The context within which Kennan had originally formulated his doctrine had changed. The economic basis of containment made sense when economic aid was Europe's most urgent need; now, it seemed clear that military assistance had to be the first order of business. In 1946 the United States enjoyed a nuclear monopoly, but in 1950 the United States simply had nuclear superiority. This made an over-reliance on atomic weapons seem increasingly dubious to many decision makers (outside of those in the air force). Threats of bombing Soviet cities with atomic weapons may have made sense in the latter 1940s, but by 1950 that policy seemed to need revision. The United States simply did not have the atomic weapons required to attack all the urban-industrial Soviet targets recommended by the air force. Logic seemed to dictate that instead of threatening Soviet cities, atomic weapons would most effectively be targeted against the Soviet Union's atomic delivery systems and its war-sustaining industries. The United States therefore began to develop targeting plans that included such targets.[5]

The Soviets were also playing an increasingly active role in world affairs by lending their active support to communist insurgencies and Marxist-based political movements, such as Eurocommunism. The United States felt compelled to develop military strategies that would not only better address the problem of a

U.S.-Soviet confrontation but would also be more responsive to the requirements of deterrence at lower levels.

NSC–68 was the first high-level attempt to systematize such strategies. Without challenging the overall objective of U.S. policy, NSC–68 challenged the way containment was being implemented. NSC–68 emphasized "the inadequacy of the Western capability to meet limited military challenges due to a lack of conventional forces, shortcomings in the Western alliance system, and the military and economic weaknesses of Western Europe."[6] NSC–68 assumed that by 1954, which it labeled "the year of maximum danger," the Soviet Union would possess a nuclear stockpile of up to 200 warheads, threatening the viability of the U.S. nuclear deterrent.[7] As a consequence, a U.S.-Soviet "standoff" could develop, where the fear of retaliation would make both the United States and the USSR more reluctant to cross the atomic threshold. Such a standoff, with the threat of a U.S. atomic response neutralized, meant that Soviet adventurism could become more likely. When the Soviets chose not to demobilize their armed forces after the war, the problem was made worse for the West. To the authors of NSC–68, therefore, it was clear that "a substantial and rapid building up of strength in the free world is necessary to support a firm policy intended to check and roll back the Kremlin's drive for world domination."[8]

NSC–68 took a much broader view of the Soviet threat than before, asserting that "the assault on free institutions is worldwide now, and in the context of the present polarization of power a defeat of free institutions anywhere is a defeat everywhere." Such a formulation, explicit in its perception of a growing number of threats to U.S. interests, could obviously not be supported by Truman's capped budgets. NSC–68 rejected the Truman administration's perception of limited resources. Its authors avoided documenting specific budget figures but privately supported $50 billion in annual defense expenditures.[9]

NSC–68 has more in common with the Clifford-Elsey Report than Kennan's long telegram or his *Foreign Affairs* article. NSC–68 posed an extremely dangerous and imminent threat and elevated the military component of containment to prominence.

In the concept of containment, the maintenance of a strong military posture is deemed to be essential for two reasons: (1) as an ultimate guarantee of our national security and (2) as an indispensable backdrop to the policy. . . . Without superior aggregate military strength, in being and readily mobilizable, a policy of containment . . . is no more than a policy of bluff.

Furthermore, NSC–68 was unambiguous about Soviet objectives and the proper Western response to the Soviet challenge.

Our aim in applying force must be to compel the acceptance of our terms consistent with our objectives, and our capabilities for the application of force should, therefore, within the limits of what we can sustain over the long pull, be congruent to the range of tasks that we may encounter.[10]

A reflection of NSC–68's influence is that many of the key ideas it espoused made their way into the national security planning of future administrations. For example, the notion of strengthening deterrence by meeting but not escalating a Soviet attack found its way into U.S. nuclear policy in the mid-1960s, in Robert McNamara's counterforce/no cities doctrine, in James Schlesinger's Limited Nuclear Options of 1974, in Harold Brown's countervailing strategy of 1980, and in numerous policy statements that emanated from the Reagan defense establishment. The need for a conventional buildup to meet an ever-growing number of commitments and interests was emphasized by President Kennedy in his strategy of flexible response and was reportedly reiterated by President Reagan in his Defense Guidance of May 20, 1982. Even Reagan's window of vulnerability scenarios, based as they were on the notion of an imminent Soviet nuclear threat, somewhat echoed NSC–68's fixation on a year of maximum danger. The Kennedy and Reagan defense programs also shared with NSC–68 a costly price tag. Truman's overall budget request (after supplemental requests) for FY1951 was over $23 billion, about a 75 percent increase from the previous year.[11]

Unlike Kennan's conception of force as but one element of national security policy, NSC–68 saw force as the *primary* element. Prior to NSC–68, Truman and Kennan favored economic initiatives, such as the Marshall Plan and aid to Greece and Turkey, to combat Soviet aggression. Where Kennan tended to make distinctions between vital and peripheral interests, NSC–68 made no such distinctions. The earlier enunciation of containment emphasized that the *potential* U.S. war production capacity deterred conflict; NSC–68 called for a massive buildup of the armed forces to convey the willingness of the United States to defend and protect its interests, thereby deterring aggression in the first place.

NSC–68 did not go uncriticized. To many, it seemed to assume unlimited expenditures, and its strategy of measured responses to aggression seemed in some ways to risk sacrificing the geostrategic initiative to the adversary. Its commitment to meet Communist aggression at any corner of the globe risked allowing the enemy to pick terrain favorable to him and potentially forcing terms of battle, which could prove decidedly unfavorable to the United States.[12]

To many, North Korea's invasion into the South and the lengthy U.S. involvement in that faraway theater seemed to vindicate the latter criticisms. The U.S. commitment in Europe helped discourage any notion of direct Soviet hostilities there. The Communist takeover in China, however, opened up a whole new theater of operations for the Communist "monolith," which was now seen to comprise both the Soviet Union and China. As John Spanier notes, the fall of China "shifted the balance of power in the Far East against the United States. The United States no longer confronted only Russia; it was now faced with the challenge of the combined power of the Sino-Soviet bloc. . . . The recovery of Europe and China's collapse, then, created a vacuum in the East and turned Russian pressure toward Asia."[13] The North Korean invasion seemed to validate both the tenets of and the criticisms engendered by NSC–68. The administration based its decision to fight in part on the conviction that all U.S. interests were vital. The war appeared to validate the perception that the Soviets would fight by proxy where direct action was precluded. Finally, the war showed that the atomic air threat would not alone deter aggression.

At the time, the United States was simply not prepared for a challenge like the one posed by the North Koreans. In June 1950, the navy had only one carrier, an amphibious group, and a small screening force of cruisers and destroyers stationed in the western Pacific. Though in early July the United States sent the Seventh Fleet to the Straits of Formosa, a protracted battle was still unforeseen. SAC could have commenced bombing campaigns, but to do so would have been an unabashed escalation of hostilities—precisely what the framers of NSC–68 sought to avoid. Moreover, the criticism that NSC–68 could lead the United States into a protracted war that it could not adequately fight seemed validated. North Korea's invasion showed that the Communists had no intention of challenging U.S. control of the seas—a traditional strength—but would challenge the United States on the ground, where it was least prepared.

Truman was committed to thwarting the Korean aggression, yet in 1950 all of the army's divisions, except one in Europe, were skeletonized. Infantry regiments had been reduced from three to two battalions and artillery battalions had been reduced from three to two batteries. Tank companies were included in each division, but the first units, which arrived in Korea on July 18, 1950, were quickly depleted.[14]

Truman's FY1951 supplementals were beneficial for all the services. For additional aircraft procurement alone, the navy and the air force were granted an additional $100 million and $200 million, respectively. The navy, having so recently identified for itself a tactical role in the air campaign, could now plan on maintaining over 8,000 planes by mid-1951.[15]

The navy also received 192 ship-construction orders in the three supplemental bills, most of which were landing craft and minesweepers. Total fighting ships in operation rose from 243 to 323, and total active naval vessels rose from 683 to 1,044. The air force, with 48 incomplete air groups, gradually expanded its request in each supplemental, for a total of 87 groups. The air force requested more than 5,000 planes over the fiscal year.

The biggest benefactor was the army. Allocations to army ordnance centers rose from $637 million to $7 billion. Army weapon increases were across the board, as additional tanks, personnel carriers, jeeps, small arms (such as the 3.5-inch bazooka, thought to be capable of piercing Soviet tanks), antiaircraft weapons, ammunition, and mobile artillery were procured.

Besides increasing the defense budget, Truman also strengthened U.S. forces in the Philippines, stepped up aid to the French against indigenous Indochinese revolutionary forces, and dispatched the Seventh Fleet into the Formosa Straits. By November 1950 hopes of a short war subsided, and the administration began to plan for a long engagement. Thus, in his budget request for FY1952, Truman identified the maintenance and supply of forces in Korea as the country's primary military requirement.[16] Truman also sought to increase the size of the armed forces to 3.5 million personnel by the end of the fiscal year, and he recommended a budget estimated at $46-billion dollars, or about a 100 percent increase from the prior year. This was divided almost evenly among the services, with the navy receiving somewhat less than the air force and the army.

In December 1950, the National Security Council (NSC) decided that the force levels set by the JCS for 1954 were to be pushed forward and met by June 30, 1952. The JCS later submitted revised estimates, calling for a 95-group air force, an 18-division army, and a navy built around 12 large carriers and 15 light and escort carriers. Most gratifying for the navy, allocations for the supercarrier and its first nuclear-powered submarine, the *Nautilus*, were included in the FY 1952 budget.[17] Its active force levels were raised to 1,116 vessels and 4,000 new airplanes. Finally the navy was acquiring the capabilities it had sought since the admirals' revolt.

Air force capabilities were also expanding. Not surprisingly, many air force leaders such as Curtis LeMay and Chief of Staff General Hoyt Vandenberg expressed some concern over how expansion would proceed. They supported expansion but not at the expense of SAC. In a memo to the other service chiefs, Vandenberg took a shot at NSC-68, arguing that "the Armed Forces cannot and should not expect this nation to build, and support indefinitely, a military structure fully prepared for all of the wartime tasks which are outlined in current war plans." Vandenberg directly related his concerns to the premises such as the "year of maximum danger" in NSC-68:

> By 1954, we will be entering an era in which atomic bombs should become much more plentiful. BUT, during the entire period under consideration, in fact, as far into the future as we now can see, our ONE MAJOR MILITARY ADVANTAGE over the USSR lies in the atomic field . . . . Facts dictate that in our current military strategy greater emphasis should be placed on air power [emphasis in original].[18]

Vandenberg recommended total air force wings be increased to 143 but amazingly advocated no increase in the number of tactical wings. As for LeMay, he was equally adamant in insisting SAC should be the air force's number-one priority. A memorandum summarizing LeMay's views indicates that in his opinion "if we concentrate on TAC air we may stop the Russian's army but we will lose the War because their industrial stockpile and production facilities will remain." In addition, LeMay was concerned that a concentration on TAC would lead to the production of "small yield nuclear bombs which would not do the job that [SAC] would need."[19] As the expansion continued and it became evident that SAC was going to grow, such opposition to the buildup declined somewhat. But it is interesting that even in the midst of the Korean War, the air force continued to seek an expansion of SAC at the expense of tactical air, which remained at 14 wings.

Although Truman sent four army divisions to Europe, the air force remained the essential component for U.S. operations in that theater. Air force leaders maintained that in the absence of rapid European rearmament, a strong SAC was vital to deter the Soviets there. Throughout the Korean War, SAC remained enormously popular within Congress. Senator Henry Cabot Lodge, appearing before the Senate Subcommittee on Military Appropriations on July 13, 1951, pushed for 150 air wings. In October the JCS accepted the air force recommendation for 143 wings, although Truman later pared this back to 133.[20]

THE KOREAN WAR

On May 1, 1950, Secretary of State Dean Acheson testified before the Senate Foreign Relations Committee that "if anything happens in Western Europe the whole business goes to pieces, and therefore our principal effort must be on building up the defenses, building up the economic strength of Western Europe, and so far as Asia is concerned, treating that as a holding operation."[21] The idea that Asia would be put on hold was consistent with the administration's "defensive perimeter" concept. Given the reliance on air power and the emasculated state of the army, the United States defined its interests in Asia in terms of where the United States believed it could effectively attack from the air, avoiding protracted and costly commitments. Thus a defensive perimeter was established in the Pacific, running from the Aleutians to Japan, through the Ryukyus (Okinawa) and to the Philippines. This formulation suggested that U.S. planners were relegating Korea to a secondary interest, outside the defensive perimeter as defined by the administration.

Thus, Korea was excluded from the U.S. defensive perimeter in large part because it was geographically inconvenient. Although the peninsula is accessible from the air on three sides, ground forces could easily be trapped there by massive numbers of Communist land forces coming over the Chinese border. Ultimately, though, it was in Korea that U.S. forces would be committed.

The North Koreans crossed the 38th parallel and invaded the South on June 25, 1950. Initially, the United States tried to stem the aggression with air and naval forces alone, but by July 18, the United States had to commit three army divisions (under the aegis of the United Nations and with UN-allied troops) to the battle. By August 2, additional amphibious ships arrived from the U.S. West Coast, and the marines immediately joined in the land battle. On July 2, only two months after Acheson's testimony before the Senate, the aircraft carrier *Valley Forge* arrived off the Korean west coast. By the end of the month, four carriers with over 200 navy and marine aircraft were on station around Korea.

The air force mobilized as well. The buildup advocated by NSC–68 was primarily to enhance conventional warfighting capabilities and was to be structured for contingencies precisely like Korea. Yet as noted, congressional sentiment favored SAC's air-attack mission, which by this time was fairly well entrenched in the air force's collective mindset. Thus, the bulk of the air force buildup was devoted to SAC.[22] Tactical air forces were largely sacrificed at the budgetary altar as the air force focused upon the strategic-bombing mission and structured its forces accordingly.

Over the next month, a defensive perimeter was established around the port city of Pusan. On September 15, UN Supreme Commander General Douglas MacArthur landed an amphibious force at Inchon, about 150 miles behind the North Korean lines. (While the war was primarily fought by U.S. forces, troops were formally sent to Korea under the aegis of the United Nations.)[23] The invasion force consisted of an army infantry division, a U.S. Marine Corps division, most of a marine aircraft wing, and supporting troops. A fleet of over 230 ships carried and supported these forces. The invasion forces drove northward, trapping about half the Korean army while the other half fled. Terms appeared favorable to the UN forces as they drove the North Korean forces upward to the Yalu River; however, this push triggered the entry of the Chinese Communist army into the war in November.

The Communists' November offensive was massive, forcing UN forces to withdraw south of Seoul. By April 1951, however, the allied forces had regrouped and pushed north to the 38th parallel. The Communists launched a new offensive, and the war degenerated into an inexorable pattern of give-and-take. MacArthur requested reinforcements and urged pressing forward. His goals were to unify Korea and to neutralize the Chinese Communist army's capacity to wage a quick and aggressive war. He did not think that the Soviet Union would directly enter the war in light of U.S. atomic superiority.

MacArthur advocated the following maneuvers: a naval blockade off the Chinese coast; air bombardment of China's industrial complex, communications network, supply depots, and troop assembly points; reinforcement of allied forces with Chinese Nationalist troops; and "diversionary action possibly leading to counterinvasion" by Chiang (the Nationalist leader) against the mainland.[24] MacArthur's proposals were ultimately rejected on three grounds: they were politically incompatible with the purposes of the Truman administration; they would require the United States to deplete resources from Western Europe; and according to the JCS, they were militarily unsound. Each of these will be briefly considered.

POLITICAL INCOMPATIBILITY

After the Inchon landing, the United States reassessed its political and military goals in the war. Initially, the United States sought a unified Korea. However, in the Sino-Soviet Pact of February 1950, the Soviet Union committed itself to supporting the Chinese if that country was directly attacked. Soviet involvement could be largely logistical, replenishing supplies and aircraft, or it could involve active participation in the war. In a more extreme scenario, the Soviets could launch a second offensive in Europe to divert U.S. fighting forces, possibly triggering a third world war. In any case, this agreement threw doubts on MacArthur's conviction that the Soviets would eschew active involvement in the conflict.

Faced with these considerations, the administration backed away from its goal of a unified Korea and reverted to seeking a truce between North and South and to restoring the status quo. The United States would seek a limited political settlement in lieu of a military victory. Such a settlement, however, was not to be obtained until July 27, 1953, three years after the war began and over six months into the administration of a new president.

LIMITED RESOURCES

Even if the Truman administration had wanted to go along with MacArthur's plans—which it did not—many U.S. military officials doubted that the United States could sustain the required effort. U.S. forces were still being rebuilt. The United States did not possess the resources to sustain a full-fledged offensive, which would almost certainly lead to a protracted ground war in Korea, and, at the same time, to assure the security of Western Europe. The United States could not afford to exhaust its resources in Korea if doing so would endanger the West Europeans.

MILITARY UNCERTAINTIES

Finally, the Joint Chiefs of Staff rejected MacArthur's proposals on military grounds. China was barely industrialized and most of its supplies came over land, so a naval blockade would have little impact. Similarly, aerial bombardment would have little effect because even a massive campaign to obliterate China's industry would do little to hinder the resupply effort from the Soviet Union. Air power, it was decided, would best serve an interdiction function against the 200 miles of logistical and supply lines in North Korea. The idea of employing Nationalist troops was dismissed because of their poor showing in the revolutionary war they had recently lost. Thus, MacArthur's approach to the conflict was rejected, and ultimately, he was recalled from Korea. The United States eventually achieved its political ends but not before three years of flesh and blood were expended in the process.

THE SERVICES IN KOREA

Besides the political constraints imposed upon the services, the problem that most hindered their effective prosecution of the war was their unpreparedness to fight it. World War II was still highly influential on their operational planning, even if that planning had been somewhat modified to exploit nuclear weapons. Army doctrine was revised in 1949 but in many ways was a restatement of its World War II planning. The navy relied on its 1947 fleet operations manual, and the air force doctrine had not been revised since 1943. The services had assumed that the next war would be global, although primarily European-based, and prepared accordingly. Hence, they were not only unprepared to fight a protracted ground war but lacked the proper doctrinal guidance for such operations.

General Matthew B. Ridgway, commander of the Eighth Army in Korea and U.S. commander in chief (CINC) in the Far East, described the army as in a state of "shameful unreadiness" at the outset of the Korean War.[25] As discussed, every division except one had been skeletonized, infantry and artillery battalions had been drastically cut, and tank companies, quickly dispatched from Europe to Korea, were unable to reinforce the war effort sufficiently. Many units sent to Korea also came from occupied Japan, depleting forces there.

Since American military planning assumed the next war would be global, according to Ridgway, "the concept of 'limited' war never entered our councils."[26] Doughty points out that

> in the initial dark and tumultuous days of this unexpected war, American soldiers paid a bloody price for this unpreparedness. . . . The combination of the terrain, weather and enemy tactics tended to hamper employment of much of the tactical doctrine and equipment of the Army which were oriented toward another World War that would be fought primarily in Europe . . . problems were encountered with the mountainous terrain, for it limited the full use of American mechanized and motorized might.[27]

Much of the doctrine in the army's FM 100-5 proved inapplicable to Korea. Plans to "envelop" the enemy (as an alternative to penetrating his defenses) and maneuvers to hold terrain by establishing an active defense were conducted, reflecting the national policy of calibrating efforts to hold, rather than overwhelm, the enemy. But the commanders responsible for such operations displayed little enthusiasm for them. Indeed, tactics were often developed on an ad hoc basis at the theater commander's discretion.[28]

In many instances, even if army leaders wanted to follow their own doctrine, the army's unpreparedness made it impossible to do so. Where the outnumbered UN troops would try to set up defensive formations, there would invariably be holes and exposed flanks. Enemy troops would infiltrate and occupy positions to the rear of the allied troops, from where they could attack command posts, support units, and artillery positions. Moreover, much of the American weaponry proved ineffective during the war. For example, the American rocket launchers were generally unable to deal with Russian T-34 tanks. They were only effective over short distances and could only penetrate limited areas of the tank hulls. The first American tanks to arrive were the very light M-24s, which were outmatched by the Soviet T-34s. American doctrine held that the best antitank weapon was a better tank, but in the early stages of the conflict, it was the Communists who were making the case.

When the Chinese entered the war, they exploited their superiority in manpower by overwhelming UN forces and operating from behind enemy lines. A portion of the attacking units would engage the rear-deployed forces while the remainder attempted to encircle the forward defenders. Most Communist attacks were at night. In these attacks, the enemy used concealment tactics and attacked from as close as possible, limiting warning time and making it difficult for the UN forces to employ effectively artillery and close air support.

In World War II, U.S. forces were generally on the offensive. In the early stages of the Korean War, U.S. forces were often forced to respond to enemy operations and were then usually forced into defensive roles. This often made for cumbersome and uncoordinated troop movements. A 1954 study of initial retrograde operations during the war concluded that "many . . . withdrawals were mob movements rather than military movements, and the men were cut to pieces."[29] The UN forces tried to develop a "main line of resistance," but the lack of equipment and manpower meant that the line was spread extremely thin, lacking the depth necessary to stop enemy attacks. In time, however, adjustments were made to increase the fighting capabilities of UN troops. Depth was accomplished by placing strong outposts forward of the main lines of resistance. Manpower levels were increased, and better equipment was produced and made available to the allied troops.

Over time, the UN forces gradually shifted toward a mobile defense. Troops were held in reserve, back from the front, to engage the enemy after he penetrated the initial line of defense. A number of tactics were developed, consistent with this new defensive doctrine. One, called the "fight and roll," was based upon the premise that, as put by Robert Doughty, "an inflexible line had little or no effect against a mass attack. Waves of troops could charge a position almost faster than they could be killed, and the smallest penetration allowed the attackers to envelop the remaining line." The defense would remain in position as long as possible to exact the highest price from the aggressor. Then, "a rapid and orderly preplanned withdrawal was conducted to a previously prepared defensive position. Although the defenders might be forced to occupy as many as five or six subsequent positions, it was 'inevitable' . . . that the surging mass would eventually halt."[30] As the tactic was carried out, local counterattacks would be launched by combined tank-infantry teams. These attacks would usually consist of massive concentrations of artillery fire. They were implemented to avoid unnecessarily exhausting valuable manpower against a much larger enemy. Another change was seen in the improved use of firepower. This resulted from better weapons—including new-generation bazookas, rifles, and machine guns—and from technical innovations. For example, battlefield-illumination techniques improved, increasing the capacity of the UN forces to fight at night. As discussed below, close and coordinated air support also contributed to the improved use of firepower.

In contrast to World War II, ammunition was not always available for the allied forces. Doughty notes that "despite the public uproar over the shortages, ammunition continued to be rationed since the long Pacific sea lines and insufficient road and rail networks compounded the delivery problem."[31] Tank divisions and transport carriers, so vital to success in World War II, played a secondary role in Korea to the infantry and artillery brigades. This was largely due to the Korean terrain, which was essentially inhospitable to major armored or mechanized unit operations, and to the need to respond quickly to the adversary's guerrilla and counterinsurgency tactics.

The Korean War did not validate the air force's doctrine of strategic bombing. The air force's emphasis on World War II–type air campaigns—if necessary, atomic—against enemy cities and industrial and war-making capacity was hardly applicable in Korea. SAC's B-29 bombers participated in limited bombing raids against North Korean targets in mid-1950 and returned to the United States in the fall. "The local peculiarities of the limited war," Robert Futrell notes, "did not permit a full exploitation of the strategic bombing function." He continues,

> because of the artificial boundaries of the conflict most of the production facilities that the Communists used to support their war effort could not be attacked. In the early months of the war the few war-supporting industries of North Korea were easily destroyed and after this very few targets could be found that would warrant a [large] medium bomber formation.[32]

Employing atomic weapons was ruled out. The North Korean forces were rarely concentrated enough to justify expending the limited atomic weapons actually available. After the Chinese entered the war, the allied forces had not yet stabilized at the demilitarized zone (DMZ) and were mostly retreating in a state of disarray. This limited options for effective counterattack involving nuclear weapons. Moreover, the European allies were emphatically opposed to introducing nuclear weapons. After the Chinese entered the war, Truman suggested that he might approve the use of atomic weapons, but this was strongly protested by British Prime Minister Clement Atlee and other European leaders.[33] Thus the air force was left to perform mostly tactical roles, such as air support for the ground forces, interdiction of enemy lines, and air transport.

The air force maintained control of the air during the Inchon invasion. Interdiction of the major lines of communication (LOCs) and isolation of the area around Inchon from enemy ground forces took place under the air superiority attained by the Fifth Air Force.[34] Under the direction of the Far East Air Force (FEAF), the Fifth Air Force developed an aggressive interdiction strategy and, in accordance with that strategy, began moving the interdiction effort northward. But the intervention of some 200,000 Chinese troops prevented the strategy from being fully implemented.

When the Chinese intervention forced the allies to retreat to Pusan, air strategy involved severing the North Korean logistical supply lines to the ground forces attempting to mount offensives at the Pusan perimeter and attacks against the ground forces themselves. At this time, when the combined North Korean and Chinese forces were striking at Pusan, deep into the South, air power was perhaps most effective. The close air support and interdiction attacks by the air force (as well as naval and marine aviation) depleted the enemy's strength and supplies, permitting the allies to maintain control of the Pusan perimeter.

The numerical superiority of the Chinese meant that direct air attacks against them might be necessary. MacArthur wanted the air forces to continue supplying close air support for the badly out-numbered allied forces and to assist in a full-scale offensive into North Korea. He planned to subject the bridges and LOCs used by the North Koreans to sustained air attack, thereby denying them their sanctuary. The North Koreans had developed a highly capable air force, but both it and the Chinese air force were decidedly inferior to the allied air forces. MacArthur's plan would have thus pitted an allied advantage—air power—against North Korean and Chinese forces, preserving the vastly outnumbered allied ground forces in the process.

The Joint Chiefs insisted that the Far East Command's air offensive go no farther than the Yalu River at the Korean and Manchurian Chinese border, unless the enemy initiated massive air attacks against the U.S.-led forces. If such attacks occurred, the allies were authorized to attack the airfields from which the attacks originated. By imposing these limits, however, the Joint Chiefs allowed the Chinese a sanctuary immediately across the Yalu River.

Air strategy shifted from close support of the ground forces to a strategy involving (1) offensive fighter patrols along the Yalu, (2) attacks against forward staging bases from which MiGs might strike Fifth Air Force airfields and the Eighth Army, and (3) intensive attacks against the main supply lines of the advancing Chinese armies.[35] On December 1, 1950, allied forces began to withdraw, and these air operations were the primary means of preventing the enemy's air and ground forces from pushing the allies out of Korea altogether. The JCS instructed MacArthur to employ maximum air power for interdiction and for attacking the advancing army. However, the Eighth Army was instructed to hold, rather than defeat or destroy, the opposing ground forces. Air power was required for this mission. This overextended resources and made interdiction missions less than optimally effective. Once the allies stabilized their retreat at the 38th parallel, interdiction became the primary mission for the Far East Air Force. After two or three weeks, it was hoped, the enemy's supplies would run out. If the Eighth Army could hold out that long, attrition would compel the Communists to forgo the offensive.

By focusing attacks on the Chinese and North Korean supply lines, the allies sought to convince the Communists that pursuing a military victory would be fruitless. The primary purpose of this strategy at this stage of the conflict was not to defeat the enemy. This would have required larger ground forces and a greater commitment of air power against enemy sanctuaries in Manchurian China. Rather, the strategy sought to *hold* the enemy's advances and prevent the Communist forces from successfully overrunning all of Korea, until a political settlement could be reached.

For the most part, therefore, air power was applied not to win but to apply maximum pressure on the Chinese to sign an armistice. The culmination of this tactic was the spring offensive of 1953 in which FEAF strategy was to inflict maximum destruction at key points, such as Pyongyang, the North Korean capital, and various North Korean power plants. Few targets were spared in this all-out effort aimed at bringing about an armistice.

THE NAVY EXPERIENCE

Korea was primarily a ground war. It was clearly not going to be fought for control of the seas; thus, the navy used its Pacific Fleet primarily to support the ground campaign. In the early stages of the conflict, however, this was not precisely the case. When North Korean troops first crossed the 38th parallel in 1950, most of the Pacific Fleet was immediately pressed into service. On July 2, the aircraft carrier *Valley Forge* arrived at the Korean west coast, and its aircraft commenced air strikes the next day. Additional amphibious ships arrived by early August.

At the start of the conflict, when allied forces were trying to establish a foothold on the Pusan Peninsula, naval air power worked closely with the air force to provide close air support for the ground troops and to attack northern targets. Together with the air force, the navy carried ground-troop reinforcements to the Naktong River line around Pusan and contributed enough firepower to permit the outnumbered ground troops to hold the line. Russell Weigley points out that before the battle for the Pusan Peninsula ended, four navy carriers—the *Valley Forge*, the *Philippine Sea*, and the smaller escort carriers *Badoeng Strait* and *Sicily*—were sending their fighters into the fray. The navy and marine forces also played vital roles in the Inchon landing, where they provided support for the First Marine Division's amphibious assault on September 15.[36]

In that operation, MacArthur drew on his World War II experience in the Japanese Islands and sought to isolate Korea from China by closing off the supply routes across the Yalu River. Carrier aircraft worked with the Fifth Air Force in trying to close off the Yalu bridges and later assumed sole responsibility for this mission. The JCS insisted, however, that MacArthur limit his attacks to the southernmost spans of these bridges, alleviating any possibility of expanding the war into China. Furthermore, navy planes were not permitted to violate Manchurian air space or even respond to fire from the Manchurian side of the border. At the time, writes Russell Wiegley,

> the Air Force had no planes that could carry a bomb load heavy enough and yet fulfill these conditions. If B-29s had attempted high-level precision bombing against the southern spans of the bridges, in the course of making their "run-ins" for adequate sightings they would have had to fly over Chinese territory as the Yalu looped far below them.[37]

Thus, these missions were assigned to the navy. Carrier-based aircraft dropped spans of three bridges and damaged four others, but the Chinese simply built more bridges. When November arrived and the Yalu began to freeze, the Chinese soon had unimpeded access over the entire river surface.

When the war settled into a stalemate at the 38th parallel, the navy withdrew into a supporting formation. Navy and marine aircraft conducted air attacks against enemy troops and their LOCs. Naval surface ships also provided gunfire support for the ground war and interdicted enemy coastal supply lines. The carriers acted as offshore air bases, and navy and marine aircraft accounted for over 30 percent of the total U.S. attacks against the enemy.

THE WAR ENDS

The spring offensive, discussed above, was largely responsible for convincing the Communists to accept the settlement terms proposed by the UN Command. But another factor may also have played a role. By 1953, General Dwight D. Eisenhower was president. He sought to pull out of Korea quickly, and the U.S. nuclear stockpile, now containing over 1300 warheads,[38] may have contributed to his decision. Throughout the spring of 1953, the Eisenhower administration secretly threatened to introduce nuclear weapons into the Korean conflict. At that time, Eisenhower also approved the transmittal of some tactical nuclear weapons to air force custody. On July 27, 1953, the armistice was signed.[39]

In reviewing the Korean War and the role of the services in that conflict, two questions merit discussion. How effective was service coordination throughout the conflict? What similarities and differences between the Korean War and World War II can be discerned, and how did these factors affect doctrinal and strategic development?

Given the interservice parochialism that so blatantly preceded the Korean War, the coordination among the services was exceptional. Once Ridgway took control of the Eighth Army, the latter was able to thwart the Chinese offensive and advance to the 38th parallel. But much of the Eighth Army's ability to advance was due to the air support of the Fifth Air Force and naval and marine aviation. Their air cover prevented the Chinese from mounting a sustained offensive, as almost 40 percent of the daily sorties were devoted to battlefield interdiction missions.[40]

Because MacArthur's experience in World War II was largely rooted in the Far Eastern theater, he was not intimately familiar with the closely coordinated air-ground operations that occurred regularly in Europe. As discussed above, in noting MacArthur's attempts to isolate Korea from China, the general tended to lean toward procedures that were effective in the Pacific Island campaigns.[41] But the campaign to turn back the Chinese led MacArthur to appreciate the importance of close coordination. It was also clear that closely coordinated interdiction operations greatly contributed to the allied forces' survival against numerically superior Communist forces.

To the army and air force leadership, therefore, the issue was not whether coordination was important, but who should control the coordinated forces. Within the Far East Command, staff representation was supposed to be equally divided among the services. But MacArthur purposely did not establish an army component command, reserving for himself the roles of Far East commander and commander of the Army Forces. Thus while the Far East Air Force and Naval Forces Far East (NAVFE) were established, MacArthur maintained some control over their direction. The Far East Command was weighted excessively with army personnel. From MacArthur's perspective, this was justified because army personnel had to do twice the work commensurate with the nature of the battle and MacArthur's dual responsibilities. Yet the imbalance created tensions and problems within the services. As General Momyer explains:

> Lieutenant General George E. Stratmeyer, the Far East Air Force [FEAF] commander, urged in 1950 that FEAF should plan the targeting of air missions for MacArthur's Far East Command [as] FEAF was the only agency with the professional ability to determine the best targets and the best way of destroying them. [MacArthur instead established] a General Headquarters [GHQ] Target Group. This group, made up of officers within the Far East Command staff, lacked the experience and depth of knowledge for targeting an air force . . . the effort was inadequate.[42]

Eventually, Stratmeyer was able to wrest control of SAC, TAC, and allied air power operating in Korea. But coordinating the navy (and the marines) with the air force, predictably, was more difficult, as the services vied for predominance in the tactical bombing roles. Fearful of sacrificing any control over naval assets, NAVFE adamantly opposed placing their forces under the control of the air component commander, even though naval aviation could assist the air force in attaining air superiority, conducting interdiction operations, and providing close air support.[43]

In the Key West agreement, it was decided that sea campaigns were the province of the sea commander and air campaigns the province of the air force. Stratmeyer argued that on this basis FEAF should control naval air (which he thought was most useful in missions supporting the air force). NAVFE responded that to secure the LOCs and control the seas, the sea commander required the ability to access carrier forces at any time. They had to be available to engage enemy naval forces. Thus NAVFE was willing to make its forces available to Stratmeyer, but he could not control them. Control would remain with NAVFE.

The problem with the navy's argument was that there really were no battles for control of the sea to speak of. Thus in a memo of July 8, 1950, the Far East Command (FECOM) chief of staff directed that for naval missions NAVFE would maintain control of naval assets but for air missions FEAF would maintain control of those forces. Since there were no real naval battles, the issue seemed to be resolved in favor of the air command. But the navy resisted this solution, and it was not until mid-1952 that the navy came to recognize FEAF as the controlling authority for all air operations. Naval officers were given greater weight in the target and mission selection process, and by late 1952 carrier-based aircraft were performing interdiction missions using the control procedures established for the Fifth Air Force and allied aircraft.[44]

The service parochialism that symbolized so much of the prewar era thus found its way into the war itself. It also reemerged immediately following the war, when both the army and the air force portrayed themselves as primarily responsible for the war's successful outcome. From the army's perspective, the air force's contribution was in providing air support for the advancing army. The real measure of success, as Ridgway saw it, was the army's ability to hold ground or to move up and down the Korean peninsula as desired.[45]

The air force rejected this argument. FEAF Commander Otis Weyland argued that "we are pretty sure that the Communists wanted peace, not because of a two year old stalemate on the ground, but to get air power off their back."[46] In 1955, an air force colonel examined the conflict from a global level of analysis, and concluded that

it would be almost impossible to pinpoint the precise degree to which our global air base system, with its substantial elements of our national air power in position in the NATO area and the Far East and with its facilities for swift and massive redeployment of our air power, had on the course of events in Korea. Certainly the Soviets had to weigh these factors, and certainly they must have been the compelling consideration in their decision as to just how far and in what ways they dared support their junior partner in Korea.[47]

The real lesson of the Korean conflict was that coordination among the services was indispensable; the full impact of this lesson, sadly, was lost in the reemergent parochialism of the immediate postwar era.

Prior to the Korean conflict, a prevailing assumption among military planners was that the next conflict would be fought much like World War II. Thus, MacArthur drew on his Japanese island-hopping strategy from that war and sought to apply the same principle—logistical isolation—to the Korean conflict. The realities of geography dispelled MacArthur's conceptions. Although MacArthur tried exhaustively, North Korea simply could not be logistically isolated from China. When certain roads or bridges were destroyed by the allied forces, new ones would be built, usually less vulnerable and less visible than their predecessors. The World War II methods MacArthur sought to duplicate—naval blockade, naval gunfire, and carrier air power to supplement land-based air power and fire power provided by ground troops, and amphibious envelopment tactics—were not nearly as successful on the Korean peninsula as they had been on the Japanese islands.

Political constraints aggravated MacArthur's efforts to pursue a total victory, which would have involved crossing the Yalu, at least by air if not on the ground. North Korea was dependent upon China for supplies and the means to wage war, yet strategic bombing of North Korea's industrial and war-making capacity was ruled out. It would have necessitated crossing the Yalu.[48]

Many of the tactics MacArthur employed in the Inchon landing can be traced to his first counteroffensives against the Japanese in New Guinea, where he had so successfully employed amphibious end-run tactics. MacArthur was to try a similar tactic in attempting to land a force at the port of Wonsan, on the east coast of North Korea. Whereas Inchon was an unquestionable success, the Wonsan operation produced a number of needless difficulties and, along with his many disputes with Truman, contributed to the general's dismissal.

For the services, the war seemed to indicate that limited wars were not only a possibility but perhaps even more probable in the future than the global war upon which so much planning was based. Interestingly, however, the Korean War did not significantly affect air force planning. Future doctrinal revisions alluded to conflict at less than total levels, but offered few substantive revisions. In fact, compared to the army and the navy, air force doctrinal development has practically stagnated in the postwar period, as later chapters show.

In Korea, U.S. forces were used primarily to force a political settlement. This was a significant break from past U.S. experience, such as in World War II, where force was employed to win the war. For the army especially, the Korean War was a unique experience. A 1954 Army Field Forces training bulletin concluded that the war "reaffirms the soundness of U.S. doctrine, tactics, techniques, organization, and equipment." Doughty notes, though, that

> Despite these disclaimers, a subtle but important change had occurred in Army thinking if not its doctrine. The Army had become accustomed to massive amounts of firepower which came at the expense of mobility. The Army had also perfected its techniques of employing firepower and the defense to inflict huge losses on an attacker. Thus the Army focused upon attrition at the expense of maneuver and its offensive spirit.[49]

This attritional orientation was to engulf army doctrine for the next thirty years.

CONCLUSION

In a July 1950 statement accompanying his first wartime request for a tax increase, Truman said, "The purpose of these proposed estimates is two fold; first to meet the immediate situation in Korea, and second, to provide for an early, but orderly, build-up of our military forces to a state of readiness designed to deter further acts of aggression."[50] Later, in June 1951, Truman also tried to reintroduce (albeit to only marginal congressional support) Universal Military Training, a plan for mandatory military conscription he had toyed with since the end of World War II.

However, the Korean conflict was growing increasingly unpopular at home, where many were questioning the point of continuing to fight it. Along with the exorbitant cost of the war, this unpopularity was to have a significant impact on the defense policies of the incoming Eisenhower administration. The fiscally minded Eisenhower rejected almost every aspect of the Truman legacy, from the increased budgets to the mobilization policy. He rejected the idea that containment required the United States to be prepared to fight in any contingency and sought to reorient containment toward deterring conflicts from occurring in the first place. Eisenhower's policy of massive retaliation is discussed in chapters 5 and 6. These chapters focus on massive retaliation as a policy most notable for its absence of a strong conventional component. Chapter 4, however, examines the salient developments in the Atlantic alliance up to 1952.

NOTES

1. All manpower (and budgetary) figures are from Office of the Assistant Secretary of Defense (Comptroller), *National Defense Estimates for FY1988/1989* (Washington, D.C.: GPO, May 1987).

2. Edward Kolodziej, *The Uncommon Defense and Congress* (Columbus: Ohio State University, 1966), p. 112.

3. Samual Huntington, "The Interim Years: World War II to January, 1950," in Raymond O'Conner, ed., *American Defense Policy in Perspective* (New York: John Wiley and Sons, 1965), p. 302.

4. Gaddis points out that "NSC–68 was not intended as a repudiation of Kennan." John Lewis Gaddis, *Strategies of Containment* (New York: Oxford University Press, 1982), p. 90. According to Paul Hammond, however, this view is incorrect. Hammond notes that Kennan saw NSC–68 as a repudiation of his view of the Soviet threat and points out that Acheson replaced Kennan with Paul Nitze as the deputy director of the Policy Planning Staff, the group charged with writing NSC–68, precisely because Kennan's views were out of step with Acheson's. Paul Hammond, letter to the author, March 17, 1989. In his historical biography of Paul Nitze, Strobe Talbott makes the same point, noting that "Kennan . . . was appalled by NSC–68." Strobe Talbott, *Master of the Game: Paul Nitze and the Nuclear Age* (New York: Alfred A. Knopf, 1988), p. 57.

5. This is best documented in David Alan Rosenberg, "The Origins of Overkill: Nuclear Weapons and American Strategy, 1945–1960," *International Security* 7, no. 4 (Spring 1983). Counterforce targeting is against an enemy's forces and other military targets; countervalue targeting is against an enemy's population and industrial capacity (usually located in cities). The new targeting emphases are discussed in the next chapter.

6. Quoted in William W. Kaufmann, *Planning Conventional Forces 1950–1980* (Washington, D.C.: The Brookings Institution, 1982), p. 2.

7. The size of the U.S. nuclear stockpile at this time is uncertain, and estimates vary widely. One source estimates the U.S. warhead stockpile at 299 in mid-1950 and 447 by mid-1951. Robert Futrell, "The Influence of the Air Power Concept on Air Force Planning, 1945–1962," in Harry Borowski, ed., *Military Planning in the Twentieth Century*, Proceedings of the Eleventh Military History Symposium (Washington, D.C.: USAF Office of History, 1986), p. 262. Futrell also says that by mid-1952 the stockpile almost doubled to 832 warheads. The Nuclear Weapons Databook, however, relying on David Alan Rosenberg's estimates based on recently declassified material, puts the stockpile of U.S. warheads (both strategic and tactical) at 450 in 1950 and 650 in 1951. Thomas B. Cochran, et al., *Nuclear Weapons Databook*, vol. 1, *U.S. Nuclear Forces and Capabilities* (Cambridge, Massachusetts: Natural Resources Defense Council, 1984), p. 15.

8. State Department Policy Planning Staff, *NSC–68*, "United States Objectives and Programs For National Security," *Foreign Relations of the United States*, (FRUS), April 14, 1950, v. I (Washington, D.C.: Department of State, 1977), pp. 283.

9. Gaddis, *Strategies*, p. 100.

10. FRUS, *NSC–68*, pp. 253 and 244.

11. Comptroller's Office, *National Defense Estimates*.

12. For an extended discussion, see Gaddis, *Strategies*, pp. 109–111.

13. John Spanier, *American Foreign Policy since World War II* (New York: Praeger Publishers, 1974), p. 70–71.

14. Robert Doughty, *The Evolution of US Army Tactical Doctrine, 1945–1976*, Leavenworth Papers no. 1, (Fort Leavenworth, Kansas: Combat Studies Institute, 1979), p. 7.

15. Kolodziej, *Uncommon Defense*, p. 136.

16. Kolodziej, *Uncommon Defense*, p. 140. The problem was that following the commitment of the United States to Korea and until the completion of the U.S. buildup, NATO was skeletonized.

The Europeans, operating under increasingly effective economies, refused to significantly increase their conventional capabilities, choosing instead the cheaper method of relying on the U.S. nuclear commitment. In early 1952, for example, the British chiefs of staff argued that the advent of nuclear weapons justified a primary reliance on atomic air power and a substantial reduction in expensive surface forces. Robert F. Futrell, *Ideas, Concepts, Doctrine: A History of Basic Thinking in the United States Air Force, 1907–1964* (Maxwell AFB, Alabama: Air University Press, 1974), p. 262. One can now question the wisdom of this sanguine attitude, in light of the actual size of the U.S. atomic stockpile at the time. This situation would recur during the Vietnam War.

17. Figures supplied by David Alan Rosenberg, "American Postwar Air Doctrine and Organization: The Navy Experience," in Alfred F. Hurley and Robert C. Ehrhart, eds., *Air Power and Warfare*, Proceedings of the Eighth Military History Symposium (Washington, D.C.: Office of Air Force History, 1979), p. 264. Allocations for the supercarrier were to be included in the budget for the next several years.

18. Memorandum by the Chief of Staff, U.S. Air Force, for the Joint Chiefs of Staff, *United States Program for National Security*, 6 September 1951, p. 1, 1017–18, 1020. (NSA).

19. Papers of Curtis LeMay, *Commanding General's Diary*, 2 September 1951. (NSA)

20. The 143 air wings were to be composed of 126 combat wings and 17 troop carrier wings. The JCS also advocated an army with 20 divisions and a navy with 409 major combat ships, including 12 modern carriers, 3 marine divisions, and 3 marine air wings. On December 28, 1951, Truman approved this buildup. Futrell, "Influence of," p. 262.

The Korean War called into question the extent to which the United States would maintain its qualitative superiority over the Soviets, as MiG-15 aircraft were encountered over Korea. The air force also pointed to a number of new Soviet aircraft, antiaircraft artillery defenses, and radar interceptors over the Soviet homeland. Futrell, *Ideas, Concepts, Doctrine*, p. 164.

21. Dean Acheson, executive session testimony, Congress. U.S. Senate. Senate Foreign Relations Committee. Hearings. *Reviews of the World Situation, 1949–1950*, (Washington, D.C., 1974), p. 292.

22. In December 1949, SAC had 72,000 men, 14 bomb groups, 610 strategic aircraft, 2 strategic fighter groups, and 6 air-refueling

squadrons. Within four years, SAC had 171,000 men, 37 bomb wings, over 1,000 strategic aircraft, 6 fighter wings, and 28 air-refueling squadrons. Greenwood, *Air Power and Warfare*, p. 236.

23. General MacArthur, as UN commander, controlled all of the allied forces. As commander of U.S. forces, his title was commander in chief, Far East. The Far East Command (FECOM) was a unified command and reported to the Joint Chiefs of Staff (JCS).

24. See, e.g., Spanier, *American Foreign Policy*, p. 91.

25. General Matthew B. Ridgway, *Soldier: The Memoirs of Matthew B. Ridgway* (New York: Harper and Brothers, 1956), p. 191.

26. Ridgway, *Soldier*, p. 140.

27. Doughty, *Evolution*, p. 7. Much of the ensuing discussion of the army in Korea derives from the excellent Doughty study.

28. Indeed, the air force and the army were to engage in lengthy internal battles over theater control—battles which go on to this day.

29. *Lessons From Korea, 1954* (Fort Benning, Georgia: Infantry School), p. 5.

30. Doughty, *Evolution*, p. 10.

31. Doughty, *Evolution*, p. 11.

32. Futrell, *Ideas, Concepts, Doctrine*, p. 179.

33. Roger Dingman, "Atomic Diplomacy during the Korean War," *International Security* 13, no. 3 (Winter 1988–89): 66.

34. General William Momyer, *Air Power in Three Wars* (Washington, D.C.: GPO, 1978), p. 168.

35. Momyer, *Air Power*, p. 168.

36. Russell Weigley, *The American Way of War* (New York: Macmillan, 1973), pp. 384–387. Weigley points out that both the Joint Chiefs of Staff and the navy initially objected to landing at Inchon. The JCS argued for a shallow water landing; they believed that Inchon was too distant from the troops marching northward from Pusan, and the two units would not be able to coordinate support. MacArthur rejected this argument on the grounds that the JCS underestimated the depletedness and therefore vulnerability of the North Koreans. The navy raised a number of logistical problems, but MacArthur rejected these, as well (Weigley, pp. 383–384).

37. Weigley, *American Way of War*, p. 389.

38. Cochran, ed., *Nuclear Weapons Databook*, p. 15.

39. When the armistice was signed, Secretary of State John Foster Dulles proclaimed: "The fight was stopped on favorable terms because the aggressor, already thrown back to and behind his place of beginning, was faced with the possibility that the fighting might, to his own great peril, soon spread beyond the limits and methods he had selected." Two contemporary historians, however, suggest that the role of atomic weapons in bringing the war to a close may have been overstated by the administration. See Roger Dingman, "Atomic Diplomacy during the Korean War," and especially Rosemary Foot, "Nuclear Coercion and the Ending of the Korean Conflict," both in *International Security*, 13, no. 3 (Winter 1988–89).

40. Momyer, *Air Power*, p. 114.

41. General James Ferguson in *Air Superiority in World War II and Korea*, Richard H. Kohn and Joseph P. Harahan, eds., Air Force Warrior Series (Washington, D.C.: Office of Air Force History, 1983), p. 73.

42. Ferguson, *Air Superiority*, p. 54.

43. Momyer, *Air Power*, p. 57.

44. Richard P. Hallion, *The Naval Air War in Korea* (Baltimore, Maryland: Nautical and Aviation Publishing Company, 1986) pp. 79–91. This episode is also detailed in Momyer, *Air Power in Three Wars*, p. 58–59.

45. In Doughty, *Evolution*, p. 12.

46. Doughty, *Evolution*. See also Futrell, *Ideas, Concepts, Doctrine*, p. 177.

47. Colonel Ephraim M. Hampton in Futrell, *Ideas, Concepts, Doctrine*, p. 177.

48. Indeed, in his 1950 book, deSeversky wrote: "Strategic air power, the decisive modern force, does not enter into the Korean equation. . . . There are no genuine strategic targets in Korea. The sources of North Korean war-making capacity lie elsewhere, in Manchuria and Russia. . . . No judgments applicable to air power in a genuine intercontinental Russo-American war can conceivably be based upon the Korean experience." deSeversky, *Air Power*, p. xxi.

49. Doughty, *Evolution*, p.12.

50. Quoted in Wiegley, *American Way of War*, pp. 395–396.

4
NATO and Coalition Defense

To many decision makers in the Truman administration, the Korean War was a "sideshow," symbolic of a much greater and more significant conflict between the United States and the Soviet Union, the focus of which would be the European theater. Even in the midst of hostilities in Korea, the administration was reluctant to withdraw forces from Europe. There was an overwhelming concern that to do so would leave Western Europe open to direct Soviet aggression. Most worrisome was the possibility that diverting forces stationed in Europe to Korea could create a vacuum in the European theater, encouraging the Soviets to open up a second front there. In part because of this concern and in part because the Korean War and the Soviet explosion of an atomic device led to increased domestic support for military spending, Truman bolstered the U.S. commitment to NATO.

Early Truman initiatives toward Western Europe included the Marshall Plan and the accession of the United States into NATO in August 1949. Truman also requested Senate approval of General Dwight D. Eisenhower to be Supreme Allied Commander, Europe (SACEUR) in January 1951 and the allocation of four additional divisions into the European theater.

As the last chapter discussed, U.S. planning also assumed that the defense of Europe would be based upon aerial bombing campaigns conducted by SAC. Such plans evolved into the "collective balanced forces" concept, often referred to as coalition defense. Each of the allies agreed to assume certain responsibilities for the defense of Western Europe. Each would cooperate in developing the forces required to attain a force structure evenly balanced between air, naval, and land-based assets. The United States would contribute strategic air power and naval forces. The Western allied naval powers, such as Great Britain, would also contribute naval forces with which to conduct naval operations on the flanks. Great Britain and France would contribute tactical air power, and the continental allies, which later included Germany, would contribute the bulk of the ground forces.

But the Korean War showed that air power alone would not deter the "full spectrum" of conflict. The Soviets' atomic capacity reduced confidence in the viability of the strategic bombing doctrine, and their overwhelming preponderance of general purpose forces in Europe led to grave doubts about the prospects of nonnuclear confrontation. In 1950, the Soviets still had 30 divisions in Eastern Europe, 100 more divisions in relative states of readiness that could be deployed from Russia alone, and over 6,000 operational aircraft. The West, on the other hand, fielded 12 undermanned divisions and under 1,000 aircraft.[1]

Upon assuming the European Command, Eisenhower worked to redress these imbalances. Under Eisenhower's supervision, over 100 air bases on the continent were built. Supreme Headquarters, Allied Powers, Europe (SHAPE), which provided a central location to facilitate coordination and integration of allied war planning and procurement, was also established. Eisenhower authorized a Central European Command, a Northern European Command, and a Southern European Command. The Central European Command was the most vital, because Soviet doctrine called for attacks across the central plane through Germany. The principal objective of Soviet planning was to insure that the war would be fought on Western European soil. In what was essentially a forward strategy, the Soviets planned a rapid mobilization into the West. Their intent was to deter the capitalist powers from initiating hostilities and specifically deter their use of air-atomic weapons—the crux of Western strategy.[2]

Eisenhower's counterstrategy for NATO was also a "forward" strategy. Its basis was to establish a defense at the Elbe River in Germany. Still not completely recovered from World War II, both the Western Europeans and the Soviets wanted to avoid having their homelands again become battlefields. Atomic weapons naturally exacerbated those concerns and encouraged forward strategies for both parties. Neither side found the vision of retreating into nuclear battlefields particularly appealing.

The four additional divisions Truman sent to Europe were to be symbols of U.S. resolve and of the U.S. commitment to its European allies. When Eisenhower arrived, there were only 12 skeletonized and unprepared divisions in Europe. Eisenhower and Truman were aware that 16 Western divisions would still be vastly outnumbered by the Soviet forces. The additional divisions were sent to Europe to create what became known as a "tripwire." Their presence conveyed the U.S. will to support its allies in the event that the Soviets launched an attack. The very fact that U.S. forces in Europe were so small, however, sent a second message: a Soviet attack could trigger an atomic response from the United States. The U.S. atomic weapons' inventory was minuscule at the time, but the Soviets presumably did not know this.

The new forces resulted in over six American divisions. Their presence showed that the United States was now committed at least to attempting to fight a conventional war in the European theater. The United States had hardly abandoned strategic bombing in its European strategy, but the emergence of bilateral atomic stockpiles made it imperative at least to try to delay using atomic weapons. Thus, an attempt would now be made to derail the Soviet attack directly. In essence, Eisenhower sought a "shield" to hold the Red Army at the Elbe while SAC prepared to attack the Soviet Union if hostilities escalated.[3] This was a reversal from prior strategy, which posited strategic bombing operations followed by land-based forces in a "mop-up" role.

The Joint Chiefs of Staff began to reassess the air force's role in theater operations. In 1950, the JCS charged the air force with the responsibility for strategic bombing, continental air defense, and tactical support of surface forces. From this evolved the target list that served as the basis for SAC planning throughout the 1950s. This target list, approved by the JCS in August, encompassed three specific tasks for the strategic air campaign: destruction of the Soviet war-making capability, blunting of the Soviet capacity to launch an atomic offensive, and retarding the advances of Soviet ground forces in Europe. These tasks were designated Delta, Bravo, and Romeo, respectively. The JCS were not trying to deemphasize the role of atomic bombing in Europe so much as attempting to enhance the air force's capacity to support ground operations there. Nonetheless, LeMay at first resisted assigning to SAC such a wide range of missions. The controversy was apparently resolved in 1951, when SAC won the right to comment on all JCS targeting plans in advance.[4]

The new target list broke with prior air force thinking in two important ways. First, in targeting Soviet war-making and atomic capacity over Soviet cities, greater emphasis was placed on counterforce over countervalue targeting. Second, the plan made provisions for tactical air missions to a greater extent than in the past. But these were still principally to be conducted by SAC, which was never enthusiastic about such missions. "If you have to employ strategic air power against tactical targets," LeMay had said, "you are not getting the full use of the weapon."[5] Thus, even though TAC was at this time granted its independence from the Continental Air

Command, as discussed below, it never attained the priority in air force budgeting as did SAC.

The challenge before the air force was to restructure its forces so that tactical air power would be available for tactical missions. This was much easier said than done. The December 1948 assimilation of TAC into the Continental Air Command had foreclosed consistent development of the tactical forces as the bulk of the air force investment was geared toward SAC. Indeed, TAC's status had been so downgraded that in June 1949 the army air forces informed the air force that they were no longer satisfied with the cooperative arrangements detailed in guiding joint manuals.[6]

In 1950, planning and procurement for the Korean War commenced under robust wartime budgets, and TAC's situation improved. In August, the Continental Air Command assigned the Ninth Air Force (Tactical), together with available fighter bomber, troop carrier, light bomber, and tactical reconnaissance units, to TAC. On November 15, the air force specified that TAC would provide for air force cooperation with land, naval, and/or amphibious forces, and in December, TAC was promoted to a major air force command.

The U.S. nuclear stockpile was growing, and naturally, disputes between TAC and SAC over nuclear missions emerged. SAC argued that it had embraced and incorporated the retardation mission and therefore should carry it out. Since SAC had a virtual monopoly on atomic weapons and their means of delivery, SAC assumed that it would prosecute retardation missions with atomic weapons. The TAC leadership argued its *raison d'être* was to carry out support and retardation missions, and TAC's nuclear capabilities should be enhanced commensurate with its new responsibilities.

PROJECT VISTA

A number of studies were undertaken in this period in an effort to resolve these and other differences between TAC and SAC. One such study was Project Vista, which was sponsored by the U.S. Army in 1951 and conducted by a number of prominent scientists, many of whom had worked on the Manhattan Project. The purpose of the study was to make the case for tactical nuclear warfare as an alternative to the strategic air campaign and, in the army's words, "bring the battle back to the battlefield." Completed in early February 1952, the conclusions of this study were disputed by SAC. To assess precisely how influential the study actually was is difficult. Many of its recommendations were for activities already undertaken. For example, Project Vista argued the United States had become too reliant on SAC, and the air forces should be restructured to emphasize tactical air and air defense. But this process had already begun, as reflected in TAC's reemergence and the reduced proportion of air wings allocated to SAC in the air force's 143-wing reorganization proposal, discussed in the next chapter.

The report argued that "any battle of Western Europe will ultimately be won or lost on the ground" and recommended an augmentation of army capabilities. This was already under way. The report also envisioned a greater role for tactical air forces. Army strategy, the report argued, should be based on forcing enemy forces into concentrations conducive to massive air strikes with atomic or conventional weapons. The report endorsed U.S. and allied tactical air power as the key to winning the next battle, emphasizing that the battle for air superiority would be of overwhelming importance.

Project Vista clearly endorsed an enhanced role for tactical air. It argued, however, that bombing large targets in the Soviet Union would be pointless because it would lead to a Soviet retaliation in kind and that air power should instead be used to "destroy the march of Russian armies" on the ground.[7] The report contended that the essential functions of the air forces would be tactical—to counter enemy operations from Eastern Europe and to prevent the enemy's use of atomic weapons in ground operations. It argued that the discriminating use of tactical nuclear weapons could offset the Soviets' superiority in manpower and divisions.

The report endorsed greater coordination between TAC and the army, recommending that the army theater commander have control over the utilization of the tactical air forces as appropriate. Project Vista recommended an increase in TAC's nuclear stockpile and in NATO tactical air units to approximately 10,000 aircraft.[8] As described by air force historian Robert Futrell, the war envisioned by Project Vista would proceed as follows:

1. TAC would concentrate primary attacks on Soviet and East European air facilities, to blunt their ability to launch atomic attacks.[9] Secondary attacks would be directed against Soviet supply depots, command and control headquarters, and other military targets.

2. After the air battle, the army would mobilize, at which time TAC (and U.S. and allied naval air forces) would focus on interdiction and support missions. At this stage, Vista envisaged some control by the field commander over TAC targeting and operations.[10]

The Project Vista report was circulated in 1952. Not surprisingly, the air force reacted adversely to its recommendations. A typical air force comment in response to the study was that "Vista represents another attempt to undermine the strength of the USAF . . . only the Air Force can reach the source of Soviet strength."[11]

Project Vista was never officially approved by the JCS, but the report was significant for a number of reasons. It established the basis of latter-day NATO strategy, relying on tactical nuclear weapons to offset Soviet–East European numerical superiority. The report walked a careful middle line between too heavy a reliance on either nuclear weapons or conventional armaments. It advocated a means of deterring (and meeting) enemy aggression that required neither an extensive conventional buildup or an untoward reliance on strategic nuclear bombing.

As Project Vista was being debated, the ministers of the NATO countries were meeting in Lisbon to determine future defense needs. Their initial plan of action was not consistent with Project Vista; the ministers envisaged a massive buildup of nonnuclear forces. Consistent with the conventional buildup under way in the United States, the allies committed themselves to the deployment of 96 divisions (75 of which were to be deployed in NATO's central front), 4,000 aircraft, and additional naval procurement. The 96 divisions were assumed to be the minimum necessary to meet the Soviet threat.

In the meantime, the Korean War dragged on without the Soviets opening the feared second front in Western Europe. The French were overcommitted in Indochina, and the British were trying to maintain a global presence. Neither could incorporate additional troop increases into already strained budgets. The allies began to backtrack from the Lisbon goals. They reduced their military budgets, cut terms of service for draftees, and stretched out arms procurements. Most important, tactical nuclear weapons began to play a major role in Europe's deterrence policies as advocated in Project Vista.

Responding to these trends and to allegations in the Western European press that the United States was somehow responsible for those trends,[12] the State Department sent the NATO ministers a secret cable, pointing out that

> U.S. defense expenditures four times total all other NATO countries combined; US with smaller population has more men under arms than all other NATO countries combined; percentage of GNP spent by US is above all others and twice NATO average; US per capita defense expenditures are six times NATO average.[13]

The Department of State was arguing that the United States could not be accused of failing to pull its weight in the NATO alliance. But Truman's time in the White House was coming to an end. As a candidate for the presidency, Eisenhower promised to bring fiscal conservatism to military procurement. The allies, however, were not inclined to step up their own commitment without some insurance of commensurate measures from the United States. This was ironic because Eisenhower had hoped the Europeans would accelerate some of their programs to relieve the United States of some of its defense burdens. But in December 1952, the Lisbon goals were reduced to about 50 divisions, and the allies came to rely almost completely on U.S. tactical and strategic nuclear strength to deter Soviet aggression.

The dispute over the Lisbon force levels was to presage numerous future occurrences where the United States would urge a greater commitment from the European allies for their own security. The allies would tentatively agree, at least to the goals, and then fail to take measures commensurate with the rhetoric, choosing instead to rely on the U.S. nuclear umbrella. Clearly, in 1952, both the United States and the allies perceived a Soviet threat from the East. But the West Europeans and the United States differed on their perceptions of the immediacy of the threat. The Europeans were still recovering from a major war fought on their own soil. Some of the allies, in particular France, were committed elsewhere and were unwilling to commit themselves to costly rearmament programs.

The U.S. atomic umbrella and the Soviet atomic capability promised a devastating war, were it actually to occur. The forward strategy was an attempt to control some of the devastation, but there was no assurance that the strategy could be successfully prosecuted. The strategy risked escalation to the nuclear level and anticipated a Soviet attack at the outbreak of hostilities. There was no way to know whether such an attack would be augmented with atomic air strikes. The Europeans made clear their justifiable concerns over atomic war on their own soil but proved unable or unwilling to pay for their own conventional rearmament.

This left the United States in the precarious position of having to justify increased NATO outlays at home to a war-wary Congress and having to assure the allies of the U.S. commitment, on the one hand, and urging the allies to undertake a greater commitment to their own defense, on the other. The allies wanted the best of two worlds. They recognized the need for a European-based defensive alliance, but they wanted the United States to pay the bulk of its costs, in terms of the resources and personnel necessary to sustain it. They were also concerned that if they increased their contributions to their own defense and appeared able to afford it, the United States might possibly decrease its commitment to their defense.[14]

While serving as Supreme Commander Allied Powers in Paris, General Eisenhower expressed concern over the Truman administration's projected military budgets. He also rejected the concept of a "year of maximum danger," writing that

> there is no greater probability of war today than there was two years ago; and no one can say for certain that there is any greater probability of deliberately provoked war at the end of this year or of next year than there is now. . . . If we do not, as American citizens, weigh this situation and reach a reasonable answer in this year's appropriations, we will be so committed to a possibly unwise military program that either we will begin to go far more rapidly down the inflation road or we will again have to accomplish a sudden and expensive contraction in that program. In this latter case, much of this year's appropriations would have, of course, gone down the drain.[15]

Consistent with these views, Eisenhower the presidential candidate promised both a fiscally conservative military program that would not jeopardize U.S. national security and a speedy conclusion to the Korean War. As president, Eisenhower was given the chance to fulfill his promises.

NOTES

1. Figures in James Lacy, *Within Bounds: The Navy in Postwar Security Policy* (Alexandria, Virginia: Center for Naval Analyses, 1983), p. 155.

2. Michael MccGwire, *Military Objectives in Soviet Foreign Policy* (Washington, D.C.: The Brookings Institution, 1987), p. 19.

3. John Spanier, *American Foreign Policy since World War II* (New York: Praeger Publishers, 1974), p. 58.

4. David Alan Rosenberg, "The Origins of Overkill: Nuclear Weapons and American Strategy, 1945–1960," *International Security* 7, no. 4 (Spring 1983): 17–18.

5. Robert Futrell, *Ideas, Concepts, Doctrine: A History of Basic Thinking in the United States Air Force, 1907–1964* (Maxwell AFB, Alabama: Air University Press, 1974), p. 155.

6. Richard Davis, *The 31 Initiatives* (Washington, D.C.: Office of Air Force History, 1987), p. 9.

7. David Eliot, "Project Vista and Nuclear Weapons in Europe," *International Security* 11, no. 1 (Summer 1986).

8. These were to include 1,500 air-superiority fighters, 3,500 all-weather interceptors, 3,000 fighter bombers, 1,500 attack aircraft, and 500 tactical bombers. Vista also recommended the army have two airborne units (one stationed in the United States and the other in Europe), and that 400 C-124 and 850 C-123 transport aircraft be procured to support this airborne force. Robert F. Futrell, *Ideas, Concepts, Doctrine,* p. 167.

9. The report estimated that approximately 50 out of 200 air bases in East Europe were capable of accepting Soviet jets, and approximately 100 atomic bombs should be dropped on them at the outset of hostilities. Eliot, "Project Vista," p. 171.

10. Futrell, *Ideas, Concepts, Doctrine,* p. 167.

11. In *Aviation Week,* July 1952, p. 9. Quoted in Eliot, "Project Vista," p. 176.

12. The argument was that the United States was failing to meet its foreign and military aid commitments.

13. Quoted in Stanley Sloan, *NATO's Future: Toward A New Transatlantic Bargain,* (Washington, D.C.: National Defense University, 1985), p. 20.

14. This situation has changed little since 1952. As Sloan has pointed out, "Some of the issues raised in the halls of Congress in the 1980s concerning US participation in the alliance bear a striking resemblance to those prominent in the [NATO treaty] ratification debate of 1949." Sloan, *NATO's Future,* p. 5.

15. Quoted in Robert Futrell, "The Influence of the Air Power Concept on Air Force Planning, 1945–1962," in Harry Borowski, ed., *Military Planning in the Twentieth Century* (Washington, D.C.: Office of Air Force History, 1986), p. 263.

5
Era III: The Absence of the Conventional

THE ABANDONMENT OF CONVENTIONAL MILITARY PLANNING

In preparing the FY1953 budget, the Truman administration requested from Congress about $52.8 billion for military outlays. This was an increase of over $6 billion from the previous year and represented Truman's greatest post-World War II budget request.[1] Each of the services was seeking to continue its wartime expansion. The air force wanted 143 wings; the army, 21 divisions; and the navy, 408 major combatant ships based around 16 carrier air groups.

Truman accepted these force levels, although he ordered the services to "stretch out" their force procurement schedules. They were told to maintain their preparedness goals but plan to meet them over a longer period of time than originally anticipated. The air force was the least hurt by Truman's stretch-out order, but all the services had to change their procurement scheduling somewhat. The air force and the navy each were allocated about one-fourth of this budget. The army received approximately half, reflecting the needs imposed by the Korean War and the refortification of the European theater.

In the summer of 1952 the Truman administration undertook a review of NSC–68. The resulting study, NSC 135/3, reaffirmed NSC–68's conclusions. The importance of maintaining the necessary capabilities to meet Communist aggression in any theater was again emphasized. Indeed, in the midst of the Korean War, no less, the document called for "a greater capability and greater willingness than have been demonstrated to commit appropriate forces and material for limited objectives, and [a U.S. commitment to] develop greater stability in peripheral or other unstable areas." Upon Eisenhower's election in November, the administration revised the conclusions of NSC 135/3, tied them to specific recommendations for action, and presented them to the incoming administration as NSC 141. NSC 141 stated that a capability for varied and flexible application of our striking power is essential both because of the wide variety of situations which may confront us and because such a capability offers the best chance to convince the Soviets that they cannot hope to destroy our striking power by surprise attack.

From the Truman administration's perspective, all global interests were equally vital and all were equally threatened. "To the greatest possible extent," NSC 141 said, "we must accordingly develop flexible, multi-purpose forces to meet the varied threats that confront us."[2]

NSC 141, together with Truman's stretched-out procurement programs, left an expensive potential legacy for Eisenhower. Had the incoming president shared Truman's world view, he would have had little need to reconceptualize U.S. national security policy or reevaluate the procurement programs then in effect. He would merely have had to board the train already set in motion by his predecessor. This, however, was not to be the case.

As a candidate, Eisenhower said much that presaged his actual policies while in the White House. Emphasizing the need to control defense spending, Eisenhower asserted that "the foundation of military strength is economic strength" and that American security was dependent "not upon the military establishment alone but rather on two pillars—military strength in being and economic strength based upon a flourishing economy." Like Truman at the time of demobilization, Eisenhower viewed a military buildup as likely to cause economic inflation, and he believed that meeting the force-level goals put forth by the three services would seriously risk bankrupting the country. Candidate Eisenhower rejected the concept of a "year of maximum danger" and argued that planning should be calibrated instead to the "long pull,"[3] over an extended period of time.

In Eisenhower's view, the means to support defense commitments were limited and had to be reconciled with budgetary restraints. He estimated that implementing the Truman administration recommendations may have resulted in $44-billion budget deficits over the next five years. Eisenhower was also wary of a strategy that depended so heavily on fighting ground wars. As Korea showed, such a strategy let the Communists set the terms of battle, which ultimately meant U.S. weaknesses would be pitted against Communist strengths. Eisenhower wanted a quick resolution to the war. It was draining the U.S. economy, no longer supported at home,[4] and fought on terms that inherently favored the opposition.

These were the views that Eisenhower brought with him into office. As president, Eisenhower rejected NSC-141, which, after all, had been put together by members of a lame duck administration who had no reason to factor the cost of their recommendations into their analysis. The new president perceived containment as practiced by the Truman administration to be overly reactive to Communist actions. "No foreign policy deserves the name," proclaimed Eisenhower in 1953, "if it is merely the reflex action from someone else's initiative."[5] The Truman strategy, he argued, sought only to preserve the status quo, to live with communism rather than to eradicate it. This, concluded Secretary of State John Foster Dulles, was "negative, futile, and immoral."[6]

Having rejected his predecessor's national security policies, President Eisenhower was faced with the challenge of developing new ones. He wanted a strategy that would exploit U.S. strengths over weaknesses, entail less costs than NSC-68, and make some distinctions between vital and peripheral U.S. security interests without conceding certain regions as outside the U.S. defensive commitment. It also had to contain some assertive elements. As Eisenhower summed it up, his own challenge was to somehow solve what he called *the great equation:* "how to maintain indefinitely a strong military force without bankrupting the country in the process."[7] Eisenhower thus initiated a "new look" at the U.S. military posture.

On October 30, 1953, Eisenhower approved NSC 162/2, "Basic National Security Policy." This document provided the basic statement of the New Look. As summarized in a memorandum from the service secretaries to the JCS, NSC 162/2 stressed

> the need for greater reliance upon our allies for the provision of indigenous forces, particularly ground forces, in countering local Communist aggressions, with greater stress upon our atomic capability as our major contribution to the needs of collective security. In the meantime, the determination and capability of the U.S. to use its atomic capability and massive retaliatory striking power should serve as the major deterrent to aggression.[8]

An essential tenet of NSC 162/2 was that a sound economy was as essential to U.S. national security as a strong military and that procuring both strong nuclear and conventional deterrents could prove economically prohibitive. In advocating the former, NSC 162/2 stated that "In the event of hostilities, the United States will consider nuclear weapons to be as available for use as other munitions."[9] The policy was unveiled in Eisenhower's State of the Union address of January 1954. The heart of the policy was the strategic air campaign, to be principally conducted by the air force's Strategic Air Command. These campaigns would almost certainly, but not necessarily, employ nuclear weapons.

In his State of the Union address, Eisenhower stated that the "services could use strategic and tactical nuclear weapons whenever it would be to the advantage of the United States to do so."[10] This did not mean that any provocation would necessarily lead to nuclear escalation. On January 12, 1954, for example, Dulles told the Council of Foreign Relations that

> local defense must be reinforced by the further *deterrent of massive retaliatory power*. A potential aggressor must know that he cannot always prescribe battle conditions that suit him . . . the way to deter aggression is for the free community to be willing and able to respond vigorously at places and means of its own choosing (emphasis added).[11]

But Dulles's critics picked up on the "massive retaliatory power" phrase used in the speech, and that phrase came to symbolize the entire Eisenhower approach. It seemingly implied nuclear escalation as a foregone conclusion. In an April 1954 *Foreign Affairs* article and in numerous public appearances, Dulles explained that his intent was not as commonly interpreted. In the *Foreign Affairs* article, Dulles insisted that "massive atomic and thermonuclear retaliation is not the kind of power which could most usefully be evoked under all circumstances."[12] But there is little question that the threat of nuclear escalation was the foundation of Eisenhower's policy.

As conveyed by Dulles, another important aspect of the policy was that in responding to an aggression, the United States would not necessarily respond to the provocation directly, as was the case under Truman. Rather, the United States would choose the place and means of response that would put the adversary on the defensive, forcing him to respond in a new theater or against an unanticipated threat. One analyst has noted, for example, that according to Dulles, if the Communists had renewed their aggression in Korea, U.S. policy would not have necessarily required bombing Moscow or Peking (although it might), but it "does mean that there are areas of importance to the aggressors in that vicinity which may have an industrial or strategic relationship to the operation which would no longer be what General MacArthur called a 'privileged sanctuary.' "[13] The prospect of such a response, it was reasoned, would create uncertainties for the enemy planners and make them more reluctant to attack in the first place.

This, then, was the essential purpose of the Eisenhower policy: to deter aggression from occurring in the first place. This was accomplished by conveying to the aggressor, through force posture, strategy, and declaratory statements, that under any circumstance the cost of initiating aggression would outweigh the benefits. A policy of meeting aggression on the adversary's terms sent the wrong message. If the adversary could draw the United States into a protracted ground war, the benefits of aggression could appear to outweigh the costs. A policy of threatening to escalate the level of violence, on the other hand, was much more forceful—especially if the escalation could involve nuclear weapons.

Thus the policy as developed by the Eisenhower administration emphasized U.S. strengths in technology and air power and deterrence over defense, and tried to do so affordably. As Dulles put it:

> The basic decision was to depend primarily upon a great capacity to retaliate instantly, by means and at places of our choosing. Now the Department of Defense and the Joint Chiefs of Staff can shape our military establishment to fit what is our policy, instead of having to be ready to meet the enemy's many choices. . . . As a result, it is now possible to get, and share, more basic security at less cost.[14]

The emphasis on cost, the final word in the Dulles formulation and so vital a factor in Eisenhower's national security policy, is no accident. An initial JCS estimate for the FY1954 defense budget was $34.8 billion—almost $20 billion less than Truman's budget request for FY1953 (actual expenditures were in fact much higher, at approximately $49 billion).[15] To a great extent, Eisenhower's defense program was influenced by domestic factors such as the budget and emerging technology and on a coherent conception of the strategic threat. By this time, it was evident that materials necessary for the production of nuclear weapons were going to be more plentiful than had originally been thought. Moreover, it was also clear that the procurement and maintenance of nuclear weapons were generally less expensive than maintaining robust conventional forces. This cost disparity was reflected in subsequent Eisenhower budgets. Because of the general growth of the overall budget throughout the 1950s, one does not see dramatic cutbacks in defense spending in the 1950s; however, there were significant decreases in the rate of growth in defense spending. The FY1954 budget saw a decrease in the rate of growth of 7.9 percent from the year before, and the budget for FY1955 saw another decrease of 15.6 percent. Furthermore, the total obligational authority for general purpose forces decreased from 45.1 percent in FY1952 to 38.7 percent in FY1954 and steadily decreased throughout Eisenhower's two terms in office. At the same time, spending for strategic (nuclear) forces rose steadily throughout the Eisenhower years.[16]

There is some question as to whether massive retaliation adequately accounted for changes in Soviet military capability. On

November 1, 1952, the United States tested a hydrogen device, and in October 1954, the Soviets followed suit. The precise size of the Soviet atomic stockpile was unknown, but it was certainly growing. This posed a fundamental challenge to massive retaliation. The Soviet nuclear capability, many argued, made conventional wars more likely. Both sides would be reluctant to resort to their nuclear weapons because of the threat of nuclear reprisal. But Eisenhower believed that such a stalemate would not develop and that the best way to deter aggression from occurring was to threaten the adversary with all the power the United States had available.

To the extent that some future contingency might require the use of conventional forces, the Eisenhower administration established a wide-ranging set of global alliances, putting the onus of developing nonnuclear forces for self-protection on the allied countries. The Southeast Asia Treaty Organization (SEATO) was formed with South Korea and Nationalist China, the Baghdad Pact (which was later the Central Treaty Organization [CENTO]) was established, and agreements were reached with a number of states in the Middle East. In all, the administration was to reach agreements with almost 150 countries.

PLANNING FOR EUROPE

At this time, the Soviets were quickly consolidating their hold over the Eastern European satellites and strengthening their divisions in those countries. Yet the administration withdrew two American divisions stationed in Europe. The administration accepted the JCS recommendations that future ground wars should primarily be fought by local, indigenous forces, supported by U.S. air and naval aviation. The United States thus came to rely on tactical nuclear weapons as the basis of its policy in the European theater.

The administration wanted the Europeans to take greater responsibility for their own defense. Eisenhower urged the Europeans to establish a European Defense Community (EDC) and accept German participation in the coalition. Yet 1953 passed without any of the six original signatories to the EDC ratifying the EDC treaty,[17] and the project lost its momentum. Eisenhower warned the Europeans that the United States would not "take any steps toward redeployment [of U.S. troops in Europe], or even talk about redeployment, until these objectives have been reached . . . the French have an almost hysterical fear that we and the British will one day pull out of Western Europe and leave them to face a superior German armed force."[18] Nevertheless from the perspective of France and the other NATO allies, the case against building up their ground forces was much more compelling than the case in favor. While advocating that NATO be protected by tactical and strategic nuclear weapons, the administration proved unwilling to contribute the forces required by the Lisbon Goals, even after the Lisbon Goals were almost halved. If the United States was unwilling to prepare for the ground war, the Europeans saw no reason to do so.

Although the Netherlands, Belgium, Luxembourg, and the Federal Republic of Germany (FRG) ultimately ratified the EDC treaty, the French resisted committing itself, and on August 29, 1954, the treaty died in a preratification vote of EDC-country ministers. By this time, the Soviet threat seemed somewhat less immediate, especially to the French,[19] and no NATO country wanted to invest in large standing ground forces.

With the death of the EDC came a flurry of other initiatives aimed at solidifying the Western Alliance. In late 1954 the occupation of West Germany ended and the FRG was recognized as a sovereign state. In return, the FRG agreed to station foreign troops on its soil. In December 1954, NATO ministers favorably considered MC/48, a report from NATO's military committee immodestly entitled "The Most Effective Pattern of NATO Military Strength for the Next Few Years." In this report the military committee advocated a heavier reliance on nuclear weapons to deter aggression. In MC 14/2, the NATO ministers formally accepted the New Look writ tactical: nuclear weapons were recognized as NATO's first line of defense, and a stockpile of theater nuclear weapons would compensate for reductions in European-based manpower. As discussed in the previous chapter, forward deployed forces would henceforth be a "tripwire." To challenge these forces would inevitably lead to a nuclear response.

On May 5, 1955, West Germany joined NATO. Soon after, the Soviets formally consolidated the Warsaw Pact Organization (WPO) with Albania, Bulgaria, Czechoslovakia, East Germany, Hungary, Poland, and Rumania. NATO then faced a unified threat from the East and the prospect of having to accelerate rearmament. But rearmament was decidedly unpopular with the Europeans and with Eisenhower, and reliance on tactical nuclear weapons had become entrenched as the basis of NATO policy.

Why did the Europeans allow their homeland to become a potential atomic battlefield, rather than attempt to match the Soviet/Pact threat on an equal basis? Perhaps because the prospect of actually going to war appeared remote, and the costs incurred in a conventional buildup seemed forbidding. On a more fundamental level, the Europeans apparently accepted the U.S. position that the purpose of military power had shifted from defense to deterrence. Atomic weapons and the U.S. nuclear commitment provided an alternative to a costly and protracted conventional buildup. But underneath the confidence in the U.S. nuclear guarantee must have been the conviction among European leaders that Europe was better off if war could simply be avoided altogether and that relying on nuclear weapons to the exclusion of other options was the best way to do so. Without adequate forces-in-being to fight the ground war, the alliance would have no choice but to resort to nuclear weapons. Aware of this, no adversary, it must have been hoped, would dare to mount a challenge in the West European theater.[20]

THE SERVICES AND THE BATTLEFIELDS

Of all the service components, the air force's Strategic Air Command most benefitted from the policy of massive retaliation. In 1949 SAC controlled 72,000 men organized into 14 bomber groups, 610 strategic aircraft, 2 strategic fighter groups, and 6 air-refueling squadrons. By the end of the Korean War in 1953, SAC had grown to encompass 171,000 men, 37 bombing wings, over 1,000 strategic aircraft (mostly B-36s and all-jet B-47s), 6 fighter wings, and 28 air-refueling squadrons.[21] This remarkable growth was to continue throughout Eisenhower's tenure and would affect the entire air force. Total wings, for example, were scheduled to grow to 137 (back up from Truman's cut to 133) by the end of FY1957, 120 of which were to be completed by June 30, 1955.[22] In this period, air force personnel levels rose to over 970,000.

Because of the heavy emphasis on air power in Eisenhower's policy, the army suffered the most severe cutbacks in allocations, personnel, and materiel acquisition. In total obligational authority for FY1955, the army received $4.5 billion less than it had in FY1954. Within a month of approving NSC 162/2, Eisenhower announced his intention to withdraw two of the U.S. divisions in Korea. However, under Eisenhower, tactical nuclear weapons took on their central role in U.S. deterrence policy, and the army was given such systems to compensate for the manpower cutbacks. For example, many of the 10,000-pound bombs of the post-WWII era were replaced by atomic Mark 7s.[23]

Army Chief of Staff General Matthew Ridgway argued vehemently against massive retaliation and an overreliance on nuclear weapons. Shortly before departing from his position as army chief, Ridgway prepared a sweeping and extensive criticism of U.S. national security planning for Secretary of Defense Charles Wilson. In this report, Ridgway argued that "national objectives could not be realized solely by the possession of nuclear capabilities, [and] no nation could regard nuclear capabilities alone as sufficient, either to prevent, or to win a war." He went on to sound what was now a long-standing army refrain: "In a situation of nuclear plenty, mutual cancellation of nuclear advantage can occur in terms of mutual devastation; or, depending on the degree of parity, in terms of mutually limited use; or, finally, in common refusal to use nuclear weapons at all."[24]

In general, the army criticized the policy as an abdication of political responsibility. According to an earlier army review of NSC 5410/1, a 1953 NSC study of U.S. global war policy, there were no sensible objectives to be gained from such drastic action. The army charged that the NSC had "failed properly to consider the implications of unlimited nuclear destruction." NSC 162/2 found the goal of liberating Eastern Europe infeasible, but it was nonetheless an oft-stated objective of U.S. foreign policy. The army argued that the air force's war plan, which had grown to include numerous targets in Eastern Europe, would neither encourage the defection of the Eastern Europeans or, if war were to occur, enhance their desirability as allies. The army questioned what role occupying forces could serve in a theater decimated by nuclear weapons and how, after the war, "liberated" (and decimated) East European countries could be integrated into the West's economic structure. Finally, army leaders argued that as perpetrators of nuclear holocaust, the United States would find itself (at the least) vilified and friendless in the postwar epoch.[25]

On December 21, 1953, the army presented its critique of NSC 5410/1 to Eisenhower, who rejected virtually all of the army's arguments. Army leaders then presented their own revised planning document that almost completely repudiated the use of nuclear weapons, "a proposal," A.J. Bacevich notes, "which must have seemed quixotic to administration officials who viewed nuclear weapons as a panacea." The army argued for "the restriction of attacks by weapons of mass destruction, if used, to selected tactical targets which would cause minimal human loss and material loss and promote the achievement of military objectives by conventional forces."[26]

Eisenhower dismissed these views out of hand. Eisenhower felt that overall, these views were "pretty close" to questioning "the prerogatives of the Commander in Chief." In his view, the mutual availability of nuclear weapons did not mean that a nuclear stalemate had developed, but that "everything in the next war would have to be subordinated to winning that war" and that he "could not conceive of any other course of action than [one] which would hit the Russians where and how it hurt most."[27]

In contrast to the army, the navy offered little overt resistance to the new administration policy. Initially, this was not the case. On December 7, 1953, CNO Robert Carney made arguments very similar to those of the army's based on the same concern that once a nuclear stalemate developed, conventional forces would become more, not less, important. Carney observed that

> we must maintain a strong U.S. air capability, including a capability for inflicting massive damage, but not neglecting our capabilities for tactical air support, control of sea communications, and vital sea areas. . . . Our Allies (must be confident) that we can and will maintain control of sea communications in the face of any threat. U.S. naval forces as now constituted are essential to maintain this vital sea control in the face of the well-recognized Soviet surface, submarine, air and mining threat . . . it is unsound drastically to cut back these forces, already bought and paid for, for the sole purpose of making funds available to enlarge other types of air power.[28]

But the navy eventually stifled its criticisms and went along. After the admirals' revolt, the navy was reluctant to run against the prevailing national security winds. In January 1954, Carney submitted a new memo to the JCS advocating that for planning purposes air power should include the navy's carrier-based aircraft. The JCS accepted this position on February 5, 1954.[29]

The navy began a number of programs aimed at fending off its own technological obsolescence and insuring for itself a role in the air campaign. In January 1954 the first nuclear-powered submarine (the *Nautilus*) was commissioned.[30] Over the next few years, navy aircraft speeds increased to supersonic levels, and missiles began to replace guns on ships and aircraft. Air-breathing guided missiles were also deployed on the decks of cruisers. In particular, the Polaris missile was developed and would soon be deployed on submarines for nuclear-attack missions. Nuclear-attack capabilities for naval aircraft were upgraded as the A3D Skyraider and A4D Skyhawk entered service.

Carriers and naval fighter aircraft remained the essence of the navy's arsenal. The navy had reopened its case for additional aircraft carriers and, as discussed in the last chapter, Secretary of Defense Charles Wilson authorized construction of new supercarriers in 1952.

This program ran unchallenged throughout Eisenhower's tenure, and in October 1956 the first new carrier *Forrestal* was commissioned. By 1961 six more carriers were commissioned, the last of which, the *Enterprise*, was nuclear powered. These supercarriers could each carry up to 12 heavy fighter-bombers and could store more than six times as many nuclear weapons as the *Midway*-class carriers commissioned after the Korean War began.

During this period, the navy maintained two types of carrier task forces. The first was built around the new attack carriers and was deployed primarily for strategic and tactical offensive missions. The second was built around the older naval ships such as the *Essex* and consisted of support carrier groups. These were deployed to perform seek-and-destroy missions against Soviet submarines. The second group could operate independently of the first group but was intended to work in support of the modern carriers, allowing them to carry out power-projection missions.[31]

Reflecting the navy's experience in Korea, power projection became central to navy planning. Soviet submarines posed the greatest threat to control of the seas, but it was felt that these could be countered at their source, rather than in the vast oceans.[32] A joint navy–air force study of the Soviet submarine threat posited four targets that needed to be attacked in the initial stages of conflict: the Soviet Union's principal shipyards, Soviet submarines, their fuel and ammunition facilities, and their bases. As James Lacy concludes,

> while the two services still disagreed on which had primary responsibility for the last of these targets, the principle that "naval" targets might range far from inland was no longer itself a matter of great dispute. From there, for the Navy, it was an easy step to a still wider range of land targets. To neutralize submarine support facilities meant carrier groups entering "harm's way."[33]

The navy vigorously promoted the atomic potential of its carriers. The navy increased the range of targets requiring "significant expenditures of nuclear weapons" and planned to use its aircraft in "offensive action (including atomic) against enemy resources that threaten[ed] control of the seas and in support of the land battle."[34] These included "missions in support of amphibious landings, defense of naval bases and forward areas, and . . . retardation of enemy advances in areas 'of primary naval responsibility.' "[35] As Korea showed, these missions could be achieved conventionally. But the navy placed them on its "atomic" targeting list and thus within the administration's strategic and funding priorities.

The navy's peacetime missions, such as showing the flag and enforcing "gunboat diplomacy," changed little. The Sixth and Seventh fleets continued to sail in the Mediterranean and the Pacific Far East, respectively. The overall participation of the navy in incidents involving a show of force decreased in this era, but the carrier's participation as a percentage of all naval involvements increased dramatically from 52 percent (from 1946 to 1948) and up to 82 percent from 1949 to 1955.

Thus, the air force had ascended to become, once again, the dominant wing of the defense establishment, and the navy had established a comfortable role for itself within the parameters of massive retaliation. Only the army remained dissatisfied with the Eisenhower strategy. In January 1955, NSC 162/2 was superseded by NSC-5501, which in turn was replaced by the administration's statement of "Basic National Security Policy," NSC-5602. These documents alluded to enhanced roles for conventional forces (as the army noted) and, along with the report of the Killian Board in February 1955, maintained that the Soviets would soon reach nuclear parity.[37] But these documents had no appreciable effect on administration thinking with respect to the procurement and funding of general-purpose forces.

MASSIVE RETALIATION IN ACTION?

The first major test of massive retaliation came in 1954. In September, just as Secretary of State Dulles was concluding negotiations on the establishment of SEATO,[38] the Chinese Communists began bombing attacks against Quemoy, a nationalist-held island off the Chinese coast in the Taiwan Strait. Soon after, attacks began on the island of Matsu. Many in the United States saw these attacks as the first volleys in an attempt by the People's Republic of China (PRC) to overrun Taiwan. The United States and the Nationalists signed a Treaty of Mutual Defense, which committed the United States to defend Formosa in the event that hostilities over the islands escalated.[39] The situation heated up throughout the first four months of 1955 but was finally defused in late April, when Zhou EnLai, the premier of the PRC, declared that the Communists wished to avoid war with the United States and proposed direct negotiations to resolve the issue.[40]

The administration argued that the Chinese backed down because of its implicit threats to escalate the conflict, possibly to the nuclear level. In a famous interview, Dulles expanded on his theory of brinkmanship and implied that this was the case. In Dulles's view,

Some say that we were brought to the verge of war. Of course, we were brought to the verge of war. The ability to get to the verge without getting into the war is the necessary art. If you cannot master it, you inevitably get into war. If you try to run away from it, if you are scared to go to the brink, you are lost. We've had to look it square in the face—on the question of enlarging the Korean War, on the question of getting into the Indo-China war, on the question of Formosa. We walked to the brink and we looked it in the face.[41]

Whether or not the United States would actually have resorted to nuclear weapons, had the crisis not abated, is questionable. It is also not certain that the threat of escalation or the diplomacy of Eisenhower and Dulles led to the Chinese capitulation.[42] The crisis in the Taiwan Strait illuminated the credibility problem inherent in the massive retaliation policy. Had the Chinese not backed down, the United States would have had to face the choice of lending support to the Nationalists, as promised in the Mutual Defense Treaty, and would also have had to come to a decision with respect to using nuclear weapons. Had the United States retracted on either of these counts, there could have been a serious loss of confidence in the United States among the SEATO signatories. Fortunately for the United States, a decision with respect to using nuclear weapons did not have to be made. What if the Chinese had not backed down?

Of course, there was no superpower war during Eisenhower's tenure. But this was not necessarily due to massive retaliation. As we now know, the Soviet stockpile in the mid-1950s was consistently overstated by national intelligence sources.[43] Even if the Soviets had wanted war with the United States (for reasons difficult to fathom), it seemed doubtful that they would have seen it in their interest to initiate one. Nor did massive retaliation prevent the occurrence of localized and regional conflicts potentially involving U.S. interests. The capture of Dien Bien Phu by the Viet Minh in Indochina marked the end of the French occupation there, and, while the United States made numerous threats to intervene on behalf of the French, these threats were not acted upon. Crisis befell the Middle East over Egyptian nationalization of the Suez Canal in 1956. In the same year, the Soviets invaded Hungary to quell nationalist uprisings. In 1958 the PRC again began to threaten the islands off the Taiwanese coast, and the marines were forced to land in Lebanon to quell a civil struggle. During this period, the United States also had to contend with the Malayan War (ended in 1954), Israel's Sinai Campaign (1956), terrorism in Cyprus (1955–1959), and rebellion in Algeria (1956–1962).

To an extent, it can be argued that these events had little or no direct effect on U.S. security, and Eisenhower's disengagement from them showed his ability to make distinctions between vital and peripheral interests. But the conflicts in the Middle East and France's problems in Indochina involved close U.S. allies. France specifically requested U.S. intervention in Indochina, and the failure of the United States to assist the French strained relations between the two allies for some time. The Soviet invasion of Hungary could have been a tinderbox. These conflicts may have merited strong responses from the United States, yet in almost all of the cases cited above, the administration sent in the Sixth or Seventh Fleet to show resolve but offered little substantive assistance.

"The Army exists for the single purpose of victory in battle and success in war. It may have the subsidiary purpose of being a deterrent,"[44] General Ridgway would repeatedly state. In its 1954 revision of FM 100-5, the army steadfastedly pictured itself as the first line of U.S. defense:

> Army forces as land forces are the decisive component of the military structure . . . during the course of military operations Army forces, because of their decisive capabilities are supported from time to time by other military components . . . Army combat forces do not support the operations of any other component. . . . The efforts of all the components are directed toward insuring the success of the land operations.[45]

But the army's views, based in large part on the Korean experience, were hopelessly out of line with an administration wanting no more Koreas. This inclination gives some clue as to why the Eisenhower policy prevailed. Massive retaliation may have failed to deter smaller, limited wars, but it did deter the United States from becoming involved in such conflicts. For a country militarily retrenching from an unpopular war, that may have been the bottom line.

QUANDARIES FOR THE AIR FORCE

Throughout the 1950s, the air force was subjected to a barrage of criticism from outside observers and from army officials skeptical over the administration's apparent overreliance on the strategic air campaign, particularly in light of the growing Soviet arsenal and the air force's alleged neglect of close air support. The army remained the most virulently critical.

In the various air force manuals produced in this period, the service made clear that it disputed the army's conception of which service contributed the decisive forces. In a manual devoted to strategic doctrine, the air force argued that the primary task of air forces participating in the strategic air campaign is the destruction of the "enemy nation's total organization for waging war." Operations directed against an enemy's deployed military forces were "diversionary."[46] In a subsequent manual, the air force position was made even more clear:

Of the various types of military forces, those which conduct air operations are most capable of decisive results. . .with air forces and modern weapons systems available, it no longer is necessary to defeat opposing armed forces as a prerequisite to conducting major operations directly against an opponent either in his sovereign territory or in any other locality.[47]

The air campaign, the manual argued, would encompass direct attacks against both the enemy's heartland (his war-sustaining capabilities) and his periphery, from where his air and surface efforts would originate. Contrary to the city-busting strategy heralded at the national level, the air force's conception of massive retaliation was now increasingly counterforce. Much greater attention was given to attacking the enemy's war-sustaining industry and his capacity to attack the United States with long-range aerial weapons. One manual, for example, stated that "the implications of a surprise air attack by an aggressor having weapons of devastating power are critical. . . .Because of the decisive potential of air weapons, the survival of the nation in total war demands that a favorable decision must be attained against an enemy's long range air forces."[48]

Thus, the new manual reflected the changes in air force thinking, which was discussed in the last chapter. To be sure, destroying the enemy's will to fight remained the primary purpose of the air campaign; but this was no longer accomplished, as was the case during the pre-NSC-68 Truman era, by destroying its population. At that time, the strategic bombing campaigns of World War II were fresh in the minds of the air force leadership; the U.S. atomic stockpile was minuscule, and there was no Soviet atomic threat. Then, there was a logic to targeting Soviet cities, which would return the most "bang for the buck." But now the new Soviet atomic threat had to be taken into account. As expressed by LeMay in a 1957 memo,

For the first six years that I commanded SAC, we didn't have to worry about winning an air power battle because the Russians had no threat against us. They did not have atomic weapons; they did not have a long range Air Force. . . .However that has now changed and. . .we must, as a matter of priority, defeat the Russian Air Force before any other military task can be accomplished.[49]

The air force also sought to demonstrate its capability to engage in "brushfire" and smaller-scale conflicts. SAC sought operational responsibility for these missions by ostensibly expanding the role of the Tactical Air Command. In May 1956, General Otis Weyland, commander of TAC, stated

> It is becoming increasingly clear that any armed conflict which may occur in the foreseeable future will most probably be of the limited or local variety. The United States must develop an effective deterrent to such local wars and must be able to support the indigenous forces of friendly countries if such a war does occur.
>
> SAC forces are not suited for and cannot cope with the essentially tactical air aspects of local wars. Nor should they become seriously involved in a local war, since they would jeopardize their effect as a deterrent to major war. Consequently, tactical air power must be the primary deterrent to local or limited war.[50]

Many factions within the air force emphatically disagreed with Weyland's views. Their arguments were primarily twofold. One was the familiar argument that "if we have the strength required for global war we could handle any threat of lesser magnitude" and that "local war is best prevented by the same means as general war."[51] The second argument against reassigning resources to TAC was a military argument. The limited range of TAC forces, it was argued, hampered their global mobility and reduced the number of targets they could reach; and they lacked all-weather strike capabilities.[52]

As such, only minor restructuring of the air force in favor of TAC actually occurred. On July 8, 1955, TAC activated the Nineteenth Air Force operating permanently from Foster Air Force Base, Texas. The rationale, as elaborated by Richard Klocko, was that

> the Air Force should establish and fund a "Ready Air Fleet" within the Tactical Air Command. Based in the United States this Ready Air Fleet would be an integrated self-supporting organization that could immediately deploy to a crisis area and operate until such time as normal operational forces could be moved into the area to augment or replace it.[53]

Some new aircraft, such as the F-105 Thunderchief nuclear-capable fighter, was procured specifically for TAC, but this was not at the expense of SAC by any means, as the overall size of the U.S. nuclear stockpile was growing exponentially in this period. By 1956 there were approximately 3,550 nuclear warheads in the U.S. arsenal, an almost 300 percent growth from 1953, when Eisenhower assumed the presidency.[54] Although it is difficult to find precise distribution figures, it is clear that some of these could be allocated to TAC without significantly disrupting SAC's targeting plans (their constant growth notwithstanding). In any case, when financial constraints forced air force wing strength to be reduced after peaking at 137 in mid-1956, most of the reduction came from TAC. The 11-wing B-52 force expanded to 14 wings as the number of shorter range B-47s were reduced.[55] In FY1956, TAC wings peaked at 28, 5 wings more than in the year before. But this growth was primarily cosmetic, as wings were skeletonized: total operational tactical aircraft in this period (1953–1956) *dropped* from 9,519 to 8,036.[56]

THE ARMY AND THE PENTOMIC DIVISIONS

The army remained steadfast in its opposition to massive retaliation but the army's views, based in large part on its Korean experience, were hopelessly out of line with an administration wanting no more Koreas. In 1955 the administration expanded the army reserve forces in lieu of a buildup of the active forces. By 1956, active army forces were being reduced dramatically, by about 100,000 men, and two of twenty divisions were eliminated. In comparison, air force end strength dropped by only half that much.[57]

Army leaders presented an alternative to massive retaliation which they called a "tridimensional" strategy. This strategy was an early elaboration of a limited nuclear war scenario. Massive air strikes would give way to a measured retaliation proportional to the military force, geographical area, and political stakes involved. To support this strategy, the army pushed for modernization of its combat equipment; a larger conventional stockpile; stepped-up guided-missile development for field, antiaircraft, and antimissile purposes; large-scale mobile air and sea transports; and an expanded tactical air support capability.[58]

But the new army strategy received scant attention. The administration continued to deemphasize the conventional force budgets for all the services, preferring to emphasize nuclear weapons and guided missiles. The administration called for 17 reorganized army divisions and, consistent with its new emphasis on missile technology, an increased number of missile and antiaircraft battalions and "atomic support commands." The administration also scheduled for the army a manpower decrement of approximately 100,000 men, to approximately 898,000.[59]

The army began to reassess its approach to the military planning and budgeting process. Clearly, some reorganization to incorporate atomic capabilities was in order, if for no other reason than to maintain some stake in budgeting decisions. To be sure, in the 1954 revision of FM 100-5 greater attention was paid to the potential impact of atomic weapons on the battlefield. Nevertheless, army thinking was still as concerned with assimilating the lessons of Korea as with the implications of the atomic bomb. As reflected in the manual, the army still viewed the new weapon cautiously: "In exceptional cases a development may possess potentialities which dictate radical revision of the conduct of tactical operations. . . .The full import and extent of changes resulting from the employment of the latest developments, the nuclear and thermonuclear weapons and the guided missiles, is not clear at this time."[60]

In this spirit, offensive tactics generally reflected the army's Korean War experience (much more thought was now given to attaining "limited objectives") and focused on nonnuclear confrontation. Offensive doctrine remained basically unchanged from the 1949 edition, continuing to stress envelopment and penetration carried out in main force and secondary operations. However, unlike its predecessor, which dedicated one paragraph to "radiological" weapons, the new manual made some effort to define the role of nuclear weapons in the next war. Essentially, atomic weapons were considered "another means of extremely powerful fire support" and were simply incorporated into operations: "The integration of atomic weapons into tactical operations does not change tactical doctrine for the employment of firepower. . .the planning and execution of offensive operations will continue to be based on the integration of fire and maneuver."[61]

In viewing nuclear weapons as no more than "extremely powerful fire support," the army made little effort to adapt its tactics to atomic contingencies. Army units were expected to fight in an atomic environment, which dictated greater emphasis on dispersion: "Plans provide for immediate movement through or around the target area. Exploiting units remain dispersed until the critical moment, then concentrate rapidly, and move to the decisive point to take maximum advantage of surprise and the enemy's disorganization."[62] Otherwise, however, there was no sense of the many potential difficulties created by an attacking force operating in an atomic environment. For example, the doctrine emphasized massing of forces for effective penetration, but massing made the army unit vulnerable to enemy attack with nuclear weapons. Conversely, dispersion reduces the attractiveness of the army unit as a nuclear target, but dispersion also makes penetration more difficult. To an extent, these issues were confronted in the manual's discussion of defensive tactics. But it was not until the Pentomic reorganization that the army began to deal with these and other such problems in earnest.

Defensive tactics evolved in a manner that began to address the problems discussed above. Defense was now seen to involve two types of operations: the *position defense* and the *mobile defense*. The position defense descended from earlier concepts and was aimed at achieving traditional army objectives such as "holding the terrain at all costs": "The concept of this defense is that the battle position will be held by defeating enemy by fire in front of the position, by absorbing the strength of his attack within the position, or by destroying him by counterattack. . . .A considerable proportion of available firepower is deployed forward."[63]

Much more innovative was the mobile defense. In describing the proper conditions dictating the employment of the mobile defense, enemy possession of atomic weapons was listed last, as if it was an afterthought. But the mobile defense was clearly the army's first concerted effort to deal with changing battlefield conditions. The aim of the mobile defense was to "canalize the attacking forces into less favorable terrain, and block or impede the attacking forces, while the bulk of the defending force is employed in offensive action at the time and place most favorable to the defender. . .the armored division is particularly adaptable to the mobile defense."[64]

Canalizing the enemy forces would force them to mass, therefore creating conditions more favorable to atomic attacks. The endorsement of the armored division reflected the general view that armor would be more suited to the atomic battlefield than infantry, a major concept underlying the Pentomic organization. Finally, the mobile defense was notable because of its emphasis on dispersion and mobility as the keys to success on the atomic battlefield. "Rapidity of movement," the manual intoned, "is an excellent defense because the enemy may take considerable time to deliver atomic. . .weapons, even after a target is located."[65]

In the Korean War, allied forces had found themselves insufficiently prepared to fend off the threat posed by the adversary's tanks. After that experience, the army went into the armored tank business. By the mid-1950s the army had produced three new tanks (the M-41, M-47, and M-48) and the M-59 armored personnel carrier and had other tanks in the latter stages of development. By 1956, four of the army's divisions were armored. Armored tanks and personnel carriers were considered ideal for employment in the mobile defense and as a mobile reserve for supporting operations. Most important, however, was their envisaged role on the atomic battlefield.

A series of army tests and two army studies, the "Atomic Field Army-1 1956 (ATFA-1)," and the PENTANNA study, seemed to confirm the utility of armored divisions on atomic battlefields. The studies envisioned a highly mobile battlefield—armored divisions prepared for atomic as well as conventional battle—and enhanced control capabilities for the division commander, permitting him to control five, instead of the traditional three, regiments. The outcome of this reassessment was a new army organization called the "Pentomic Divisions," a reorganization that ushered in a new era of the atomic battlefield. The Pentomic Divisions were rooted in the U.S. tradition of emphasizing technology over manpower as the decisive factor in the land war,[66] the increasing availability of tactical nuclear weapons, and the army's determination to play a greater role (and attain a bigger piece of the budget) in the military planning process.[67] In October the Pentomic Divisions were introduced to the public by Army Chief of Staff Maxwell Taylor.[68] In December the army recommended that all its divisions be reorganized for atomic operations.

Each new armored division consisted of five self-contained and independent units, including the support elements based with the regimental combat team. The basic component of the division was the infantry battle group. Each battle group contained five rifle companies, a combat support company, and a headquarters and service company. The division commander controlled the battle groups, although special task forces of two or more battle groups could be formed under an assistant division commander. The division also included an armored battalion of five tank companies, a cavalry squadron of three troops, and direct and general support artillery battalions. All of the army divisions were affected by the reorganization, but the infantry divisions most adversely, each losing about 3,000 men.[69] The armored divisions were augmented with atomic and conventional firepower and a stronger aviation detachment.

At all levels of the Pentomic organization, emphasis was placed on "strategic mobility," flexibility, and dispersion. The atomic war zone was now viewed as much wider and deeper than in the past. Furthermore, army leaders recognized that large troop concentrations would be too lucrative a target for the enemy. Combat units, therefore, had to be highly mobile, dispersed, and organized with considerable gaps between units. Each unit had to be self-sustaining so that atomic attacks would be disruptive but not necessarily fatal.

Even within units, tactical mobility was emphasized. Tactical mobility could range from foot mobility to the use of trucks, armored personnel carriers, and aircraft. In short, being able to concentrate or disperse quickly was the key to success and survival on the atomic battlefield. In the offense, atomic weapons could destroy major enemy concentrations while highly mobile infantry and armor forces could rapidly exploit deep into the enemy's position. In the defense, some penetration between the dispersed defensive positions by the enemy was unavoidable. However, once his attack was disrupted by the series of battle positions, he would be vulnerable to the defender's atomic weapons or to counterattacks on his flanks or rear.[70]

To enhance mobility, the development of aviation assets was made a high priority. Fixed-wing aircraft and helicopters took on integral roles. Helicopters, it was anticipated, would "expedite and improve ground procedures in forward areas of the battlefield." Transport capabilities would be developed with the goal of being able to swiftly move entire companies.[71]

At this time, the army accelerated production on a number of new atomic artillery and missile systems, most of which had been under development since the early 1950s. Some systems, such as the 280mm atomic cannon, had already been deployed, but this was a huge, highly immobile, and vulnerable piece of equipment, hardly suited for the mobile battlefield. Thus, the 280mm cannon was augmented with the Corporal, which had an 80-mile range and a 30-inch warhead, and with the Hermes, which had an 80- to 150-mile range and a 44-inch warhead. Missile development—for space exploration, long-range attack, and air defense—became a top priority and intensified the competition in this area between the army and the air force.[72]

Conceiving the Pentomic Divisions was one thing; actually implementing the ambitious changes the concept required proved to be quite another. Over time, numerous problem areas emerged:

- *Equipment:* Much of the equipment which the Pentomic Divisions were to employ simply was not available in the late 1950s. This included communications and radar devices, and aircraft that were essential for maneuver and control.

- *Mobility:* Problems were encountered in trying to make the heavily armored equipment that the divisions required transportable by air. In 1957, moreover, DoD stipulated that as the army increased its airlift capabilities other forms of army transportation would be reduced.

- *Firepower:* In Doughty's words, "The delayed delivery of some of the new. . .weapons caused the new division to lack the destructive capability and staying power required against an enemy armed with modern weapons." The Pentomic Divisions were to be flexible enough to fight a conventional or nuclear war, but it was doubtful that they could sustain prolonged activity.

- *Manpower:* The army assumed that the Pentomic concept would compensate for the reductions in manpower. Yet the army's manpower levels were severely cut back during Eisenhower's second term, from 1,026,000 in 1956 to 862,000 in 1959.[73] Divisions were reduced to 15. The army believed that firepower could replace manpower but not to the extent that such severe cutbacks warranted.

- *Practicability:* There was some question as to whether the army was oversimplifying operations on the atomic battlefield. Typically, the army planned for the battle to proceed conventionally until defeat seemed likely. The army would then resort to nuclear weapons. Numerous generals and analysts charged that the implications of fighting such a war had not been adequately thought through.

- *Organization and structure:* Operational command of a division designed for optimum flexibility proved next to impossible. Absent an intermediate echelon, the division commander had to oversee up to sixteen subordinate units. In tests, the divisions proved unable to sustain themselves during continuous operations, and "commanders resorted to stripping combat units to bolster service support elements too weak to support the division."[74]

The Pentomic Divisions were conceived for two reasons. One, the army sought to ensure for itself a proportionate role in the military planning process and a greater share of total military outlays. Two, army leaders were concerned over the growing nuclear capability of the Soviet Union, which made organization and doctrine for the atomic battlefield seem imminent.[75] But the problems in implementing the Pentomic Divisions outweighed the potential benefits, and the concept ultimately gave way to more traditional army doctrines. By the end of the decade, both the massive retaliation doctrine and the Pentomic Divisions were largely discredited.

Toward the end of Eisenhower's second term, some rethinking of massive retaliation took place. But the concept remained the central organizing principle of Eisenhower's national security policy, despite some recognition on the part of U.S. officials that air power was not the panacea of a deterrent it was originally envisaged to be. A serious effort to reformulate national security policy was not to occur until 1961, after John F. Kennedy assumed the presidency. Nonetheless, the later Eisenhower years did see a "new new look" to U.S. national security policy aimed at deemphasizing the U.S. reliance on the strategic air campaign and, in 1958, a major reorganization of the defense establishment. It is to that period that we now turn.

NOTES

1. Figures are from Office of the Assistant Secretary of Defense (Comptroller), *National Defense Budget Estimates for FY1988/ 1989* (May 1987), p. 72.

2. Both documents quoted in John Lewis Gaddis, *Strategies of Containment* (New York: Oxford University Press, 1982), pp. 124–125.

3. In James Lacy, *Within Bounds: The Navy in Postwar American Security Policy* (Alexandria, Virginia: Center for Naval Analyses, 1983), p. 163.

4. According to Ole R. Holsti, Gallup polls showed that in August 1950, 66 percent of the American public supported the U.S. entry into the war in Korea, but by October of 1952, only 37 percent did. Ole R. Holsti, "Public Opinion and Containment," in Terry L. Deibel and John Lewis Gaddis, eds., *Containment: Concept and Policy*, vol. 1 (Washington, D.C.: National Defense University Press, 1986), p. 77.

5. Quoted in Gaddis, *Strategies*, p. 146.

6. Quoted in John Spanier, *American Foreign Policy Since World War II* (New York: Praeger Publishers, 1973), p.102.

7. Quoted in Edward Kolodziej, *The Uncommon Defense and Congress* (Columbus: Ohio State University, 1966), p. 181.

8. Note by the secretaries to the Joint Chiefs of Staff, *Military Strategy and Posture*, 10 December 1953, p. 1084. (NSA).

9. Quoted in H.W. Brands, Jr., "Testing Massive Retaliation," *International Security* 12, no. 4 (Spring 1988): 149.

10. Kolodziej, *Uncommon Defense*, p. 186. This provides an interesting contrast to Eisenhower's early thinking as commander of U.S. armed forces in Germany. In a memo to the JCS dated January 21, 1946, Eisenhower wrote that the atomic bomb "makes war unendurable. Its very existence should make war unthinkable." In the following paragraph, Eisenhower again endorsed a philosophy which ran counter to his future policies as pres-

ident: "The atomic bomb cannot stand alone in the nation's arsenal. To put all our reliance on that one powerful weapon is to court disaster." Dwight D. Eisenhower, *Statement of the Effect of Atomic Weapons on National Military Organization*, January 21, 1946. (NSA).

11. John Foster Dulles, Speech before the Council of Foreign Relations, January 12, 1954.

12. John Foster Dulles, "Policy for Security and Peace," *Foreign Affairs* (April 1954): 356, 358.

13. In Lacy, *Within Bounds*, p. 189.

14. John Foster Dulles, "The Evolution of Foreign Policy," Department of State *Bulletin*, January 25, 1954, quoted in Lacy, *Within Bounds*, p. 168.

15. Note by the secretaries to the Joint Chiefs, p. 1089. (NSA).

16. Figures from Richard Cohen, *National Defense Spending Patterns: Implications for Future Nuclear Weapons R&D Funding* (Washington, D.C.: Washington Defense Research Group, December 1987), various charts.

17. Great Britain, France, the Netherlands, Belgium, Italy, and Luxembourg.

18. Quoted in Stanley Sloan, *NATO's Future: Toward A New Transatlantic Bargain* (Washington, D.C.: National Defense University Press, 1985), pp. 21–22. At a press conference, Dulles warned the Europeans that a failure to ratify "would force from the United States an agonizing reappraisal of its foreign policy." While the effect of Dulles's press conference is unknown, there is some evidence that it backfired. One official of the French Foreign Ministry reportedly concluded that "the press conference had finished EDC, that it must have been deliberate, that the problem was now to save the Atlantic Alliance, that some new way would have to be found to tie Germany to the West, perhaps through NATO, and finally that France would have to do some painful rethinking of its own policies" (Sloan, p. 22).

19. What is interesting is that the French, who actively discouraged ratification, had originally proposed the treaty. A number of reasons for the French turnaround have been posited. Besides a relaxed perception of the Soviet threat, they include unwillingness to take on new commitments after defeat in Indochina and likelihood of struggle in Algeria; concern over aggressiveness of new U.S. policies; political pressure from French Communists against a weak French government; and France's fear of a

resurgent West Germany. On these points see Sloan, *New Trans-atlantic Bargain*, pp. 25–27.

20. The context within which these decisions were made should be kept in mind. In 1954, World War II was only nine years past. Consider the formidable impact that a comparably limited war fought in a remote theater about 17 years ago—Vietnam—has on U.S. military planning today. Then consider what the impact of a hypothetical war fought in the United States and leaving the United States largely decimated and fought only ten years ago—1980—would be. This was the situation confronting the Europeans in 1954.

21. John Greenwood, "The Emergence of the Postwar Strategic Air Force, 1945–1953," in Alfred Hurley and Robert Ehrhart, eds., *Air Power and Warfare*, The Proceedings of the 8th Military History Symposium (Washington, D.C.: Office of Air Force History, 1979), p. 236.

22. This figure actually represents a decrease from the original JCS recommendation for 143 wings, but the JCS estimated a $42-billion budget, much larger than Eisenhower was prepared to accept. On October 16, 1953, Defense Secretary Charles Wilson formed the Everest committee to determine how the United States could conform to the JCS force recommendations at reduced cost. The committee recommended that the number of air force fighter wings be reduced to 137.

23. Specifically, the Mark 7 was deployed on the *CORPORAL* (1953), the *HONEST JOHN* (1954) and the third modification of the *Atomic Demolition Munition* (ADM-B, 1954).

24. Matthew Ridgway, Memorandum to the Secretary of Defense, 27 June 1955, pp. 2, 3. (NSA).

25. In A.J. Bacevich, *The Pentomic Era: The U.S. Army between Korea and Vietnam* (Washington, D.C.: National Defense University Press, 1986), p. 28.

26. Bacevich, *The Pentomic Era*, p. 29.

27. Bacevich, *The Pentomic Era*, p. 31. Eisenhower conceded that "we can't tell what we will do after we achieve a victory in what will be total and not in any sense limited warfare."

28. CNO Robert Carney, memo to the Joint Chiefs of Staff, quoted in David Alan Rosenberg, "American Postwar Air Doctrine and Organization: The Navy Experience," in Hurley and Ehrhart, *Air Power and Warfare*, p. 268.

29. Rosenberg, "American Postwar Air Doctrine," p. 268.

30. At this time, the significance of the nuclear-powered submarine was not yet fully appreciated. It was perceived as potentially useful "in the vanguard of carrier Task Forces," serving as "scouts, missile carriers, and radar pickets." H.G. Rickover, remarks at commissioning of USS *Nautilus*, San Francisco, October 27, 1953, quoted in James Mullen, *The Evolution of U.S. Naval Strategy, 1945–1975* (unpublished paper prepared for the Army War College, Carlisle, Pennsylvania, 1974), p. 17. The missile carrier mission had not yet emerged as a significant strategic naval function.

31. Lacy, *Within Bounds*, p. 212.

32. This concept would emerge in the Reagan administration's maritime strategy. See chapter 10.

33. Lacy, *Within Bounds*, pp. 207–208.

34. Rosenberg, "American Postwar Air Doctrine," p. 269, quoting official naval documents.

35. Quoted in Lacy, *Within Bounds*, p. 209.

36. Barry Blechman and Stephen S. Kaplan, *Force Without War* (Washington, D.C.: The Brookings Institution, 1978), p. 48.

37. In 1954 Eisenhower appointed the Killian Board, under the chairmanship of James Killian of the Massachusetts Institute of Technology (MIT), to study U.S. national security policy. The report of the board, *Meeting the Threat of Surprise Attack*, was released to the president in February 1955.

38. SEATO was a treaty organization much like NATO in its basis in collective security. It involved the United States and a number of friendly Asian nations.

39. Indeed, much controversy was engendered by the fact that the treaty failed to commit the United States to the defense of the islands themselves.

40. Brands, "Testing Massive Retaliation," p. 147.

41. In James Shepley, "How Dulles Averted War," *Life* XL (January 16, 1956): 78.

42. A current historian, for example, had studied newly declassified archival records and concluded that "war was avoided due more to Chinese Communists' caution than to the diplomatic skills of Eisenhower and Dulles." Gordon H. Chang, "To The Nuclear Brink," *International Security* 12, no. 4 (Spring 1988): 122.

43. See, John Prados, *The Soviet Estimate* (Princeton: Princeton University Press, 1986).

44. Ridgway, "Speech Before the Council of Foreign Relations," 14 February 1955, in Bacevich, *Pentomic Era*, p. 50.

45. Department of the Army, Field Manual (FM) 100-5, *Operations* (Washington, D.C.: 1954), p. 4-5.

46. Air Force Manual (AFM) 1-8, *Strategic Air Operations* (Department of the Air Force, 1 May 1954), p. 2.

47. Air Force Manual 1-2, *United States Air Force Basic Doctrine* (Department of the Air Force, 1 April 1955), p. 10.

48. AFM 1-2 (1955), p. 7.

49. General Curtis LeMay, memo, "Capabilities and Employment of SAC," February 4, 1947, p. 5. (NSA).

50. Robert Futrell, *Ideas, Concepts, Doctrine: A History of Basic Thinking in the United States Air Force, 1907–1964* (Maxwell AFB, Alabama: Air University Press, 1974), p. 207.

51. Air Force Secretary Donald Quarles in October 1956 and Air Force Director of Plans General John D. Cary in March 1957 both quoted in Futrell, *Ideas, Concepts, Doctrine*, p. 227.

52. Ibid. One exception to the third point was the tactical Matador missile.

53. Richard Klocko, "Air Power in Limited Military Actions," summarized in Robert Futrell, ibid., p. 226.

54. Thomas B. Cochran, William P. Arkin, and Thomas Hoening, *Nuclear Weapons Databook*, vol. 1, *U.S. Nuclear Forces and Capabilities* (Cambridge, Massachusetts: Ballinger, 1984), p. 15.

55. Robert Futrell, "The Influence of the Air Power Concept on Air Force Planning, 1945–1962," in Harry Borowski, ed., *Military Planning in the Twentieth Century*, Proceedings of the Eleventh Military History Symposium (Washington, D.C.: USAF Office of History, 1986), p. 266.

56. Jeffrey Record, *Revising U.S. Military Strategy: Tailoring Means to Ends* (McLean, Virginia: Pergamon-Brassey's, 1984), p. 103, appendix E.

57. Appendixes C and E in Record, *Revising*, pp. 101, 103. It may seem surprising that air force personnel dropped at all. This was a period of fiscal constraint, however, and the relative drop compared to the army is the essential figure.

58. Kolodziej, *Uncommon Defense*, p. 230–231.

59. For FY1957, army active-duty end strength was approximately 998,000 personnel. Comptroller's Office, *National Defense Budget Estimates*, p. 124.

60. FM 100-5 (1954), p. 8.

61. FM 100-5 (1954), p. 96.

62. FM 100-5 (1954), p. 96.

63. FM 100-5 (1954), p. 121.

64. FM 100-5 (1954), p. 120.

65. FM 100-5 (1954), p.131. The 1956 and 1958 revision of Army field regulations contributed few changes to the development of the atomic battlefield. They further emphasized the deeply intertwined relationship between mobility, dispersion, and atomic warfare and said that the commander should consider their use complementarily.

66. The definitive discussion on this point remains Russell Wiegley, *The American Way of War* (New York: Macmillan, 1973).

67. Although this book is fundamentally a history of conventional planning, the Pentomic Divisions are discussed because an essential purpose of this study is to communicate conceptions of the battlefield throughout the postwar era. The Pentomic Divisions are an important part of that history.

68. Robert Doughty, *The Evolution of US Army Tactical Doctrine, 1946–1976*, Leavenworth Papers no. 1 (Fort Leavenworth, Kansas: Combat Studies Institute, 1979), p. 17. The name Pentomic Divisions came from the repeated use of the number five in the concept and the orientation toward the atomic battlefield. Much of the following discussion is from the Doughty study and from Bacevich, *Pentomic Era.*

69. Doughty points out that most of the manpower reductions came in command and control personnel, because one of the main purposes of the reorganization was to increase the "foxhole strength" of each division. Doughty, *Evolution*, p. 17.

70. Doughty, *Evolution*, p. 18.

71. Futrell, *Ideas, Concepts, Doctrine*, p. 178.

72. This competition came to a head in the Thor-Jupiter IRBM controversy of 1956. The air force and the army were each developing its own intermediate-range ballistic missiles (IRBMs)—the Thor and the Jupiter, respectively—and each wanted sole jurisdictional control over its missile. Defense Secretary Wilson ruled in favor of the air force, giving the air arm sole jurisdiction over IRBM deployment. The army was permitted to develop Jupiter, but when fielded, the missile would come

under air force control. In 1957, new Defense Secretary McElroy allowed the army to develop a new missile, the Pershing.

73. Comptroller's Office, *National Defense Budget Estimates*, p. 124.

74. Bacevich, *Pentomic Era*, p. 134.

75. Much deliberation was given to tactics on the atomic battlefield. One typical article that appeared in the June 1956 issue of *Army* offered advice such as "the circular hole is a bit more difficult to dig by hand, but mass production of such atomic foxholes seems feasible except by troops digging in under atomic fire." Colonel Henry E. Kelly, "Dig That Atomic Foxhole," *Army* 6, no. 6 (June 1956).

6
The New New Look

LIMITED WAR AND THE NEW STANDARD OF SUFFICIENCY

In 1957 the NATO ministers once again reduced the Lisbon goals, from 50 active-and-ready reserve divisions to a 30-division standing force in Europe's central region. In many ways, this was the last act of the New Look and of strict adherence to the nuclear-oriented massive retaliation as the basis of U.S. security policy.

As alluded to in the previous chapter, a number of events in late 1956 and 1957 led to stepped-up criticism of massive retaliation. One particularly important event occurred in the summer of 1956. On July 26, the Egyptian leader Gamal Abdel Nasser announced his intention to nationalize the Suez Canal, guaranteeing passage of all ships except Israel's. On October 25, the Israelis launched an attack on Egypt in the Sinai Peninsula. A day later British and French forces joined the Israelis in the effort.[1]

The United States opposed this intervention and eventually persuaded the British, French, and Israeli forces to withdraw.[2] Nevertheless, the event enhanced Nasser's prestige among the Arab states in the region and encouraged him to attempt additional pan-Arabic initiatives. Jordan was urged to establish an economic and military union with Egypt and Syria. In the spring of 1957, the Egyptians, hoping to facilitate the rise of a pro-Egyptian government in Lebanon, organized riots against the Lebanese government. Nasser stepped up his rhetorical attacks on Western governments, in particular the United States, and made a number of diplomatic overtures to the Soviet Union.

Spurred by the Suez Crisis, in early 1957 the Eisenhower administration pledged the United States to defend the Middle East against "overt aggression from any nation controlled by international communism."[3] The Eisenhower Doctrine, as the proclamation came to be known, was meant to signify a new U.S. willingness to intervene directly on behalf of its allies. This broke from past policy, which was based on building up local indigenous forces and backing them with U.S. nuclear power, and in a 1958 crisis, the United States went so far as to send a marine landing-force to Lebanon.

But other events in the latter 1950s were putting into question the viability of Eisenhower's policies. In August 1957, the Soviets announced that they had developed an intercontinental missile capability. In October they launched Sputnik, an artificial satellite that orbited the Earth and seemed to confirm the August announcement. The implication of Sputnik was that, given the Soviets' intercontinental reach, the United States was now as vulnerable to attack from the Soviet Union as the Soviet Union was from U.S. bases in Europe and around the Soviet periphery. The Gaither Committee, appointed by Eisenhower in early 1957 to examine the viability of implementing civil defense, presented its report almost immediately after the Sputnik launch. Entitled "Deterrence and Survival in the Nuclear Age," the Gaither report argued that

- a "missile gap" between the United States and the Soviet Union was widening in the Soviets' favor;
- SAC aircraft forward deployed at European bases were vulnerable to preemptive Soviet attack and would find it increasingly difficult to penetrate the evergrowing Soviet air defense batteries;[4]
- the United States should institute a comprehensive civil defense program; and
- the United States should increase defense spending on conventional as well as strategic forces.

The report added to the Sputnik-induced fears of a "missile gap" and precipitated near-hysterical public and congressional demands for increased defense spending.[5]

The report recommended over $44 billion in additional defense expenditures and primarily on this basis was rejected by Eisenhower. By July 1957, the nation was running a deficit of approximately $273 million. In addition, the nation entered into a recession in 1957–1958, and prices were rising steadily. Not wishing to cut domestic spending or raise taxes, Eisenhower looked to the defense budget, planned at $42 billion for FY1958, as a source of possible budget cuts.

At the same time, the Soviets continued to build up their own atomic arsenal and atomic delivery capability. The military superiority upon which massive retaliation rested was eroding, and the threat of massive retaliatory attacks seemed increasingly less credible as Soviet atomic capabilities improved. The administration responded to these adverse trends in two ways: first, a new standard of sufficiency replaced superiority as the basis of planning, and second, limited atomic-war concepts replaced the threat of total war inherent in massive retaliation.

In the nuclear age, it was now ordained, power would be measured in terms of one's absolute capabilities, rather than one's capabilities relative to the adversary. A hint of the president's emerging views was seen in a conference he held in November 1957 with Gaither and other members of the Gaither Committee, just prior to the release of the Gaither report. The members of the committee made clear their problems with the present state of military affairs. Eisenhower agreed with the committee members that military strength is most sensibly measured relative to the capabilities of one's opponents', but in his view, the United States was "getting pretty close to absolutes" when it could inflict up to 50 percent casualties on the enemy.[6] A new administration perspective was thus beginning to emerge: power would be measured in terms of *sufficiency*, as Assistant Defense Secretary for Research and Development (R&D) Donald Quarles explained:

> Neither side can hope by a mere margin of superiority in airplanes or other means of delivery of atomic weapons to escape the catastrophe of [nuclear] war. Beyond a certain point, this prospect is not the result of *relative* strength of the two opposed forces. It is the *absolute* power in the hands of each, and in the substantial invulnerability of this power to interdiction.[7]

By embracing the sufficiency standard, the administration could justify cutbacks for all the services. In formulating the FY1958 budget, the navy—whose manpower levels in 1957 had risen from 669,925 to 677,108 men—was instructed to cut back to just over 641,000. Its total number of combatant ships fell from 743 to 677 (although the navy actually gained two carriers in this period). The army suffered the most drastic cuts, losing almost 100,000 personnel (from 997,994 to 898,925) and three full divisions. This time around, even the air force came under the budget knife, as some cuts in the tactical forces were levied. The service's total wings fell from 137 to 117. From 1957's 919,835 personnel, the air force dropped to 871,156. Tactical wings began a steady three-year decline (from 25 to 24, down to 18 by 1960), and operational aircraft fell from 7,115 to 6,054.[8]

In the 1960s, massive retaliation would be wholly repudiated by the Kennedy administration. But in the late 1950s, the Eisenhower administration remained steadfastly committed to nuclear weapons as the basis of security policy. The U.S. tactical nuclear weapon stockpiles had grown consistently throughout the 1950s, but in the last years of the decade their role in administration planning became increasingly prominent. Their ascendency in the planning process was directly tied to the rise of limited nuclear war as a planning concept. In October 1957, Secretary of State John Foster Dulles argued that the development of tactical and battlefield atomic weapons meant that resorting to nuclear weapons "need not involve vast destruction and widespread harm to humanity" and that

> in the future it may thus be feasible to place less reliance upon deterrence of vast retaliatory power. It may be possible to defend countries by nuclear weapons so mobile, or so placed, as to make military invasion with conventional forces a hazardous attempt. For example, terrain is often such that invasion routes can be decisively dominated by nuclear artillery.

Dulles went on to say that a conventional aggression would very likely be met with a direct and limited nuclear response. As a result, "would-be aggressors will be unable to count on a successful conventional aggression, but must themselves weigh the consequences of invoking nuclear war."[9] Such thinking was reflected in NSC 5810/1, the National Security Council's 1958 statement of *Basic National Security Policy*. In contrast to past statements of policy, 5810/1 acknowledged that "uncertainty is growing whether U.S. massive nuclear capabilities would be used to defend free world interests." In the same vein, 5810/1 acknowledged that an overreliance on the strategic air campaign could undermine deterrence. Where past statements of policy took the view that such a capability ensured deterrence at lower levels, it was now argued that

> the prompt and resolute application of the degree of force necessary to defeat such local aggression is considered the best means to keep hostilities from broadening into general war. . . . When the use of U.S. forces is required to oppose local aggression, force will be applied in a manner and on a scale best calculated to avoid hostilities from broadening into general war.[10]

This modified approach to military planning (sometimes called the New New Look) was directly applicable to developments in Europe, where the conventional force balance continued to weigh heavily in favor of the Soviets. General Lauris Norstrad, allied commander in Europe, noted that if in Europe "we have means to meet less-than-ultimate threats with a decisive, but less-than-ultimate response, the very possession of this ability would discourage the threat."[11]

Certainly, the New New Look was consistent with the trends demonstrated by the army's Pentomic Divisions. Limited war now meant battlefield engagements combining some nonnuclear weapons and tactics with tactical nuclear weapons, employed to achieve traditional military ends. In that sense, the New New Look was an attempt to bring strategy back into the military calculation. For the navy, the new theories meant a continuation of existent policies. In all the crisis situations in which the navy had been involved in the past decade, none had escalated to the nuclear level (most involved only a "show of force"). In spite of Eisenhower's cutbacks, the navy's position with respect to procurement was relatively secure, most likely because the Polaris missile was gaining popularity among many military planners as an effective alternative to the air force bombers. Work was also under way on new carriers, new strategic submarines, and a variety of antisubmarine warfare programs as well.

The air force, experiencing significant budget cuts for the first time since the pre–Korean War era, had to adjust its posture somewhat. The adequacy of SAC as a deterrent seemed threatened as the worldwide bases from which SAC operated became increasingly vulnerable to Soviet attack and as the navy's Polaris missile program continued to grow.[12] These problems were obviously deeply intertwined, given that the navy was offering the Polaris as the means of resolving the vulnerability problem. Nonetheless, the attention now being given to air force vulnerability led to changes in air force alert policies and to reductions in the number of forward-based aircraft. But the challenge from the navy also led to much internal dissension within the air force itself and to fundamental changes in air force planning and procurement.

At first, the air force resolved that its mission was simply to educate the public on the differences between tactical low-yield and thermonuclear high-yield atomic weapons. But the extent to which the air force should, in a limited war, rely on nuclear explosives of any sort became the topic of considerable intraservice debate. One faction, led by Air Force Chief of Staff General Thomas White, endorsed the use of small tactical atomic weapons to support battlefield operations. In a speech on December 4, White summed up the air force's position:

> Just as nuclear delivery capability constitutes a deterrent to general war, so can this total firepower deter local war. The right measure of this total firepower can, in turn, resolve local conflict if we fail to deter the aggression. . . . We deter with our total capability, including all lesser facets thereof; we will elect to use that portion required and best suited to the resolution of the particular conflict.[13]

Proponents of this view generally pointed to the high performance potential of SAC's bombers in performing bombing missions, and to the increasing hardness of enemy targets. But General Otis Weyland, the commander of the Tactical Air Command, dissented from this view:

> I can visualize local war situations arising where the threat of only atomic retaliation would severely prescribe the U.S. bargaining position at the conference table and turn the mass of human opinion against us; whereas possessing a conventional retaliation could place world opinion on our side. . . . I do not foster a large and expensive program, but rather a modest program designed to meet the limited requirements of a local war. . . . I, therefore, believe our policy must be to continue retention and modernization of a conventional capability.[14]

But at this point in time TAC was still largely subordinated to SAC and, while Weyland's views were not ignored altogether, they did not have much impact on air force planning. Thought was given to the use of nuclear weapons in limited roles, but the notion of building up the conventional forces was rejected, if only because such a buildup would require resources that could otherwise be devoted to nuclear weapons procurement and upkeep.

TAC took on a more preeminent role in air force planning but not to the extent that SAC's primacy was challenged. TAC's principal contribution to the planning process was the basing plan it proposed as an alternative to SAC's forward-based global network. It was clear that forward-based air forces were becoming increasingly vulnerable to attack, especially as the Soviet nuclear arsenal continued to grow. TAC's solution to this problem was forward and rear deployments, with a minimum number of highly alert units in forward areas and the remainder in safer, rear-area bases located in the United States. TAC thus proposed to keep two squadrons of a fighter group in the United States while rotating the third squadron at bases throughout Europe. In the event of hostilities, the two U.S. squadrons would immediately be deployed overseas to join the squadrons on alert in the forward area. The biggest obstacle to TAC's plan was in generating adequate refueling capabilities. To this end, TAC secured the KB-29 tankers released by SAC when SAC converted its forces to KC-97s and KC-135s. TAC also equipped KB-50 tankers with multiple refueling probes.[15]

Under General Weyland, TAC requested a number of additional aircraft while simultaneously increasing its dependence upon new air-delivered missiles. By the end of the decade, however, TAC may have asked for too much. SAC's leadership privately criticized TAC for developing duplicative capabilities. In FY1959 the air force was asked to absorb further cuts, and consequently, TAC suffered the brunt of the cutbacks. White announced that the majority of cuts would come "mainly through the inactivation of tactical air wings," and TAC's 24 wings were cut to 18.

In 1958, two events occurred that further laid bare the inviability of massive retaliation and planted the roots of the Kennedy administration's fundamental reevaluation of the U.S. military posture. The first was the U.S. intervention, in the summer of 1958, in the civil war between the Christians and the Muslims in Lebanon. The Muslims sought closer relations with the Arab republics; the Christians sought to maintain Lebanon's independence and confirm that country's ties with the West. Along with British paratroopers, the United States landed about 14,000 marines in Lebanon. By October, the situation stabilized, and both the British and the U.S. troops withdrew.

The Lebanon experience showed that situations could arise where U.S. conventional forces could be successfully called upon. By any standard, it would have been totally unacceptable to introduce nuclear weapons in the Lebanon crisis (there is no evidence that this was seriously contemplated) or to bomb the Soviet Union. Yet the United States took a considerable risk in hoping that the conflict could be ended quickly. Had the situation not quickly quieted, the United States would have resorted to its conventional, not its nuclear, forces. This would have tainted the credibility of the massive retaliation policy.

As always, there was the question of the Soviets. Under Nikita Khrushchev their rhetoric became especially bellicose as they worked to solidify their role as an influence in the Middle East. They actively sided with Arab nationalist movements, the Lebanese Muslims in particular. Had the Soviet Union directly entered the conflict, the United States would have had to make the hard choices massive retaliation required. Fortunately, the situation was quickly contained, but some skepticism emerged over whether the United States would be willing to stand up to a superpower challenge in the Middle East and whether U.S. nonnuclear forces were sufficiently ready to adequately sustain such an involvement.

The second event was the Soviet announcement in November 1958 that the four-power occupation of Berlin would end in six months, and control over East Berlin and the supply routes and roads leading into West Berlin would be transferred to the East Germans. The Soviets' motives were to gain formal recognition of the East German state by forcing the United States and the other Western powers to deal directly with the East Germans, and to force the assimilation of West Berlin into its sphere of influence.[16]

Diplomacy temporarily resolved the Berlin crisis. At a summit between Eisenhower and Khrushchev in September 1959, Khrushchev agreed to withdraw the Soviet ultimatum (the six-month period having already elapsed at any rate) in return for an American commitment to renegotiate the issue at a four-power summit. The crisis was momentarily defused, although it was to heat up again under Kennedy (as discussed in the next chapter).

Like the problem in Lebanon, the Berlin crisis raised questions about the credibility of the U.S. commitment to Europe. West Berlin was ostensibly protected by the U.S. nuclear umbrella. Would the United States have threatened nuclear escalation if the crisis continued? If not, how would that affect the U.S. credibility as the leader of the Western alliance? If so, what would that say about U.S. policy?

Proclaiming battlefield nuclear weapons to be instruments of deterrence could be effective when no challenger had many such weapons. In December 1954, when the allies agreed in MC 14/2 to base their security on tactical nuclear weapons in lieu of building robust conventional forces, the Soviet atomic stockpile was still small and the tactical nuclear stockpile minuscule. The possibility of tactical nuclear warfare in the European theater was of concern to NATO planners, but they were generally confident that NATO forces could absorb the brunt of an atomic attack.[17] As the Soviet tactical nuclear stockpile grew, however, this assumption was increasingly put into question.

Now, the possibility of the United States being self-deterred emerged. Clearly, threatening strategic nuclear escalation over Berlin would have been a questionable tactic. From the European perspective, threatening to fight a limited atomic war was no more appealing. Such a war would be devastating. To the Europeans, the distinction between limited atomic war and global thermonuclear war was virtually meaningless. Some of the Europeans were suspicious that a doctrine for limited nuclear war was a deliberate effort to keep nuclear war on European soil and away from the continental U.S. Yet NATO's conventional forces were so skeletonized that threatening purely nonnuclear responses was not credible.

As mentioned, Eisenhower was not about to implement all the recommendations of the Killian Board, which he rejected on the basis of cost. But Sputnik raised an immense furor in the United States, and partially in response to it, Eisenhower announced some adjustments in the U.S. force structure in his 1958 State of the Union address. Eisenhower endorsed improvements in firepower, equipment, and conventional forces; eschewed an over-reliance on single-system strategies, such as embodied by SAC; and called for balanced tripartite forces to optimize deterrence. As the year went on, Eisenhower submitted three budget supplementals. One was an addition to the FY1958 budget then in effect; two were for the proposed FY1959 budget.

However, the supplementals were essentially geared toward improving strategic programs, such as missile and heavy bomber procurement and improved command and control for air defense. Despite his rhetoric and calls for preparedness across a spectrum of conflict, Eisenhower remained committed to a constrained defense budget and continued reliance on nuclear weapons. In submitting their FY1960 budget, administration spokesmen argued that a strategic bomber force of 43 wings, in combination with intermediate-range ballistic missile (IRBM) units to be stationed in Turkey, Italy, and the United Kingdom, would sufficiently deter Soviet aggression.[18] There was simply no administration support for increased conventional force levels. By FY1960, army end strength was down to just over 850,000 men and 14 divisions. Navy personnel and force levels dropped to 617,984 men, 615 combatants, and 23 fleet carriers. Lastly, the air force was reduced to 814,752 men, 18 tactical air wings, and only 4,787 aircraft.[19]

Predictably, conventional military planning stagnated in this period. Even after the Berlin and Lebanese crises, conventional force levels dropped, so there was little incentive to develop comprehensive new plans for their employment. The air force was now committed to limited nuclear war planning, and missions were primarily divided between SAC and TAC. The navy quietly sailed along. Absorbed in development of Polaris, ASW capabilities, and new carriers, war planning was a low priority. The army had grudgingly organized itself into Pentomic Divisions,[20] and, suffering the most severe manpower cutbacks, was reluctant to attempt serious doctrinal refinement.

In its continued emphasis on nuclear weapons, the New New Look brought few substantive changes from massive retaliation. Eisenhower's policies seemed to limit U.S. military options to the early introduction of nuclear arms, and this became an increasingly questionable proposition. As one analyst has noted, European conventional war was ruled out "if for no other reason than the receding size of the Army and Marine Corps and the paucity of the funds allocated for non-nuclear modernization and procurement, to air and sea lift, and to tactical air power, precluded such a confrontation beyond a limited probing action."[21]

According to Eisenhower's critics, the policy lacked credibility and was unable to meet the vast array of alliance commitments the United States had established throughout Eisenhower's tenure. Massive retaliation, critics such as John F. Kennedy argued, may or may not have deterred adversaries of the United States but it did seem to deter the United States from acting decisively in crises. Thus, after assuming office in 1961, Kennedy proceeded to initiate sweeping changes in U.S. defense planning. Kennedy's policies are discussed in chapter 7.

THE 1958 REORGANIZATION ACT

As president, Eisenhower was particularly disturbed by what he perceived to be a persistent inability among the services to cooperate in setting force requirements and in planning for the execution of military operations. For example, both the army and navy were at odds with the air force over missile procurement; the navy and the air force heavily disputed roles and missions for strategic forces; and the army and air force continued to scrap over battlefield issues such as interdiction and close air support. Eisenhower was concerned that this inability to cooperate would emerge in military operations.

Throughout the 1950s, various efforts were made to work out acceptable command and procurement arrangements. The Pace-Finletter agreement of October 2, 1951, (named after the army and air force secretaries who negotiated it) took an early stab at the issue of organic army aviation, which had been left unclarified by the Key West agreement. In the Pace-Finletter memorandum, organic army aviation was defined as army aircraft used within the army combat zone, which was determined to be 50 to 75 miles in depth. The functions for such aircraft were specified, and it was stated that such aircraft should not duplicate air force functions. An agreement reached one year later redefined the combat zone to be 50 to 100 miles in depth, and limited organic army aviation to no more than 5,000 pounds. A 1956 agreement clarified roles and missions relating to tactical missile development and air defense and put further restrictions on organic army aviation.[22]

But these clarifications did not resolve the thorny issue of theater command. The army insisted that in a conflict it would best know how covering air assets should be allocated, so the theater army commander should maintain control over such forces. The air force insisted that air power was indivisible, that TAC would provide all the cover the army would need, and that ultimate control had to remain in the hands of the theater air commander.

The problem was that there was no overarching authority to guide either force procurement or, in the event of hostilities, the use of force. Both the secretary of defense and the JCS were proving ineffectual in providing the necessary direction. The service chiefs tended to look after the needs of their own service first. Whatever joint planning was agreed upon tended to be elaborate compromises, seeking to encompass the stated requirements of all the service secretaries without requiring much sacrifice from any. And most importantly, the JCS did not control the purse strings; money for training and equipping the armed forces went to the services themselves. There was little incentive among them to compromise on roles and missions, because that may have brought with it some cutbacks on already constrained budgets.

Eisenhower's concern, thus, was that the disjointedness that dominated service planning in peacetime would hinder effective operations in war. In a message to Congress dated April 3, 1958, Eisenhower clarified his concerns:

> First, separate ground, sea and air warfare is gone forever. If ever again we should be involved in war, we will fight it in all elements, with all services, as one single concentrated effort. Peacetime preparatory and organizational activity must conform to this fact. Strategic and tactical planning must be completely unified, combat forces organized into unified commands, each equipped with the most efficient weapons systems that science can develop, singly led and prepared to fight as one, regardless of service. The accomplishment of this result is the basic function of the Secretary of Defense, advised and assisted by the Joint Chiefs of Staff and operating under the supervision of the Commander-in-Chief.
>
> Additionally, Secretary of Defense authority, especially in respect to the development of new weapons, must be clear and direct, and flexible in the management of funds. Prompt decisions and elimination of wasteful activity must be primary goals.[23]

To enhance the overall unity in the armed forces and to strengthen the organizational and operational structure of the military establishment, Eisenhower recommended a number of detailed reforms in a proposal dated April 15, 1958. By early August, these proposals were passed by Congress with few substantive changes. The 1958 act

- strengthened the authority of the secretary of defense over both the Department of Defense and the military services.
- strengthened the unified and specified commands by clarifying their statutory mandate and including the word "combatant" in

their title. They were henceforth "unified or specified combatant commands." In the language accompanying the act, Congress noted that "forces assigned to such unified combatant commands shall be under the full operational command of the commander of the unified combatant command or the commander of the specified combatant command."[24]

- removed the services from the direct chain of command in military operations. The operational channel would now run from the commander in chief and the secretary of defense directly to the unified commanders, thereby bypassing the military components.

- strengthened the JCS, which was made responsible for providing the military advice that heretofore had been provided by the staffs of the service components. The Joint Staff was increased from 210 to 400 officers, and the prohibition against voting by the chairman of the JCS was removed.[25] The marine commandant was made a member of the JCS although his role was limited to affairs that directly affected the marine corps.

The 1958 Reorganization Act was sweeping but proved to be largely ineffectual. Eisenhower wanted to enhance the secretary of defense's authority with respect to delegating combat missions and avoiding redundancy in planning. But many members of Congress were skeptical about doing this, because of concerns that doing so would weaken their own voice in these matters. As a result, a compromise was reached whereby the secretary of defense was given authority to determine combat functions, but his decisions were subject to legislative veto. The act inadequately enhanced the authority of the JCS, and essentially did little to improve the force procurement process. Perhaps the greatest flaw in the act was that it provided the JCS with no budgetary authority. Because there was no need to justify force requirements to the JCS, there was no incentive for the services to justify their force requirements in terms of their contribution to multiservice operations. Moreover, the service components remained responsible for supplying, equipping, and training forces, so the tendency to view force requirements from a service perspective remained unchanged. Finally, the act failed for a fundamental reason: the service chiefs saw their allegiance to the JCS as secondary to their responsibility to their respective services. As Frederick Hartmann and Robert Wendzel point out, the service chiefs "saw the JCS arena primarily as one in which they could enhance overall national security while preserving the roles and missions and position and responsibility of their own services. . . .

Because the chiefs gain their real power from control of their services, they are not going to, in effect, turn the power over."[26]

Thus, little came of the 1958 reorganization. Although in ensuing years, clarifications and amendments to the act would attempt to further strengthen the hand of the secretary of defense and the JCS and to further clarify service roles and missions, the next major attempt at reorganization would not occur until 1986. That reorganization is discussed in chapter 10. For now, we turn our attention to the Kennedy administration and its major revision of U.S. national security policy known as flexible response.

NOTES

1. The French sought Nasser's downfall because of his aid to Algerian rebels. The British did not trust Nasser and felt that his attempt to assert power over the Western-oriented nations of the Middle East had to be addressed. The British were also concerned over the potential effects of nationalization of the canal on the flow of Middle Eastern oil.

2. Probably, to enhance U.S. prestige, to align itself with anticolonialist instincts rampant in the Middle East, and to deny the Soviets a potential foothold.

3. Department of State, *Bulletin* 36 (January 21, 1957): 86.

4. In 1953 the Soviets possessed approximately 2,000 interceptor aircraft. This figure steadily increased through the latter 1950s, and by the early 1960s, had doubled. In this period, Moscow also established a ring of surface-to-air missiles (SAMs) around Moscow and other key Soviet cities. See Michael M. Boll, *National Security Planning: Roosevelt through Reagan* (Lexington: University Press of Kentucky, 1988), p. 83.

5. It should be noted that defense spending in dollars actually rose throughout this period. This was to cover the cost of inflation.

6. General A.J. Goodpaster, "Memorandum of Conference With the President," November 7, 1957, p. 2. (NSA).

7. In Samuel Huntington, *The Common Defense: Strategic Programs in National Politics* (New York: Columbia University Press, 1961), p. 101.

8. These figures are distilled from Jeffrey Record, *Revising U.S. Military Strategy: Tailoring Means to Ends* (McLean, Virginia: Pergamon-Brassey's, 1984), pp. 101–103.

9. James Lacy, *Within Bounds: The Navy in Postwar American Security Policy* (Alexandria, Virginia: Center for Naval Analyses, 1983), pp. 234–235.

10. National Security Council, NSC 5810/1, *Basic National Security Policy*, May 5, 1958, p. 5. (NSA).

11. In Lacy, *Within Bounds*, p. 235.

12. Polaris was gaining acceptance as an alternative to SAC for a number of reasons. One, the navy was promoting the invulnerability of sea-based forces relative to SAC's bombers. This was an important argument at a time when the growing Soviet arsenal was raising fears of a debilitating Soviet attack. Two, the navy was espousing a strategic targeting theory known as finite deterrence, which emphasized the importance of the capacity to destroy a set number of Soviet targets. This contrasted to the air force's ever-growing target lists and fit comfortably with the sufficiency doctrine current at the time. Three, in the aftermath of Sputnik, U.S. missile programs were looked at with increasing favor.

13. Robert Futrell, *Ideas, Concepts, Doctrine: A History of Basic Thinking in the United States Air Force, 1907–1964* (Maxwell AFB, Alabama: Air University Press, 1974), p. 234.

14. Futrell, *Ideas.*

15. Futrell, *Ideas*, p. 265.

16. The Soviets' desire to see West Berlin assimilated into East Germany can be traced to West Berlin's psychological impact as an impediment to complete Soviet dominance in Eastern Europe and as an island of capitalism in a sea of socialism; their desire to close the escape route of many East German *intelligentsia* and *literati* into the West; and, as Spanier notes, to cut off Western intelligence operations in West Berlin. "There was a constant flow of information about the West from West Berlin into the Russian-controlled satellites; this defeated one of the major purposes of the iron curtain, which was to stop incoming information that might lead to comparisons of the Communist and free systems." John Spanier, *American Foreign Policy since World War II* (New York: Praeger Publishers, 1974), p. 132.

17. The actual size of the Soviet arsenal at this time (1954) is not known. National intelligence estimates approximated 200 Soviet weapons. However, U.S. war planners assumed that the bulk, if

not all, of these weapons would be committed to the intercontinental battle between the United States and the Soviet Union. See John Prados, *The Soviet Estimate* (Princeton: Princeton University Press, 1986), pp. 21–22.

18. Edward Kolodziej, *The Uncommon Defense and Congress* (Columbus: Ohio State University, 1966), p. 288.

19. Record, *Revising,* p. 103.

20. Doughty quotes a General Garrison H. Davidson: "Ground commanders everywhere breathed a sigh of relief when they were no longer faced with the grim possibility of having to employ [the Pentomic Division] in combat." In Robert Doughty, *The Evolution of US Army Tactical Doctrine, 1945–1976,* Leavenworth Papers no. 1 (Fort Leavenworth, Kansas: Combat Studies Institute, 1979), p. 22. Bacevich similarly quotes a General Paul L. Freeman: "Every time I think of the . . . Pentomic Division, I shudder. Thank God we never had to go to war with it." In A.C. Bacevich, *The Pentomic Era* (Washington, D.C.: National Defense University Press, 1985), p. 135.

21. Kolodziej, *Uncommon Defense,* p. 325.

22. The "Memorandum of Understanding between the Secretary of the Army and the Secretary of the Air Force, October 2, 1951," and the "Memorandum of Understanding Relating to Army Organic Aviation, November 4, 1952," and the "Memorandum for Members of the Armed Forces Policy Council, November 4, 1952," are discussed in *Defense Organization: The Need for Change,* Staff Report to the Committee on Armed Services, United States Senate (Washington, D.C.: GPO, October 16, 1985), p. 436. On March 8, 1971, the 5,000-pound restriction on army aviation was removed.

23. Dwight D. Eisenhower, "Special Message to the Congress on Reorganization of the Defense Establishment," April 3, 1958, in *Public Papers of the President,* vol. 65, p. 271.

24. Department of Defense Reorganization Act of 1958, Senate Report No. 1845, July 17, 1958, Section 1, reprinted in John Norton Moore and Robert F. Turner, *The Legal Structure of Defense Reorganization,* memorandum prepared for the President's Blue Ribbon Commission on Defense Management (Washington, D.C.: GPO, January 15, 1986), p. 25.

25. Moore and Turner, *Legal Structure,* pp. 26–27. A 1949 amendment to the National Security Act created the role of the chairman, Joint Chiefs of Staff.

26. Frederick H. Hartmann and Robert L. Wendzel, *Defending America's Security* (McLean, Virginia: Pergamon-Brassey's, 1988), pp. 173–174.

7

Era IV: Limited War in Theory—Flexible Response

FLEXIBLE RESPONSE: A NEW NATIONAL POLICY

In the final years of the Eisenhower presidency, administration spokesmen increasingly endorsed the notion of limited and controlled responses to conflicts, but as the last chapter discussed, programs to provide the armed forces with commensurate capabilities were not high priorities. There were some marginal increases in spending for nonnuclear forces, reflecting first, that they had been basically neglected for about five years, and second, that such forces were increasingly being integrated into operations with nuclear weapons. But from Eisenhower's perspective, the costs associated with conventional rearmament were forbidding, and he remained steadfastedly unprepared to initiate a major buildup of nonnuclear forces. Thus, whether the plans to use them involved massive attacks or controlled tactical responses, nuclear weapons were the essence of military planning in the Eisenhower administration.

General Maxwell D. Taylor, the army's chief of staff during Eisenhower's second term, was an outspoken critic of massive retaliation. In 1956, he testified that "as parity is approximated in numbers and types of atomic weapons between East and West, every effort will be made on both sides to avoid general atomic war . . . [The U.S. would face] pressures on soft spots about the Soviet periphery through subversion, guerilla action . . . coups d'état, [and] small scale wars." A proper response to these types of challenges, he continued, would be "a land operation with a very limited role, if any, for heavy weapons of mass destruction."[1]

Eisenhower rejected Taylor's prescription, but his successor in the White House took heed of Taylor's words—especially as expressed in Taylor's 1959 book *The Uncertain Trumpet*.[2] Along with Walter Rostow's 1961 statement of "Basic National Security Policy," prepared during Rostow's tenure as head of the State Department's

Policy Planning Staff, that book was the Kennedy administration's "blueprint" for military policy and strategy formulation.

Two events in 1961—the Bay of Pigs landing and the second Berlin crisis—contributed to Kennedy's ongoing reassessment of U.S. defense policy and force structure. In April 1961, a small band of Cuban exiles landed in Cuba at the Bay of Pigs and attempted to overthrow the Castro regime. The United States actively supported the exiles, and their failure was a major diplomatic and political embarrassment for the United States. Questions were raised over the U.S. capacity to conduct such operations and over the wisdom of the exercise in the first place.

The Berlin crisis was a continuation of the 1958 events in Berlin and was yet another Soviet attempt to resolve the issue of occupied Berlin. At a Vienna summit with Khrushchev in early 1961, Kennedy warned the Soviet premier that the United States would take whatever steps it viewed as necessary to protect the security of West Berlin. But Khrushchev reimposed the six-month deadline for the withdrawal of occupying forces.

The Soviets ultimately backed down from their six-month threat, but on August 13, the Soviets began to erect a wall around West Berlin, cutting off access to the East and violating Berlin's four-power occupation status. The young administration gave some thought to the prospects for strong military action but, in the end, went no further than calling up the reserves and retaining some weapon systems that were previously scheduled to be phased out. But as Secretary of Defense Robert McNamara pointed out in a memorandum to the president, "Often only small improvements in effectiveness resulted from these increases."[3]

Simply put, the administration had no confidence that the forces bequeathed it could support a protracted engagement, were a conflict over Berlin to escalate or expand. As McNamara later pointed out, "the need to call up the reserves during that period [of the Berlin crisis] confirmed our belief that much more fundamental changes would have to be made if our general-purpose forces would meet our long-range objectives."[4] These crises proved to Kennedy that much greater emphasis had to be placed on the procurement of general purpose forces flexible enough to be used in a wide variety of roles. In particular, Kennedy wanted forces useful for limited operations at the lower end of the conflict spectrum, that is, operations that involved the use of military force but did not require a full-scale mobilization for all-out war. In the new administration's view, such crises did not require a full-scale nuclear threat to be resolved, and such a threat was probably not credible in any case.

These events reinforced the view among many in the new administration that massive retaliation was a politically and militarily shortsighted policy and that a greater balance between nuclear and conventional forces was required. Many in the administration also questioned Eisenhower's extensive alliance system, which came to consist of about 45 formal treaty obligations and numerous informal arrangements with other countries. Kennedy had no intention of reneging on existing U.S. commitments, but he was wary of taking on new ones. In his view, Eisenhower's alliances left the United States overcommitted to the preservation of the existing international order. The interests of the United States, Kennedy proclaimed, were best served

> by preserving and protecting a world of diversity in which no one power or no combination of powers can threaten the security of the United States . . . [there is] one single, central, theme of American foreign policy . . . and that is to support the independence of nations so that one bloc cannot gain sufficient power to finally overcome us.[5]

Kennedy also argued that massive retaliation deterred the United States from responding to a spectrum of provocations without deterring potential U.S. adversaries. Massive retaliation really offered little choice, Kennedy told the American people in 1961, between "humiliation and all out war."

Kennedy's prescriptive policy was called flexible response. McNamara pointed out that "a careful review of the dangers confronting our nation indicated that our armed forces had to have an increased capability for countering all forms of aggression, from thermonuclear to subversion."[6] As such, flexible response aimed to enhance the ability of the United States to meet conflict "across the spectrum of violence," ranging from counterinsurgency to protracted global war. But it emphasized the importance of robust nonnuclear forces. As symbolized by his administration's resurrection of Maxwell Taylor, who was appointed the chairman of the Joint Chiefs of Staff, Kennedy accepted the basic tenet of Taylor's thinking: in an era of nuclear stalemate, conventional conflicts become more, not less, likely. Conventional forces were therefore needed to deter and defend against aggression and to provide the U.S. response options short of nuclear escalation.

TWO-AND-A-HALF WAR PLANNING

In 1962, military planners from the JCS and the services initiated a study of U.S. conventional requirements. They determined that

there were sixteen theaters where conflict could potentially develop.[7]
U.S. ground and tactical forces would be required in eleven of the
theaters, with separate garrisons in Alaska and Panama. Fifty-five
army divisions and 82 tactical fighter attack wings would be needed.
However, these plans assumed simultaneous attacks in all sixteen
theaters. Reassessment indicated that more realistically, planning
should encompass

1. a Soviet attack on Western Europe;
2. a Chinese attack in Korea or Southeast Asia; and
3. a smaller scale contingency—i.e., a conflict in Cuba or a localized
   conflict such as the Lebanese situation of 1958.

Given these scaled-down expectations, planning proceeded on
a less drastic level, for "two and a half," instead of sixteen, simultaneous theaters. Revised plans established requirements for 28
divisions and 41 fighter attack wings.[8] Altogether, planning in the
Kennedy administration was based on five elements: NATO, South
Korea, a strategic reserve, flexibility, and mobilization.[9] Each of
these is considered below.

NATO

Europe remained the primary focus of U.S. planning. Early in the
administration, a policy directive issued by McGeorge Bundy, the
president's national security adviser, made this clear: "The political
nexus between North America and Western Europe—i.e., the Atlantic
Community—is and must continue to be the foundation of U.S.
foreign policy. NATO is the principal form which this coalition takes.
It is of first importance to the U.S. to maintain its coherence and
strength."[10] The wisdom of relying so heavily on the U.S. strategic
shield was challenged by the administration, as discussed in detail
at the end of this chapter. Critics of the "tripwire" policy pointed
to the growing Soviet stockpile of strategic and tactical nuclear
weapons, the increasingly common interalliance feuding over nuclear weapons control schemes,[11] and the independent nuclear forces
of France and Britain, the growth of which sometimes appeared to
threaten alliance cohesion. At this time there were also about 125
Warsaw Pact Organization (WPO) divisions in East Germany, Poland,
and Czechoslovakia, of which 22 were Soviet. The prospects of
mounting a successful conventional defense of Europe for an extended period did not appear particularly promising, either.

Part of McNamara's response to this problem was to increase levels of tactical nuclear weapons, and it was under Kennedy that the numbers of theater nuclear weapons peaked. Much more attention, however, was now paid to enhancing NATO's capacity to respond to a provocation in the theater with nonnuclear forces. Moreover, McNamara maintained, the Warsaw Pact's conventional superiority could partly be countered by better distribution of nonnuclear resources: "NATO naval forces in some areas, for example, already exceed our needs. Several hundred million dollars might well be shifted to more urgently needed ground forces over the next five years." On this basis, McNamara sought to implement flexible response in the European theater:

> We would be keying the size and composition of our combat-ready forces to comparable, forward-deployed forces of the Warsaw Pact. Second, we would be setting mobilization and deployment schedules in accord with what the Pact, and specifically, what the USSR, could do. Third, we would be introducing into our planning the kind of flexibility required by our new political guidance; that is, we would have plans both for different levels of mobilization and for the whole range of military contingencies.[12]

The buildup of general purpose forces which immediately followed the second Berlin crisis reflected the new administration's concern with adequate conventional preparation in Europe. The level of U.S. personnel stationed there increased from approximately 379,000 in 1960 to 417,000 in 1961. To fight the naval battle on Europe's flanks, the United States established antisubmarine warfare barriers patrolled by U.S. submarines and backed by U.S. patrol boats and carrier forces far forward in the Greenland–Iceland–United Kingdom (GIUK) gap and in the Spitsbergen-Norway areas. This included the deployment of 9 CVS carriers outfitted for ASW and 104 attack submarines. To support a central European ground battle, additional tactical aircraft were also deployed.

SOUTH KOREA

By the early 1960s, South Korea was heavily fortified at the DMZ by South Korean security forces, and U.S. planners considered withdrawing the two remaining U.S. divisions there. These forces would be placed in a strategic reserve, as discussed below. As a symbol of the U.S. commitment to defend South Korea against a renewed attack from the North, several fighter attack wings would remain near the DMZ. The administration also wanted to call home the marine amphibious force (a division and an air wing) in Okinawa, the Twenty-fifth Infantry Division in Hawaii, and brigades stationed in Alaska and Panama. Not all of these plans were realized, as discussed below.

STRATEGIC RESERVE

Even if the United States were to attain the capacity to fight two-and-a-half wars in the theaters it viewed as most troublesome, a persistent problem remained. What if trouble arose in other areas of the world, such as the Middle East, Southwest Asia, or North Africa, where the United States did not maintain a strong peacetime presence? To resolve this problem, a strategic reserve was established. The strategic reserve was based in the continental United States (CONUS) and consisted of "specially tailored expeditionary forces [which] could be dispatched quickly to trouble spots, wherever they may be."[13] The strategic reserve was to consist of 9 active-duty divisions and 14 active-duty fighter attack wings, backed by 9 reserve divisions and 12 fighter attack reserve wings, respectively. In theory, at least, the advent of the jet, fast-deployment logistics ships, a large fleet of cargo jets, and a minimum of overseas deployments and prepositioned supplies would provide the strategic reserve forces with flexibility and mobility.[14]

FLEXIBILITY AND MOBILIZATION

The administration assumed 23 days for mobilization, 30 days maximum warning of an attack. It was recognized, however, that forces capable of meeting any contingency worldwide were not likely to be attained, and *flexibility* became the administration's watchword. Funding levels for airlift and sealift began to increase, on the theory that inadequate force levels could be compensated for by an ability to get extant forces to a crisis quickly. Numerous ideas to enhance the flexibility of U.S. forces were considered. One idea, which was later somewhat adopted by the Carter administration, was for sufficient equipment for three divisions to be stored in Germany for U.S.-based divisions that required quick deployment to Europe. Alternatively, a mix of fast-deployment logistics ships and transport aircraft could be procured to airlift units and equipment based in CONUS to threatened overseas areas. Ultimately, it was decided that a mix of 31 fast-deploying logistics ships and a heavy aircraft force of 280 C-141s and 129 C-5As would be procured. These could deliver either 300,000 tons of equipment or the equivalent of eight divisions by airlift over 4,000 nautical miles. It was estimated that this would provide reinforcement for NATO for 23 days. It was also decided to station an additional 300,000 tons of equipment worldwide.

The administration never met its ambitious goals. One division remains in Korea; two brigades were removed from Europe, but three brigades and six fighter squadrons were added; and the strategic reserve never grew to its projected size. As the Vietnam War would later demonstrate, U.S. forces never attained the level of flexibility hoped for by administration planners.[15]

Nor did the administration meet the specific criteria it established in its early planning exercises. Yet there is no question that the administration initiated a trend favorable to conventional force procurement and planning. Of course, nuclear weapons were not by any means radically deemphasized in Kennedy administration planning. Indeed, McNamara grappled publicly with nuclear doctrines, first supporting a doctrine aimed at avoiding cities (counterforce/no-cities) and gradually embracing assured destruction (AD), a doctrine primarily based on the destruction of urban assets.[16] While the rate of growth of U.S. strategic forces diminished under Kennedy and McNamara, the strategic nuclear stockpile grew, and the rate of growth of the tactical nuclear stockpile rose considerably. But in many ways nuclear planning was kept distinct from, and in some ways subordinated to, conventional planning. Both nuclear doctrines were not only attempts to grapple with the state of mutual nuclear threat in which the United States and the USSR found themselves but to control service nuclear force procurement requests. McNamara urged nuclear missile development for all the services but even questioned those programs, once "sufficient" levels of deterrent forces were, in McNamara's view, reached.

The Kennedy administration's conventional force orientation was reflected in its defense budgets. For FY1961, Eisenhower's budget request for nonnuclear forces represented a drop of 2 percent from the previous year. After Kennedy's 1961 supplementals, the defense budget for FY1961 reversed this trend, inching upward 1.6 percent from FY1960. Kennedy's FY1962 budget brought spending for general purpose forces upward a full 3.6 percent after inflation.[17]

In 1962 manpower levels rose in all the services.[18] Army divisions had been skeletonized during the Eisenhower years, but now this process was reversed. Equipment and ammunition levels were increased to enhance their capability to sustain actual combat. The number of navy fleet carriers rose slightly, from 24 to 26, but the number of fleet combatants rose from 624 to 754. Only the air force suffered cutbacks as the number of tactical wings fell from their

1961 peak of 25 skeletonized wings to 22, and total aircraft fell from 4,074 to 3,921.[19] These trends continued in FY1963 as military outlays topped $53 billion.[20]

PLANNING, PROGRAMMING, AND BUDGETING

Under McNamara, the Pentagon experienced yet another top-down effort to streamline its planning and procurement practices. McNamara came quickly to the conclusion that some overreaching authority was required to control service planning and budgeting, which he saw as uncoordinated and wasteful. Yet another reform to strengthen his own office, such as the 1958 Reorganization Act, was not what was required. As he put it, "The effective management of the Department's resources was not the lack of management authority. The National Security Act provides the Secretary of Defense a full measure of power. The problem was rather the absence of the essential management tools needed to make sound decisions on the really crucial issues of national security." He thus oriented his reforms to improving service planning and budgeting. With respect to planning, for example, McNamara observed that

the three military departments had been establishing their requirements independently of each other. The results could be described fairly as chaotic: Army planning, for example, was based primarily on a long war of attrition; Air Force planning was based, largely, on a short war of nuclear bombardment. . . . The two [approaches] combined could not possibly make sense.[21]

The services, he argued, set their own programs and made their case, with little coordination between them. It seemed logical that if their planning could be better integrated, redundancy could be eliminated, overall efficiency of force employment could be enhanced, and savings could be attained.

McNamara proceeded to distinguish forces precisely on the basis of roles and missions. Budget line items were grouped into programs that included forces that would operate together regardless of service. As McNamara described it, "The Navy strategic forces, the Polaris submarines, are now considered together with the Air Force Strategic Air Command; Navy general-purpose forces are considered together with the Army and Marine divisions and the Air Force Tactical Air Command."[22] In short, the services would be required to justify their forces in terms of their contribution to the total military effort. From McNamara's perspective, this meant eliminating redundant weapons systems if a single system could do the job or, even better, could perform a number of functions—the essence of flexibility. For example, McNamara argued, "We could use certain elements of the strategic retaliatory forces and continental air and missile defense forces for particular limited war tasks and, of course, all our forces would be employed in a general war."[23]

Another related major component of the McNamara reform was to institute a new budgeting process known as the Planning, Programming, and Budgeting System (PPBS). PPBS was aimed at improving both the way DOD assessed service procurement requests and the way the services formulated their requests. The aim was, first, to key procurement decisions to national security requirements, rather than to an arbitrary budget ceiling, and second, to assess new systems relative to other systems in the same context, or their contribution to national security. They would thus be judged in terms of cost-effectiveness relative to other systems that could potentially perform the same roles and missions.

PPBS has evolved over the years, but it remains fundamentally unchanged from its inception in 1961. Its essence, as noted by Amos A. Jordan and William A. Taylor, Jr., "lay in its division of weapon systems and forces into output related programs, incorporation of cost and force projections for each program in a [Five Year Defense Plan] . . . and linking of the planning and budgeting processes. It . . . provided a systematic method for focusing attention on key issues."[24]

The key document in the PPBS is the five-year defense plan (FYDP), which provides an eight-year projection of force requirements and five-year cost and personnel projections. This document, which is revised annually, is intended to provide a basis for the annual planning and budgeting cycle upon which all service and DOD planning could be based. The essential tool of PPBS is systems analysis, involving the use of statistical data to evaluate competing programs on the basis of cost and effectiveness.

Under McNamara, PPBS was a source of constant controversy and criticism. Many of the systems analysts were young, computer-oriented "whiz kids" with little experience in evaluating military weapons systems. But McNamara saw this as an advantage; he believed they were more objective in their assessments of new systems than traditional military analysts. Under McNamara, an Office of Systems Analysis was established, answerable directly to the secretary of defense. This led to a process highly centralized within DOD and drew more fire from some service officials. Moreover, some legislators also criticized **PPBS** because in its complexity and detail, it presented Congress with too many decisions—a criticism that seems somewhat ludicrous today, when congressional involvement in the planning and budgeting process is commonplace.

But PPBS proved unable to resolve the disparate war plans submitted by the CINCs of the various unified commands in conjunction with the 1958 reorganization, and proved inadequate in judging certain multipurpose systems. For example, the experimental tactical fighter (TFX) was judged to be cost-beneficial because it was designed for both navy and air force missions. But it proved difficult to bridge service requirements for this aircraft; the plane was embroiled in controversy from the start and was never jointly produced.[25] As for the service planners, they were incensed, certain that McNamara had total disregard for their views.

With experience, thus, it became clear that PPBS had limits. But PPBS has become well entrenched not only in DOD but among the service planning staffs as well. It is simply accepted as the way the military establishment plans its forces and budgets and has undergone little change since 1962.

SERVICE PLANNING IN AN ERA OF CHANGE AND CRISIS

Kennedy's effort to create a better balance between nuclear and conventional forces had significant effects on force procurement and planning for all the services. As James Lacy has noted, the new orientation

> meant that the Air Force could no longer starve its tactical air capability for close support of ground troops, or its air transport for troop movement, as had been the case in the 1950s. For another, it meant that (the) Army . . . would have to reemphasize "sustainability" if it were to have any credible conventional war capability . . . it meant that the Navy, with its 1950s' emphasis on nuclear attack forces (aircraft carriers and Polaris submarines) would have to place still greater emphasis on ASW and a much-neglected emphasis on troop and equipment overseas movement and escort capability.[26]

The air force's once preeminent position in the defense hierarchy was becoming increasingly precarious. The McNamara defense budgets were gradually beginning to shift toward the army. All of the services were developing missile capabilities, and the dominance of the strategic bomber in nuclear deterrence was coming under increasing challenge, particularly from the navy's Polaris. McNamara was beginning to question openly the utility of a strategic bomber at all.

On April 24, 1962, the air force issued a position paper, "The USAF Concept for Limited War." In listing ten maxims to guide USAF planning, the paper grudgingly noted the administration's new orientation. "Insofar as possible," began the final maxim, "military forces should be designed with the range, mobility, flexibility, speed, penetrative ability, and firepower delivery that can perform in cold, limited, and general war situations."[27] But in most respects, the paper restated traditional air force positions. After all, the old dogmas had proven remarkably successful, both in procuring air forces and in elevating the air force to its lofty position in U.S. military planning. Thus, the air force continued to emphasize the importance of its role in the strategic realm. The position paper restated the importance of superior forces to "disarm the enemy even if the highest threshold of war is crossed" and went on to argue that,

since limited war against Communist forces is not a separate entity from general war, our strategy and forces for limited war should not be separated from our overall strategy and force structure. The artificial distinction of limited war forces for this war and general war forces for that war destroys the inter-acting strength of our forces that will provide force superiority and continuous deterrence at any level of conflict.[28]

Consistent with its longstanding adherence to the "indivisibility" of air power, the air force sought to blur distinctions between nuclear and conventional forces, between strategic and tactical roles and missions, and between the weapons systems such roles and missions required. However, as discussed, McNamara proceeded to distinguish forces precisely on such criteria. He was now turning his analytic eye toward the air force. The rapid missile development that transpired throughout the Kennedy administration was predicated, in part, on the assumption that the manned bomber would no longer be the essential component of strategic deterrence.[29] Against Soviet air defenses, McNamara argued, the bomber might not always get through. By 1962, McNamara had foreclosed production of additional B-52s and B-58s and rejected the air force's request for the new B-70. The only new bomber McNamara sought was the experimental TFX, which would have both nuclear and nonnuclear capabilities.

The air force integrated flexible response and many other McNamara concepts into its doctrine. Air Force Operations Manual

(AFM) 1-1 as revised in 1964 no longer argued that nuclear strength deterred every level of conflict; now, a robust nuclear capability was seen as sufficient to deter general (nuclear) war, but it was emphasized that a "range of capabilities" was required to deter at lower levels:

> At the highest level of conflict . . . our continued assured capability to deliver unacceptable damage and retaliation should be sufficient to convince the enemy that deliberate, all-out attacks on our industries and population would be futile. At less than all-out levels of aggression, whether or not an enemy is deterred depends on his calculation of the capabilities we are likely to employ in each situation.[30]

Deterrence as an end unto itself was not just passingly referred to, as was the case in past manuals, but was now discussed in great depth. The manual distinguished between deterrence and defensive missions, saying that the air force must be prepared to fight a general nuclear, tactical nuclear, conventional, or counterinsurgency war. Entire chapters were devoted to the latter two categories, with the discussion of the air force's role in counterinsurgency probably signifying the greatest change in the service's rhetoric. Almost the entire discussion was devoted to security assistance and advisory air force functions; only two paragraphs were dedicated to describing direct air action against insurgent forces. They stressed that "maximum advantage should be taken of friendly air capabilities" and that the primary military role for the air force in such operations was interdiction.[31] As for conventional operations, much greater attention was paid to the requirements for close air support and interdiction, two areas that had generally been given nominal consideration in past manuals.[32]

In light of the new attention being paid to nonnuclear operations, air force planning again focused on the Tactical Air Command (TAC). In the February 1963 "Clearwater" study, the air force suggested a new basing mode for TAC forces, based upon a revision of the combination forward and rear deployment plan TAC had conceived in the late 1950s (this plan is discussed in the previous chapter). McNamara supported the findings of the Clearwater study, which fit in well with the strategic reserve concept and, he hoped, would "result in manpower, spare parts, and foreign exchange savings." Procurement for airlift and other systems to support the new plan was accelerated.[33] What the air force did not anticipate was that the army, somewhat disgusted with the air force's continual dragging of its collective feet on close air support, would launch a concerted effort to attain responsibility for its own cover and protection—this time with the support of the secretary of defense. This led to a major clash between the army and the air force. Before examining this incident, however, it is important to look at the evolution of army doctrine in this period, to understand the context within which this confrontation between the two services occurred.

THE ARMY MOVES FORWARD

For the army, the new national emphasis on conventional war planning "across the spectrum of violence" led to a virtual renaissance in force planning. The flaws of the Pentomic Divisions were widely recognized within army planning circles, and as early as January of 1959, new concepts were under consideration. The most prominent of these was called MOMAR I (Modern Mobile Army 1965–1970). MOMAR was an attempt to align army doctrine with the limited-war fixation of the Eisenhower administration. The army envisioned divisions with increased conventional firepower, less reliance on nuclear weapons, and even greater mobility than the Pentomic Divisions. MOMAR envisaged only two divisions—a heavy (armored) division and a medium division designed for sustained, flexible, and mobile operations under any set of circumstances.

MOMAR is notable, however, not because it attained some balance between nuclear and nonnuclear forces; this was what MOMAR planners intended. The MOMAR divisions, nonetheless, maintained a heavy reliance on battlefield nuclear weapons. As John Midgley has pointed out, "MOMAR was an alternative to the Pentomic Divisions' inflexibility and inadequate conventional firepower. However, the absolute nuclear firepower of the MOMAR heavy division greatly exceeded that of the Pentomic designs; this was essential if the Army was to incorporate the full range of new weapons."[34] Thus, MOMAR was most notable because it was the army's first realistic effort to integrate battlefield nuclear weapons into its planning. But not all army planners embraced MOMAR. According to its critics within the army, the heavy mechanized divisions were unsuited for many parts of the world, and MOMAR was too complex and inflexible to meet the army's future needs. Its two-division structure limited its practical capacity to engage in nonnuclear conflicts.

In any case, there was little support within the army for major reorganization, and MOMAR never really entrenched itself as a viable basis for planning. This left a vacuum in army doctrine, which would be filled by a new plan called ROAD (Reorganization Objectives Army Division) 1965. The problems encountered with the Pentomic

Divisions and MOMAR primarily derived from their inattention to the requirements of the *non*nuclear battlefield. ROAD, however, emphasized flexibility and mobility and was designed for fighting on nuclear or nonnuclear battlefields. ROAD also brought a uniformity to the division structure. At the time of the Pentomic reorganization, for example, infantry and airborne divisions were organized in accordance with the Pentomic structure, while the armored divisions maintained the structure that had been developed in World War II. ROAD established a fourth division type—the mechanized infantry—and organized all four divisions under a single structure.

The essence of ROAD was flexibility. ROAD's basic structure consisted of a division base to which various types and numbers of combat battalions could be added or removed, depending upon the exigencies of the battle. As explained in a March 1963 army pamphlet, "In the new division structure, the brigade has no *organic* battalions. Its authorized strength consists only of the brigade headquarters. The division *attaches* battalions to each of its brigades—how many and what kinds of battalions depends on the brigade's mission or situation at a particular time."[35]

In addition to the division and brigade headquarters, the new division structure consisted of a support command, an aviation, signal, and engineer battalion, a military police company, an armored cavalry squadron, and division artillery. The division artillery consisted of variously configured missile and howitzer battalions and batteries, the precise mix dependent upon the type division and projected needs. The ROAD divisions were also augmented with the Davy Crockett nuclear weapon, which lifted a relatively small atomic warhead (with a yield of approximately .02 KT) a short distance, up to 6,000 meters. The Davy Crockett provided the divisions with some organic nuclear capability.

But ROAD was predominantly designed for the nonnuclear battlefield. In a memorandum to McNamara, Army Secretary Elvis Starr described three advantages ROAD offered for meeting conventional requirements. These were

> first, flexible forces of division size and smaller tailored with greater discrimination to the varying requirement of fluctuating world environments. Second, improved capabilities for limited war. Third, improved non-nuclear capabilities (while slightly increasing nuclear capabilities) providing to the decision maker a wider range of alternatives and an improved capability to apply measured force.[36]

Not all army leaders were entirely satisfied with ROAD, but even the critics found it preferable to the Pentomic Divisions or the short-lived **MOMAR**. McNamara approved the **ROAD** concept, and divisions were restructured commensurate with the concept.

ROAD brought changes in both defensive and offensive battlefield tactics. Envelopment continued to grow as the basis of offensive operations, reflecting the army's growing interest in maneuver and counterinsurgency. The helicopter was further incorporated into army planning to enhance the overall mobility and flexibility of army units, leading to a greater role for airmobile operations. Where the Pentomic Divisions emphasized armored tactics and capabilities, the new concept stressed the capability to perform a variety of operations employing diverse forces. In FM 7-20, *Infantry, Airborne Infantry, and Mechanized Infantry Battalions*, the army stated that "(a) mechanized infantry battalion in an armored division is normally employed to support the advance of tank elements. In the infantry and mechanized divisions, the reverse is true—armored elements are used primarily to support the advance of infantry elements."[37]

The emphasis on the mechanized and airborne forces was intended to enhance the commander's flexibility and maneuverability on the battlefield. According to FM 7-20, the mechanized divisions would have a "sustained capability for rapid movement," and the airborne infantry battalions would have "the capability to conduct frequent airborne assaults." Soldiers would quickly commence combat and just as quickly disperse. These alterations in doctrine would help the soldier fight on the conventional battlefield and could also be applied in counterinsurgency and other "lesser strife" situations.[38] New systems, such as the M-114 lightly armored personnel carrier, were developed to enhance the overall mobility of the ROAD brigades. Such tracked vehicles provided cross-country mobility, protection from small arms and fragmentation, and some protection from the effects of nuclear weapons.

Significant changes were also seen in emerging defensive concepts. Under the Pentomic organization, defensive operations were conducted principally at the division level. In the more flexible ROAD, the mobile defense could be conducted by brigades. The position defense was replaced with an area defense, signaling the need for a defense in depth and emphasizing that, as one analyst has noted, "key terrain did not necessarily have to be occupied since enemy nuclear weapons might easily eliminate defenses on such obvious positions. In the area defense, nonetheless, there was a subtle increase in the emphasis placed on destroying or ejecting the enemy from the defender's position."[39]

ROAD was the most sweeping reorganization since the Pentomic Divisions, and it also proved to be much more enduring. Although army doctrine has evolved much since the early years of the Kennedy administration, the basic ROAD configuration has remained fairly constant, and although elements of ROAD have been discarded, ROAD's four division types are still the basis of army division organization (in the 1980s, as chapter 10 discusses, a new "light division" structure has been added). And flexibility and maneuverability remain the standards by which all future reorganizations have been judged.

FLAP OVER ARMY AVIATION

As noted above, airborne infantry battalions were increasingly incorporated into army plans. Such battalions were useful for newly emerging army concepts, but they also served another army purpose: they enhanced the army's ability to organically control air support operations in the theater. It was not long, therefore, before these battalions became the source of new clashes between the army and the air force over tactical air responsibilities.

In a memorandum to the Department of the Army dated April 19, 1962, McNamara requested army planners to take a "bold new look at land warfare mobility." McNamara urged that the study stress innovation and the development of a plan "for implementing fresh and perhaps unorthodox concepts which will give us a significant increase in mobility." Typical of his approach to military matters, McNamara justified the study principally in terms of cost-effectiveness:

> We have found that air transportation is cheaper than rail or ship transportation even in peacetime. The urgency of war time operations makes air transportation even more important. By exploiting aeronautical potential, we should be able to achieve a major increase in effectiveness while spending on airmobility systems no more than we have been spending on systems oriented for ground transportation.[40]

Lieutenant General Hamilton Howze, an outspoken advocate of employing helicopters on the battlefield, was selected to head the study. The air force, aware of Howze's predilections, formed its own board under the guidance of Lieutenant General G.P. Disosway, to prepare the air force response to the Howze Board's conclusions. After exhaustive conceptual development, testing, and wargaming, the Howze Board released its final report on August 20; the Disosway Board released its evaluation of the Howze Board report on September 14.

The Howze Board recommended additional aircraft for all ROAD divisions, armored cavalry regiments, and artillery corps. The board also recommended the creation of two army units, the most salient feature of which was air mobility. The first unit was an air-assault division containing 459 aircraft, including 87 Iroquois attack helicopters. The second was an air-cavalry combat brigade with 316 aircraft, of which 144 were attack helicopters. Thus, given that they were smaller than the air-assault divisions yet more heavily loaded with attack aircraft, the brigades were the key to truly enhancing overall battlefield mobility and flexibility. The board also recommended the formation of air-transport brigades and corps aviation brigades, all under the command of the army. Finally, the board recommended that by FY1970, up to six of the army's 16 divisions could be reorganized as air-assault brigades.[41] However, all the new organizations envisaged in the Howze Board were consistent with ROAD.

To the members of the Howze Board, there was simply no question but that the future battlefield environment would require mobility and that the helicopter could best provide that mobility. This was seen to be the case in offensive, defensive, or retrograde operations. For example, in conducting offensive operations, the board noted, "Helicopter-borne infantry, originating from positions well to the rear [say twenty-five miles] can be delivered rapidly and with very precise timing to any given area. This affords such a force great latitude in the selection of the point of thrust against the enemy and enhances greatly the possibility of surprise."[42]

The Howze Board recommendations naturally encountered much resistance from the air force, who saw the recommendations as a rather blatant attempt by the army to usurp air force missions. In fact, the Howze Board was quite unequivocal in that respect, insisting that "the Army airmobility program as recommended by the Board does not lessen in any way the importance or the magnitude of Army requirements for support by the Air Force." The board went on to state that the air force should retain all of its missions, including close air support. However, the board argued that "fighter-bombers now in the Air Force system are designed primarily for (missions other than CAS)," and as a result air force assets were "not responsive to many of the day-to-day legitimate requirements of the Army for close air support." Therefore, at least part of the close air-support mission had to be conducted by army aircraft, both rotary and fixed wing. Only aircraft directly controlled by the army, it was argued, could achieve the necessary coordination with infantry, armor, tanks, and the other army components. Finally, while the Howze Board cut back the air force's responsibilities for close air support, it recommended a greater role for intertheater, troop carrier, and long-haul intratheater airlift. Thus, the air force would be responsible for bringing men and materiel to the battle area; the army's utility and cargo aircraft (helicopter and aircraft equipped for vertical and short takeoff and landing, or V/STOL), would then deliver the cargo and troops to the front lines.[43]

The air force argued, somewhat correctly, that the army was cutting into its missions. The army responded that no duplication of missions was intended. From the army's perspective, air power would augment the army in doing

> what armies have always had to do from time immemorial—close with and destroy the enemy, or break his will and force his surrender . . . air power involves air-to-air combat, the gaining of air superiority, air strikes deep in the enemy rear with strategic objectives, interdiction of the battle area, close air support by high speed tactical aircraft, strategic airlift of Army and other forces. Army aviation is not any of these.[44]

But dividing the close air-support mission (thus opening the door for a gradual takeover of this mission by the army) and contracting the air force transport mission were unacceptable to the air force. As stated in the Disosway report, the air force view was that the army proposals had insufficiently considered coordinated service functions and essentially laid the foundation for a second tactical air force. To make matters worse for the Howze Board, various elements within the army questioned the sweeping nature of its recommendations. For example, Army Chief of Staff General Earle Wheeler questioned the army's need for extensive air-assault divisions. He argued, ironically in light of subsequent events, that they would only be useful against relatively unsophisticated defense environments, such as might be found in Southeast Asia, rather than against the sophisticated air and missile defenses that existed in Europe.[45] This was true, but to the Howze Board, this was one of the great benefits of enhancing air mobility. And it was precisely because of this perceived utility that army aviation flourished in the Kennedy era.

At this time, however, McNamara was only partially receptive to the Howze Board's recommendations. McNamara authorized an additional 15,000 men to the army's FY1964 end strength to form a provisional air-assault battalion. But in McNamara's view, the air force could use its new C-130 and C-141 transport aircraft to directly deliver cargo to the ground troops, thus putting into question the need for the army's proposed Caribou transport plane. The systems analysts in the Pentagon assessed the Caribou relative to the air force's C-130, and the C-130 came out on top. McNamara questioned the report on a number of logistical issues as well and ordered that additional testing be undertaken to support the Howze Board's concepts.

Testing continued throughout 1964. During this period, McNamara made a number of decisions, mostly deleterious to the army, over future airmobile force composition. The army's Mohawk surveillance aircraft was deleted from the FY1965 budget, and proposed purchases of the Caribou were reduced. As for roles and missions, the JCS decided that the army would control helicopters to support battlefield maneuvers, but the air force would retain the close air-support function.[46]

The extensive recommendations of the Howze Board were never fully implemented, although the helicopter was, of course, deeply integrated into battlefield planning and operations, particularly in the Vietnam War. In February 1965, the army commenced preliminary development for an advanced aerial fire-support helicopter. In July an existing infantry division at Fort Benning, Georgia, was reorganized into the First Cavalry Division (airmobile). In short time, this division was deployed to Vietnam.

THE NAVY

As was the case with the army, navy planning also underwent some transition during the era of flexible response. Since World War II, the navy had come increasingly to emphasize power projection as the basis of its planning—a process encouraged by the massive retaliation policy. McNamara envisaged the navy turning back toward its traditional sea-control missions. Indeed, in October 1962, the navy performed just such duties, in the Cuban Missile Crisis.

In the early fall of 1962, U.S. intelligence discovered the Soviets and Cubans constructing approximately 70 launching sites for medium- and short-range nuclear ballistic missiles in Cuba. This event brought the two superpowers to "the brink of war" and was the most serious crisis in the post-World War era.

Why the Soviets began building the launching sites in Cuba is still uncertain.[47] In any case, on October 22, 1962, Kennedy announced a naval quarantine around the Cuban periphery. The quarantine forces consisted of the ASW carrier *Essex* and various cruisers, destroyers, and land-based reconnaissance and patrol aircraft. Marine forces were flown to the U.S. naval base at Guantanamo Bay to counter possible Cuban action, and additional marines were deployed on amphibious ships in case they were needed. Air support came primarily from the attack carriers *Enterprise* and *Independence*. Along with TAC and various squadrons of marine aircraft, no less than eight carriers participated in the quarantine operation.[48]

The crisis was resolved on October 28, when Khrushchev began to withdraw the missiles in the face of U.S. ultimatums and assurances that the United States would not again invade Cuba, among other factors. The quarantine was called off on November 20, when Khrushchev began to withdraw remaining Soviet strategic bombers.

The navy's success in the Cuban Missile Crisis influenced McNamara's efforts to see the navy reoriented toward sea control, although other factors also bore upon the secretary's thinking. To McNamara, there was less of a requirement for a large carrier force oriented toward atomic bombing missions, given the advent of the Polaris missile force. The success of the carrier in Cuban Missile Crisis operations and the gradual appearance of a Soviet blue-water navy reinforced his view that the carrier force should be geared more toward conventional missions.

Predictably, McNamara's views with respect to the carrier were not looked upon kindly by navy planners. McNamara was increasingly skeptical over the role of the carrier in strategic nuclear deterrence. The defense secretary's perspective has been summed up well by Lacy:

> The strategic mission was a clumsy one for attack carriers. The sea space in the Mediterranean and Scandanavian areas in which the ships had to operate in order to launch heavy aircraft against "deep" inland Soviet targets was restricted. Carrier aircraft never did achieve the range and payload of land-based planes. In execution, the strategic mission left little room for maneuvering: heavy attack planes launched from a carrier for deep penetration attacks had to return to it, and this limited the carrier's options for getting out of "harm's way" in the meantime. Moreover, carrier task forces had the additional wartime mission of supporting ground forces on NATO's flanks, and were also expected to attack Soviet submarine pens and maintain air superiority over the peripheries. There was no natural concordance in these disparate tasks.[49]

McNamara's view was that SAC's strategic bombers were better suited to the long-range attack mission (even given the vulnerability of overseas basing) and that the carriers should concentrate their resources on other missions, described below. Thus, cost, vulnerability, and an increasing concern over ASW to counter the growing Soviet submarine threat were the basis of McNamara's concerns.

Over time, the Pentagon developed detailed plans for the employment of naval forces in nonnuclear missions. In the secretary's

1969 statement to Congress, he explained that "our war at sea strategy is based on the rapid employment of ASW forces . . . between the enemy submarines and their potential targets. . . . In an all-out war we would be able to destroy a very large proportion of the Soviet submarine force in a few months."[50] The strategy was premised on the assumption that preventing Soviet attack forces and submarine forces from reaching the open waters was the key to controlling the seas. Accordingly, multiple ASW barriers, comprised of submarines and both land- and sea-based ASW aircraft, would be established along U.S. and allied sea lines of communications (SLOCs), ports, and coastal areas to prevent Soviet submarines from reaching the open seas. Submarines already deployed would be deprived of replenishment and reinforcement. Thus, to reach North Atlantic shipping lanes,

> the Kola-based Soviet Northern fleet of submarines would have to "run" multiple barriers of U.S. submarines and patrol aircraft, the latter aided by information from the passive underseas Sound Surveillance System (SOSUS). And, if it did reach the North Atlantic, the Russian submarine would be vulnerable to search and attack operations by land-based aircraft.[51]

ASW missions against Soviet submarines were to be accomplished in conjunction with direct attacks against the Soviet fleet, to prevent the Soviets from effectively fielding these forces. Missions included attacking the enemy's naval forces in his ports, blockading his ports and naval forces, providing support for amphibious assaults with gunfire from surface warships and carrier-based aircraft, providing air support for land-based operations, and providing close-in protection of United States and allied convoy ships.[52] Naval forces were required to maintain control of the ocean between CONUS and the theater of conflict, and two carrier task forces were to be maintained in both the Mediterranean and the Pacific at all times. These plans led to an estimated requirement of 607 ships (excluding SSBNs [strategic ballistic missile, nuclear-powered submarines]) centered around 15 carrier task forces, 266 surface warships, and 102 amphibious assault vehicles.[53]

To carry out these plans, the carrier's role in the strategic campaign was to be cut back significantly. On February 22, 1963, McNamara requested the navy to justify the carrier in terms of its ability to carry out tactical and nonnuclear missions. McNamara was also skeptical over the need for additional nuclear-powered carriers, which were estimated as one-third to one-half more expensive to build than traditional oil-burning ships. McNamara rejected the navy's request for a new nuclear-powered carrier and decreed that, henceforth, new carriers would rely on traditional propulsion methods. Although one nuclear-powered carrier was later authorized (the CVAN-68)[54], McNamara pushed to reduce the number of carriers from 15 to 13.

These decisions led to a new round of naval officer resignations, including Secretary of the Navy Frank Korth, and public protest from navy planners. However, the question was not one of funding cutbacks but funding allocation, and these decisions, although dramatic, were not as schismatic as those that precipitated the admirals' revolt. Gradually, the navy began to reorient its forces to accommodate the new planning. Navy aircraft originally designed for strategic missions were reoriented toward conventional fighter, reconnaissance, and ASW roles. ASW capabilities for the carriers and their aircraft were also enhanced as older ASW helicopters and aircraft were replaced by models, such as the SH-3A Sea King helicopter, with greater range and improved antisubmarine detection equipment. Additional ASW fighter squadrons were formed when hostilities in Indonesia and North Vietnam threatened U.S. ASW patrols in Southeast Asian waters.

It is notable that as U.S. involvement in Vietnam deepened, carrier-based aircraft were employed for the power projection missions McNamara had been skeptical about.[55] On April 15, 1965, naval aircraft were used to support ground forces in South Vietnam, and by early 1966, five carriers were dedicated to missions there. There was only a nominal North Vietnamese navy to contend with, and plans to lock it up at its ports were not really applicable. In his FY1966 budget report McNamara conceded as much:

> Naval airpower played a critical role in Southeast Asia combat operations during fiscal year 1966. In the early stages of the conflict, before even temporary facilities could be constructed to permit large scale land-based air operations, the Navy's aircraft carriers were able to move into position and provide the required strike and support capabilities.[56]

Over time, a second nuclear-powered carrier was authorized, McNamara withdrew his opposition to the fifteen carrier force, and over half the carrier fleet was deployed in the Pacific. By the end of the decade, three nuclear-powered carriers had been authorized.[57]

EVOLUTION IN EUROPEAN DOCTRINE

Europe remained the ostensible centerpiece of the administration's policies, but there is no question that other regions of potential conflict were now playing important roles in planning for national security. This corresponded with a number of factors, including the growth in army aviation "useful in unsophisticated defense environments such as might be found in Southeast Asia," the activation of the First Cavalry Division, and the priority now placed on maintaining a strategic reserve. Mostly, however, this trend grew from the U.S. involvement in Southeast Asia. The rapid growth in U.S. active forces that began about 1965 was primarily due to Vietnam, rather than to a heightened sense of threat to Europe. Indeed, as the U.S. involvement in Vietnam grew, forces and equipment were diverted from Europe to meet requirements in Southeast Asia. U.S. personnel stationed in Europe dropped from 417,000 in 1961 (at the time of the Berlin crisis) to 363,000 in 1965 (and 291,000 by 1970).[58]

In March 1966, the French announced that within four months they would withdraw from the NATO military alliance. DeGaulle resented the overarching control of the United States over NATO policy making, particularly with respect to theater nuclear weapons. Under his leadership, France built the *Force de Frappe*, the independent French nuclear deterrent. Militarily, the effect of DeGaulle's decision was considerable. Some communications and supply lines were threatened, and as Stanley Sloan emphasizes, in a confrontation with the Warsaw Pact "the infrastructure for supporting NATO's front lines and for bringing in new supplies and reinforcements would be closer to the front and more vulnerable to enemy interdiction."[59] Moreover, NATO could no longer count on the 500,000 troops and equipment that France had supplied.

Politically, moreover, the French pullout was especially damaging. The French were publicly questioning the depth of the U.S. commitment to Europe at a time when the United States was reducing its presence there. At this time, the Soviets had 31 combatready divisions in Eastern Europe plus another 60 half-strength divisions in western Russia. These were augmented by 58 Pact divisions, 35 of which were considered combat ready. The West, however, only had the equivalent of just over 20 divisions, most of which were understrength, available for immediate mobilization to the central region, plus approximately 16 divisions mobilizable from the U.S. reserve. By the late 1960s, there were less than 5 NATO divisions in the central region, but these included the French forces.[60] The situation became more dire as French manpower decreased.

To further complicate matters, Soviet doctrine for war in Europe underwent a fundamental change in the mid-1960s. In January 1960, the Soviets announced that their military planning would deemphasize large-scale conventional forces in favor of nuclear weapons. Consistent with this decision, the Soviets designated their strategic rocket forces (SRF) as their primary component and announced that personnel levels in the armed forces would be reduced from 3.6 million to 2.4 million over the next two years. But in 1966, the Soviets reversed themselves. As the Sovietologist Michael MccGwire has noted, that year saw an

> underlying shift from the fundamental assumption that a world war would inevitably be nuclear and would mean massive strikes against the homelands of the two superpowers to the idea that nuclear escalation was not inevitable, that a world war might be waged with conventional weapons, and that the homelands of the United States and the Soviet Union might be spared nuclear attack.[61]

The Soviets must have reasoned that France's withdrawal from NATO further tilted the correlation of nonnuclear forces in their favor. The flexible response doctrine, which would soon be formally adopted by NATO, made clear that the United States was going to enhance its capacity to fight without immediately resorting to nuclear weapons.[62]

There is little evidence, however, that the basis of Soviet offensive operations in Europe—the quick and decisive blitzkrieg—changed in any way. As James Lacy has described this operation,

> The anticipated rate of advance is in the order of 70 miles in a 24-hour period. The emphasis is on high speed attacks, speedy crossing of river lines, the employment of airborne and helicopter-borne forces ahead of the advance, efficient cross-country movement, fighting with open flanks and striking by night as well as by day. The basic attack form will be "off the march" (without prior concentration) and the "meeting engagement" . . . the accepted form of action, both of them high-speed maneuvers. . . . If not effectively countered, this would put the Red Army at the Rhine in less than 48 hours and at the channel ports within a week.[63]

That a Soviet attack would proceed in a blitzkrieg-like fashion seemed confirmed by the Soviets' invasion of Czechoslovakia on August 20, 1968. Within 24 hours, every major city and airport in that country was overrun. At least 22 divisions participated in this operation.[64]

Whether Pact forces could proceed at a rate of 70 miles a day was questionable, of course, as was the notion that the Soviets could sustain such an effort in the face of a concerted Western response. And it is not certain that the lessons of the Czechoslovakian operation can be applied in any depth to a Pact-NATO confrontation. But inside the alliance, NATO's ability to respond effectively to Soviet aggression was viewed as increasingly tenuous in light of France's withdrawal from the alliance and the reductions in U.S. force levels.

In a 1967 document generally referred to as MC 14/3, NATO formally adopted flexible response as its official doctrine for Europe. This reflected the administration's desire to reduce NATO's dependence on the U.S. strategic umbrella, which many Europeans no longer found believable, and its view that at least some attempt to contain the Soviet blitzkrieg should be made. The formal adoption of flexible response for the European theater may also have been partially spurred by the new Soviet doctrine promulgated in 1966 (which in itself was partly a response to the change in U.S. national security policy under Kennedy). The effect of the Soviet decision on the WPO force structure would not be seen until the 1970s, but numerous Soviet pronouncements and articles in military journals made clear that some such shift was under way.

NATO still adhered to a forward strategy, but the tripwire concept was deemphasized. That concept mandated that a Soviet invasion into the West would trigger a swift response involving nuclear weapons. Instead, NATO adopted a three-stage strategy. The first stage, *direct defense*, called for responding to the Soviet attack conventionally, without escalating the level of violence. If direct defense was failing, NATO operations would progress to the second stage, called *deliberate escalation*. This could involve "opening up new fronts or other forms of conventional counter-attack—options sometimes referred to as 'horizontal escalation.' But it is generally assumed that escalation would entail using nuclear weapons, albeit in a limited way."[65] It is important to note, however, that deliberate escalation does not necessarily imply that battlefield nuclear weapons would be introduced into the conflict and that conventional operations would be abandoned. Deliberate escalation means that NATO would consider a range of options involving nuclear and nonnuclear forces to be conducted sequentially or simultaneously, the mix of which to be decided by NATO command. Only as a last resort would the third stage of the strategy, *general nuclear response*, be invoked. This stage would involve the use of strategic nuclear weapons and would include direct attacks against the Soviet Union.

NATO remained largely unprepared to carry out the direct defense of Europe for a sustained period of time; estimates for effective direct defense ranged from 30 to 90 days at best. To a degree, this was part of the strategy. The Soviets would know that relatively early on, NATO would have to consider the introduction of nuclear weapons. In that period, they could reconsider their attack objectives and turn back, if the risk in proceeding and triggering the inevitable nuclear response was judged to be too great. But NATO's limited capacity for direct defense also incurred considerable risk for the West, in particular the West Germans, upon whose soil nuclear weapons would be used. NATO's inadequate conventional forces meant that nuclear weapons would have to be resorted to quickly, probably more quickly than the West Europeans (or anyone else) would prefer.

Faced with this dilemma and the continuing withdrawal of American troops in Europe, the allies briefly considered rearmament. Instead, however, NATO endorsed the Harmel Report, a 1967 study initiated at the urging of the Belgian Foreign Minister Pierre Harmel. In that report, the alliance reiterated its support for collective defense but also backed East-West negotiation and cooperation as a basis for settling their differences. The West Europeans also endorsed strategic arms-control talks between the superpowers and in June 1968 issued a "declaration of mutual and balanced force reductions," urging negotiated reductions in NATO and Warsaw Pact general purpose forces. This declaration paved the way for the Mutual and Balanced Force Reduction (MBFR) Talks.

Whatever the merits of these political initiatives, the conventional imbalance in favor of the East remained an inadequately addressed reality. The MBFR Talks did not actually get under way until 1973, and no progress came of them. They were formally abandoned in February 1989. New talks got under way soon after.

NOTES

1. Maxwell Taylor, "Statement to Senate Armed Services Committee," 20 February 1956, in A.J. Bacevich, *The Pentomic Era: The U.S. Army Between Korea and Vietnam* (Washington, D.C. National Defense University Press, 1986), p. 44.

2. General Maxwell D. Taylor, *The Uncertain Trumpet* (New York: Harper and Bros., 1959).

3. Robert McNamara, Memorandum for the President, subject: Recommended Department of Defense FY'63 Budget and 1963–67 Program, October 6, 1961, p. 11. (NSA).

4. Robert McNamara, *The Essence of Security: Reflections in Office* (New York: Harper & Row, 1968), p. 79.

5. John F. Kennedy, "American University Address," June 10, 1963, in John Lewis Gaddis, *Strategies of Containment* (New York: Oxford University Press, 1982), p. 201.

6. Robert McNamara, *Statement on 1966 Defense Budget*, pp. 94–95, in James Lacy, *Within Bounds: The Navy in Postwar American Security Policy* (Alexandria, Virginia: Center for Naval Analyses, 1983), p. 288.

7. William Kaufmann, *Planning Conventional Forces, 1950–1982* (Washington, D.C.: The Brookings Institution, 1982), p. 7.

8. Ibid.

9. Ibid., pp. 9–14. In his book, Kaufmann states that planning "went something like this." In a telephone interview with this author, March 30, 1987, Kaufmann confirmed that defense planning evolved to follow the five guidelines delineated.

10. National Security Memorandum No. 40, subject: *Policy Directive Regarding NATO and the Atlantic Alliance*, April 24, 1961, p. 1. (NSA).

11. A number of nuclear-sharing schemes were considered in the early 1960s, but only one came close to being implemented as policy. The multilateral force was an effort to address European reservations over the U.S. monopoly on nuclear decision making. "The Multilateral Force (MLF) would have been a force of 25 surface ships, each carrying eight Polaris missiles, manned and funded by multinational crews and assigned to the NATO supreme commander. The United States would have retained veto power over use of the MLF weapons." Stanley Sloan, *NATO's Future: Toward A New Transatlantic Bargain* (Washington, D.C.: National Defense University Press, 1985), p. 40. For an extended discussion see John Steinbruner, *The Cybernetic Theory of Decision* (Princeton: Princeton University Press, 1974).

12. McNamara, *Essence of Security*, p. 45.

13. Kaufmann, *Planning Conventional Forces*, p. 8.

14. Kaufmann, *Planning Conventional Forces*.

15. This is not to suggest, however, that the success or failure of the United States in Vietnam can be attributed to the level of "flexibility" in U.S. forces; this is one factor among many. An evaluation of the Vietnam War is in the next chapter.

16. The theory of assured destruction holds that nuclear deterrence is accomplished by the possession of an invulnerable nuclear force configured for retaliatory missions. Generally, a retaliatory mission is construed as a countervalue (city-busting) mission.

Because of its invulnerability, an adversary contemplating a nuclear first strike will be deterred. He knows he could not escape his own devastation. The more certain is the level of invulnerability of one's force, the more stable the deterrent. Mutual assured destruction holds that when two parties maintain nuclear stockpiles and the above conditions obtain bilaterally, both parties are deterred.

The doctrine of counterforce/no-cities (C/NC) holds that deterrence is maximized by a capability to demolish an opponent's nuclear-strike force. Unlike assured destruction, however, C/NC also provides a basis for nuclear war-fighting. The doctrine holds that in response to a nuclear attack the United States calibrates its response to the size of the initial attack, avoiding attacks against an opponent's cities but withholding a reserve force sufficient to respond to the opponent's counterattack. These forces are a threat, to be used against the opponent's cities if he launches a countersalvo. The opponent is thus faced with the choice of continuing his attack or negotiating a settlement. According to proponents of the theory, he will choose the latter. He will attempt to negotiate a favorable settlement rather than sacrifice his cities. According to critics, however, the opponent will choose the former. Negotiating a settlement in the midst of a nuclear war will be seen as impossible; and the opponent crazy enough to start the nuclear war will presumably be crazy enough to continue it, by definition too irrational to bargain.

17. Figures from Richard Cohen, *National Defense Spending Patterns: Implications for Future Nuclear Weapons R&D Funding* (Washington, D.C.: Washington Defense Research Group, December, 1987).

18. Figures are given in comparison to FY1961. *Army:* 1,066,404 from 858,622; *navy:* 666,428 from 627,089; *air force:* 884,111 from 821,151. Figures are from Jeffrey Record, *Revising U.S. Military Strategy: Tailoring Means to Ends* (McLean, Virginia: Pergamon-Brassey's, 1984), pp. 101–103.

19. Ibid., pp. 101–103.

20. Unless otherwise indicated, budgetary figures are from Office of the Assistant Secretary of Defense (Comptroller), *National Defense Budget Estimates for FY 1988/1989* (Washington, D.C.: GPO, May 1987), various graphs and tables.

21. McNamara, *Essence of Security*, p. 90.

22. McNamara, *Essence of Security*, p. 90.

23. Lacy, *Within Bounds,* pp. 288–289.

24. Amos Taylor and William Jordan, Jr., *American National Security* (Baltimore, Maryland: Johns Hopkins University Press, 1984), p. 187. A thorough discussion of PPBS is in Frederick H. Hartmann and Robert L. Wendzel, *Defending America's Security* (McLean, Virginia: Pergamon-Brassey's, 1988), chapter 9, "The Defense Resource Allocation Process."

25. Both the navy and the air force saw the TFX as a potential encroachment on their roles and missions. From the navy's perspective, a long-range fighter could pose a threat to its carrier-based aircraft, but the air force argued that outfitting the TFX for conventional missions would take away from its capacity to perform nuclear missions. The services ultimately were able to jointly recommend a bid from Boeing for TFX development, but the Office of the Secretary of Defense (OSD) ignored this recommendation and approved a bid from General Dynamics, further adding fuel to the fire. The TFX controversy is detailed in Robert J. Art's *The TFX Decision: McNamara and the Military* (Boston: Little, Brown, and Company, 1968), pp. 45–46.

26. Lacy, *Within Bounds,* pp. 288–289.

27. In Robert Futrell, *Ideas, Concepts, Doctrine: A History of Basic Thinking in the United States Air Force, 1907–1964* (Maxwell AFB, Alabama: Air University Press, 1974), p. 349.

28. Futrell, *Ideas, Concepts, Doctrine.*

29. "Now what is the role of the bomber after you place 1,000 to 2,000 missiles on the Soviet Union? What have you left to mop up? . . . If it is not a mop-up operation what is the role of the bomber?" McNamara, quoted in ibid., p. 374.

30. Air Force Manual (AFM) 1-1, *Basic Aerospace Doctrine of the United States Air Force,* 1964, p. 1-2.

31. AFM 1-1 (1964), chapters 5 and 6. See in particular p. 6-2.

32. AFM 1-1 (1964), pp. 4-2, 5-2, and elsewhere.

33. This is detailed in Futrell, *Ideas, Concepts, Doctrine,* pp. 379–382.

34. John Midgley, *Deadly Illusions* (Boulder, Colorado: Westview Press, 1986), p. 98.

35. Department of the Army Pamphlet 355-200-13, *The New Army Division Structure* (Washington, D.C.: GPO, 18 March 1963), p. 2.

36. Memorandum for the Secretary of Defense from the Secretary of the Army, *Army Plans for Reorganization of its Divisions and*

Reserve Components, 19 July 1961 CS 320 (1961), in Midgley, *Deadly Illusions*, p. 109–110.

37. FM 7-20, *Infantry, Airborne Infantry, and Mechanized Infantry Battalions* (Washington, D.C.: Department of the Army, 28 May 1965), p. 81.

38. The doctrine still provided guidelines for fighting on the atomic battlefield. Dispersion and mobility were emphasized as the key to effectuating *rapid* mobilization and dispersion.

39. Robert Doughty, *The Evolution of US Army Tactical Doctrine, 1945–1976* (Fort Leavenworth, Kansas: Combat Studies Institute, 1979), p. 23.

40. Robert McNamara, "Memorandum for Mr. [Elvis] Starr," April 19, 1962, reprinted in U.S. Army Tactical Mobility Requirements Board (Howze Board), *Final Report*, Fort Bragg, 20 August 1962.

41. "Brief by the President of the Board," in Howze Board, *Final Report*, p. 6.

42. Howze Board, *Final Report*, p. 22.

43. Howze Board, *Final Report*, p. 70–72.

44. Lieutenant General Dwight Beach, Army Combat Development Command, quoted in Futrell, *Ideas, Concepts, Doctrine*, p. 416.

45. Futrell, *Ideas, Concepts, Doctrine*, p. 415.

46. See, e.g., Mark Perry, *Four Stars* (Boston: Houghton Mifflin, 1989), p. 123.

47. The Soviets were most likely motivated by some combination of the following factors: to force a resolution of the Berlin situation through a deal; to weaken U.S. status in Europe (if the United States failed to respond to the Soviet initiative, the Western allies' confidence in the U.S. ability to respond to an aggression in Europe could be further eroded); to weaken the ability of the United States to act in its "backyard," i.e., Latin America; and to be able to cover most of North America with their missile force, still much smaller than the U.S. missile force.

48. Norman Polmar, *Aircraft Carriers* (New York: Doubleday, 1969), pp. 661–662.

49. Lacy, *Within Bounds*, p. 316.

50. McNamara, "Statement on the 1969 Budget," in Lacy, *Within Bounds*, pp. 330–331.

51. Lacy, *Within Bounds*, p. 331.

52. Kaufmann, *Planning Conventional Forces*, p. 12. Elements of this strategy reemerged in the Reagan administration's Maritime Strategy. See chapter 10.

53. Record, *Revising*, p. 26. The navy possessed 971 ships in 1964, but it was evident to navy planners that the older ones were not going to be replaced on a one-on-one basis.

54. As the *N* designates, this was a nuclear carrier. According to Trewhitt's semi-authorized biography, McNamara later felt that he had "yielded too soon" on the carrier issue. "The evidence is strong," writes Trewhitt, "that the President left him no choice." Henry L. Trewhitt, *McNamara: His Ordeal in the Pentagon* (1971), pp. 154–157, quoted in Lacy, *Within Bounds*, p. 318.

55. This is discussed in the next chapter.

56. Robert McNamara, *Department of Defense Annual Report*, FY1966, p. 23.

57. Lacy, *Within Bounds*, pp. 328–329.

58. Record, *Revising*, appendix F, p. 104.

59. Stanley Sloan, *NATO's Future: Toward A New Transatlantic Bargain* (Washington, D.C.: National Defense University Press, 1985), p. 37.

60. Lacy, *Within Bounds*, p. 344. All told, the French had two mechanized divisions that remained in NATO force calculations.

61. Michael MccGwire, *Military Objectives in Soviet Foreign Policy* (Washington, D.C.: The Brookings Institution, 1987), p. 29.

62. See on these points MccGuire, *Military Objectives*. The evolution of Soviet thinking from the inevitability of nuclear war to the possibility of conventional conflict is detailed on pages 25–35.

63. John Erickon, *Soviet Military Power* (1971), p. 70, in Lacy, *Within Bounds*, p. 348.

64. See on this point William L. Lewis, *The Warsaw Pact: Arms, Doctrine, and Strategy* (New York: McGraw Hill, 1982), p. 154.

65. Laurence Martin, *NATO and the Defense of the West* (New York: Holt, Rinehart & Winston, 1985), p. 38.

8

Limited War in Practice: Vietnam

PRELUDE TO WAR

An essential aspect of flexible response involved planning for *counterinsurgency*, defined in a 1963 army field manual as "those military, para-military, political, economic, psychological, and civic actions taken by a government to defeat subversive insurgency."[1] Kennedy's interest in developing the doctrine and capabilities for operations at the lower end of the conflict spectrum came in part from his interpretation of the "lessons" of the Bay of Pigs and from China's successful "people's war" of 1949. Kennedy was also influenced by Khrushchev's January 1961 proclamation that worldwide and limited wars were to be avoided but "wars of national liberation" would be actively supported by the Soviet Union. This was judged to be evidence of a Communist campaign to exploit anti-colonialist movements occurring worldwide. Upon returning from his 1961 meeting with Khrushchev, Kennedy observed:

> In the 1940s and early fifties, the great danger was from Communist armies marching across free borders, which we saw in Korea. . . . Now we face a new and different threat. We no longer have a nuclear monopoly. Their missiles, they believe, will hold off our missiles, and their troops can match our troops should we intervene in these so-called wars of national liberation. Thus, the local conflict they support can turn in their favor through guerillas or insurgents or subversion. . . . It is clear that this struggle . . . of the new and poorer nations will be a continuing crisis of this decade.[2]

"We are opposed around the world by a monolithic and ruthless conspiracy that relies primarily on covert means for expanding its sphere of influence," Kennedy warned, and as historian John Lewis Gaddis has noted, "the struggle had been switched from Europe to Asia, Africa, and Latin America, from nuclear and conventional weaponry to irregular warfare, insurrection, and subversion."[3]

155

Kennedy originally sought to employ counterinsurgency in support of worldwide guerrilla and revolutionary movements. But Khrushchev's support of such movements and the many global commitments and alliances the United States had undertaken made it axiomatic that these forces would be used to support friendly governments trying to stay in power. It is thus understandable that when formally asked in 1961 by the South Vietnamese government to assist in its civil war, the United States agreed to step in. This was consonant with Kennedy's rhetoric, and by increasing the number of U.S. advisers in Vietnam, the United States attained firsthand knowledge and experience in counterinsurgency techniques.

For their part, the services configured some elements of their forces for counterinsurgency operations. The air force developed a combat unit of "air commandos" specifically designated for low-intensity engagements. This unit was dubbed Jungle Jim. A deployment from this unit (Farm Gate) was one of the first sent to South Vietnam in an advisory role and ultimately saw limited action.[4] As discussed in chapter 7, the army had organized the Eleventh Air Assault Division at Fort Benning, Georgia, to test the concepts advocated by the Howze Board. At the same time, U.S. Army helicopter pilots were testing airmobile concepts in a counterinsurgency environment in Vietnam. These tests continued through July 1, 1965, when the First Cavalry Division (Airmobile) was activated.[5]

Army doctrine also evolved to reflect the new priorities. The 1962 version of the army's field manual FM 100-5 featured an entire chapter on operations involving irregular forces,[6] and numerous other manuals were produced detailing counterinsurgency doctrine and tactics. A new spirit of combativeness and confidence was emanating from the army. FM 31-15, *Operations Against Irregular Forces*, reflected this new spirit, admonishing that "a defensive attitude . . . permits the guerilla to concentrate superior forces, inflict severe casualties, and lower morale."[7]

THE VIETNAM WAR: THE STRATEGY OF GRADUATED RESPONSE

President Kennedy was initially skeptical over whether the American people would support an active interventionist role in Southeast Asia and hoped to avoid a direct combat role for U.S. troops based there. In his view, the South Vietnamese had not shown sufficient

commitment in marshaling their military resources against the guerrillas from the North to justify an escalation of the U.S. commitment
beyond the advisory level. He was not about to fight South Vietnam's
war. Kennedy sought to establish fighting units trained to perform
counterinsurgency operations within the South Vietnamese Army.[8]

Kennedy questioned the reliability of Ngo Dinh Diem, the South
Vietnamese president, as a U.S. ally. He believed that Diem's authoritarian rule over the South and his violent suppression of his
Buddhist critics made him unworthy of U.S. support, and in August
1963, acquiesced in (if he did not actually authorize) plans for his
overthrow. Kennedy had hoped that a new regime would bring some
democratic reform, but soon after the overthrow Diem was assas-
sinated and the instability in the South increased. The Thieu regime
that eventually succeeded Diem was barely less authoritarian and
only marginally more successful in rallying the South against the
guerrillas. Tensions between the North and South continued to
escalate, and by the end of 1963, over 16,000 American advisers
were in Vietnam.

By this time, the Viet Cong were operating in most of the South.
Much of the weaponry at their disposal consisted of captured American and French arms. However, it was becoming obvious that the
level of arms provided by the North was steadily increasing. This
led the JCS to step up their planning for active and direct U.S.
military involvement. In a memorandum to the president dated
January 22, 1964, the JCS argued that

> the aid now coming to the Viet Cong from outside the country in
> men, resources, advice and direction is sufficiently great in the ag-
> gregate to be significant—both as help and as encouragement to the
> Viet Cong. It is our conviction that if support of the insurgency from
> outside South Vietnam in terms of operational direction, personnel,
> and material were stopped completely, the character of the war in
> South Vietnam would be substantially and favorably altered.[9]

The JCS were essentially arguing for a two-level interdiction
campaign. On one level, the United States would attack the supply
lines that ran from the North to the South. These attacks would be
aimed at cutting off the flow of supplies to the Viet Cong (VC)
guerrillas. Critical points in North Vietnam would be directly attacked to cut off infiltration routes into the South. These attacks
would involve aerial bombardment and would occur "using US
resources under [South] Vietnamese cover, and with the [South]
Vietnamese openingly assuming responsibility for the action."[10] On
the second level, the lines of communication over which external
parties (such as the Soviet Union) funneled supplies to the North

would be attacked. The JCS sought to isolate North Vietnam by mining its harbors and attacking shipping and other selected lines of communication. The JCS recognized that the second level of attack would involve a major escalation of the war; nonetheless, they were generally convinced that the war could not be won without a concerted effort to cut off supplies flowing to the North.

Arguing for a concentrated attack on North Vietnamese targets, the air force presented the administration a list of 94 key bombing targets located in the North. USAF Chief of Staff Curtis LeMay argued that anything less would not have a decisive impact and that ground forces should be deployed only if these attacks failed to resolve hostilities favorably. Army Chief of Staff Earle Wheeler also agreed that isolating the North was critical to winning the war, although in his view the war would ultimately be won by ground troops originating in the South and working their way northward. Ground forces thus had to be deployed at the onset of operations.

The view from the executive branch was quite different. At the outset, President Kennedy and his secretary of defense Robert McNamara wanted to emphasize counterinsurgency operations. In particular, McNamara objected to a bombing campaign that would expand the war along the lines recommended by the JCS. If anything, his views were more consonant with the army's, which he felt were less provocative and permitted the most opportunities for counterinsurgency and graduated reprisals. Thus, the strategy which emerged, "graduated response," was mostly army-oriented. As described by Brigadier General David Palmer, "Civilian planners wanted to start out softly and gradually increase the pressure by precise increments which could be unmistakenly recognized in Hanoi. Ho Chi Minh would see the tightening pattern, the theory went, and would sensibly stop the war against South Vietnam in time to avoid devastation of his homeland."[11]

Elements of counterinsurgency and graduated response were apparent in General William Westmoreland's plan for operations in Vietnam. But General Westmoreland had replaced Paul Harkins as the commander of U.S. Military Assistance Command, Vietnam, and was more amenable to conducting operations that went beyond counterinsurgency. This is reflected in one of his early strategic assessments:

Phase One: Commit those American and allied forces necessary "to halt the losing trend" by the end of 1965.

Phase Two: "During the first half of 1966," take the offensive with American and allied forces in "high priority areas" to destroy enemy forces and reinstitute pacification programs.

Phase Three: If the enemy persisted, he might be defeated and his forces and base areas destroyed during a period of a year to a year and a half following Phase II.[12]

The essence of this plan, it would turn out, was to wear the enemy down. The second phase, emphasizing the pacification of war-torn areas within the southern region (discussed below), meant the United States would continue to concentrate its resources in the South, bolstering the fighting capability of friendly indigenous forces and providing combat support as required (at this time, the U.S. role in Vietnam was still primarily advisory). If air attacks against the North proved necessary, they were to occur as close as possible to the DMZ that separated the North and the South.

On August 2, 1964, a North Vietnamese patrol boat was reported to have attacked the USS *Maddox*, a destroyer cruising in the Tonkin Gulf. On August 5, U.S. carrier-based aircraft commenced air strikes against the North's torpedo boat anchorages and oil dumps above the 17th parallel. This operation, Momyer points out,

> set the pattern for our future air strategy. Until the bombing halt of 1968, our overall air strategy was one of "tit for tat," or graduated escalation, with targets being released [by the President] for attack a few at a time depending upon the activities of the North Vietnamese. Furthermore, the rationale for selecting targets was oriented toward achieving some particular effect upon the ground war in South Vietnam, not toward destroying the will of the North Vietnamese to fight.[13]

On August 7, Congress passed the Tonkin Gulf resolution, which stated in part that the

> Congress approves and supports the determination of the President, as Commander in Chief, to take all necessary measures to repel any armed attack against the forces of the United States and to prevent further aggression.
>
> The United States is, therefore, prepared, as the President determines, to take all necessary steps, including the use of armed force, to assist any member or protocol state of the Southeast Asia Collective Defense Treaty requesting assistance in defense of its freedom.[14]

This resolution basically insured that Johnson would have a free hand in conducting operations in Southeast Asia.

On February 8, 1965, the Communists attacked a U.S. military adviser's compound at Pleiku, killing 9 and wounding 76. One day prior to this attack, McGeorge Bundy had written a memorandum to the president urging a policy of "sustained reprisal" against North Vietnamese transgressions. The policy was firmly rooted in the language and thinking of flexible response, as the following passage from the memo shows:

It would be important [to] insure that the general level of reprisal action remained in close correspondence with the level of outrages in the South. We must make it clear at every stage both to Hanoi and the world, that our reprisals will be reduced or stopped when outrages in the South are reduced or stopped—and that we are not attempting to destroy or conquer North Vietnam.[15]

Bundy recommended that this operation involve "air and naval actions" against selected targets in the North, and on February 13, 1965, Johnson approved Rolling Thunder, an aerial operation against such targets. Air attacks were mostly confined to regions of the north that were below the 19th parallel.[16] Nonetheless, Rolling Thunder represented the first major expansion of the war and the beginning of the end of the administration's efforts to fight a strictly counterinsurgency war. To be sure, counterinsurgency would for some time remain an important component of the total U.S. effort. But over time such operations would be gradually supplemented by more traditional operations, and later phased out almost completely.

Rolling Thunder was kept under strict civilian control, its execution supervised "from the highest levels"—i.e., the White House.[17] Eventually, Rolling Thunder grew in intensity, geographic coverage, and targets. But the operation at all times remained within politically determined parameters. In writing about Rolling Thunder, General Bruce Palmer, who served as Westmoreland's deputy in Vietnam, has argued that "with respect to the air war, U.S. political leaders, particularly in the 1965–1967 period, kept very tight control over American military leaders. As a matter of fact, President Johnson would not delegate this control to anyone outside the White House, and for most of his presidency remained the target officer."[18]

Rolling Thunder commenced on March 2, 1965. Originally, the air force argued for attacks against the North Vietnamese LOCs below the 17th parallel and against a limited number of targets in Hanoi. However, the civilian leadership chose to keep the strikes limited to logistical targets close to the DMZ and denied the air force request to expand the target set deep into the North.

In part, Rolling Thunder was politically motivated: it was viewed by the administration as a means of bolstering the morale of the South Vietnamese government. Militarily, the administration hoped that Rolling Thunder would convince Hanoi to either negotiate a settlement of hostilities or cease its insurgency operations in the South in exchange for a bombing halt. But Rolling Thunder's aerial attacks were generally followed by "negotiating pauses," which gave the North Vietnamese time to adjust to the bombing and reconstitute its supply lines to the Viet Cong. The VC guerrilla activities in the

South were thus able to continue relatively unabated. Hostilities continued to escalate, and on March 8, 1965, two marine corps battalions landed at Da Nang airfield, representing the first major contingent of U.S. non-advisory personnel to be deployed in battle. With McNamara's urging,[19] Johnson approved General Westmoreland's request for 44 additional battalions. The United States was now fully committed to a combat role.

By this time, the JCS had evolved a concept for the war comprised of three military tasks:

1. to cause the Democratic Republic of Vietnam (DRV) to cease its direction and support of the Viet Cong insurgency;
2. to defeat the Viet Cong and extend the control of the Government of Vietnam (GVN) over all of South Vietnam; and
3. to deter Communist China from direct intervention and to defeat such intervention should it occur.[20]

To achieve these ends, the JCS recommended

immediate initiation of sharply intensified military pressures against the DRV, starting with a sharp and early attack in force on the DRV, subsequent to brief operations in Laos and U.S. low-level reconnaissance north of the boundary to divert DRV attention prior to the attack in force. This program would be designed to destroy in the first three days Phuc Yen airfield near Hanoi, other airfields, and major POL [petroleum, oil, lubricants] facilities . . . and to afford the GVN respite by curtailing DRV assistance to and direction of the Viet Cong. The follow-on military program—involving armed reconnaissance of infiltration routes in Laos, air strikes on infiltration targets in the DRV, and then progressive strikes throughout North Vietnam—could be suspended short of full destruction of the DRV if our objectives were earlier achieved.[21]

This program involved expanding the war into Laos and Cambodia, building up forces in Thailand,[22] and blockading North Vietnam. In time, all of these steps would be taken. At this point, however, the JCS agenda was much too aggressive for the civilian leadership, who still wanted to avoid escalating the conflict. McNamara did not reject the program outright but accomplished the same when he refused to endorse it.

With respect to proper U.S. military operations in Southeast Asia, this incident typically reflected the divergent views of McNamara and the military. In McNamara's view, U.S. objectives in the war were to drive the North from the South and preserve the South's sovereignty. To the military, these were admirable goals but did not go far enough. Admiral Thomas Moorer, a former JCS chairman, expressed the position of the military leadership when he said, "We should have fought the war in the North, where everyone was the enemy. . . . But Lyndon Johnson didn't want to overthrow the North Vietnamese government. Well, the only reason you go to war is to overthrow a government you don't like."[23] From the perspective of the military, the United States should have been actively pursuing no less than the elimination of the North Vietnamese government. This would have required a greater commitment to employ the land forces against the North Vietnamese regular army.

The JCS continued to push for intensified air and naval bombardment against the North Vietnamese heartland. Such a strategy would exploit U.S. air power and, the JCS argued, allow the U.S. to capture the initiative in the conflict. On the one hand, the JCS argued that fighting the war on the ground surrendered the initiative to the North. They could fight where and when they wanted and retreat into the jungles or sanctuaries in Laos and Cambodia as they chose. McNamara, on the other hand, fastidiously argued that the war was essentially an army operation. Upon his urging, Johnson limited the scope and intensity of the air and naval bombardment and increased the role of the land forces. But Johnson's attempt to fight the war within self-imposed limits was faltering. By 1966 Johnson had committed 470,000 troops into Vietnam with no end to the conflict on the horizon.

By 1968, McNamara had personally reassessed the U.S. role in the war. DOD's systems analysts found that the kill ratios between the enemy and the U.S. and South Vietnamese favored the North, that the bombing of the North's supply routes had escalated four times with little notable success, and that the damage inflicted upon the North was far outweighed by the damage to U.S. bomber forces. Finally, they concluded that "despite the presence of 500,000 American troops, despite the expenditure of more bomb tonnage than the United States had dropped in all of World War II, despite estimated enemy casualties of up to 140,000 men in 1967, the North Vietnamese could continue to funnel at least 200,000 men into South Vietnam indefinitely." The systems analysts further concluded that "the notion that we can 'win' this war by driving the (Viet Cong and North Vietnamese Army) from the country or by inflicting an unacceptable rate of casualties on them is false."[24] McNamara subsequently urged a five-part program involving the leveling off of ground forces at about 470,000, stabilizing the Rolling Thunder program, pursuing a negotiated settlement and a simultaneous pacification program, and setting up an infiltration barrier across the neck of South Vietnam near the 17th parallel and across the infiltration trails in Laos.[25]

The JCS vigorously objected to McNamara's limitations. They argued that political prohibitions against attacks on enemy sanctuaries and supply lines at their origins in the North had hindered army operations, because there was no significant effect on the enemy's LOCs or on the North's ability to receive replenishment from the outside. They also argued that the graduated nature of the U.S. bombing attacks made it too easy for the North to adjust and regroup in their aftermath. The JCS recommended that the United States escalate the number and pace of air campaigns against all militarily significant targets in the North and repeated all their earlier recommendations. But the political leadership remained hesitant to expand the war, and while there was some expansion of the target set, most of the JCS recommendations were rejected.[26]

On January 31, 1968, the North Vietnamese launched the Tet Offensive, a massive attack involving both army regular forces and the Viet Cong, against the South. The Tet Offensive involved a series of attacks on 34 of 44 South Vietnamese province capitals, approximately 64 district towns, and almost every autonomous city in South Vietnam. It took 26 days for U.S. and South Vietnamese forces to recapture the town of Hue and other key cities, and in the aftermath of the attack, Westmoreland requested over 200,000 additional troops.

Johnson was now confronted with the reality that existing U.S. force levels were inadequate even to achieve his limited aims. U.S. and South Vietnamese troops repelled the Tet Offensive, but it was now clear that to achieve Johnson's objectives, U.S. troop strength would have to be greatly increased—by year's end, troop levels would reach 540,000. Johnson did not want to abandon South Vietnam, but it was clear that the strategy of graduated response was not working, and there was no indication that the North was prepared to negotiate a settlement.

On the urging of Clark Clifford, who had replaced the beleaguered and disillusioned McNamara as secretary of defense, Johnson stabilized U.S. troop levels and determined that greater reliance would again be placed on the South Vietnamese to fight what was essentially their war. Johnson sought to negotiate a cease-fire that would allow the United States to extricate itself honorably and enable the South Vietnamese to determine their own future, free of outside interference. These principles, which had precipitated U.S. involvement in the first place, would take on greater significance in the Nixon administration as the basis of what became known as Vietnamization.

VIETNAMIZATION

On March 31, 1968, President Johnson ordered a partial bombing halt, proposed settlement talks with the North Vietnamese, and announced in a stunning television address that he would not seek reelection. On November 5, Richard Nixon was elected president in a narrow contest in which the war was a highly contested issue.

By this time, public sentiment in the United States was turning decidedly against the war. The United States was successful in repelling the North and turning back the Tet Offensive. But the televised reporting from Southeast Asia brought the violence of the war into the living rooms of the American people, and a growing segment of the American population came to question the government's rosy pictures of progress in the war effort.

Given this eroding domestic support for the war, Nixon found himself in a dilemma. He campaigned on ending the war honorably and quickly, but he was not willing to abandon South Vietnam. Since Johnson called the bombing halt, the North Vietnamese had been shipping materiel and supplies into the northernmost provinces of South Vietnam and into Laos and Cambodia. They were apparently preparing for a major offensive, and it became evident that a wholesale U.S. withdrawal would spell the demise of the South. Nixon felt it necessary to address the North Vietnamese buildup, but he realized that the public and Congress would not support an increase in the land-based forces.

The Nixon administration developed a two-track policy, which came to be called Vietnamization. The first track involved a gradual withdrawal of U.S. land-based forces. Nixon reiterated that the South Vietnamese would have to prosecute the war on the ground themselves, while the United States would provide economic and military support. This support would come primarily from the air force and the navy, and U.S. ground troops would be gradually withdrawn from Southeast Asia. In 1969, 60,000 U.S. soldiers were brought home.

The second track of Vietnamization was to intensify the air campaigns against the North Vietnamese. Pursuant to JCS recommendations, these air strikes included limited raids within North

Vietnam, attacks on North Vietnamese Army (NVA) supply and surface-to-air missile (SAM) air defense sites and, commencing on March 18, 1969, attacks against NVA sanctuaries in Cambodia. These operations continued with little respite through May 26, 1970, and were augmented with lower-scale TACAIR fighter-bomber operations that lasted until 1973. On February 17, 1970, B-52s were used in Laos against approximately 15,000 North Vietnamese personnel and supply depots located there. These operations continued until April 20, 1972. Operations in both Laos and Cambodia involved ground forces but exclusively in reconnaissance and support roles. These operations were highly controversial; protests against the Cambodian operations led to the killing of four students at Kent State University (Ohio) by the National Guard. Nonetheless, in accord with Vietnamization, U.S. troops were returning home throughout the entire period. Air power had become the essential component of the U.S. effort.

Throughout 1970 and 1971, the scope and intensity of the air attacks rose steadily. But they were primarily directed against targets around the 17th parallel and were ineffective in stopping the flow of supplies from the North. In January 1972, the North Vietnamese Army launched a massive invasion into the South. On March 30, the NVA rolled across the DMZ and simultaneously attacked from the Central Highlands and from the area around An Loc, a region only 50 miles north of Saigon, the South Vietnamese capital. The NVA strategy was to sever the provinces to the north of Saigon from the capital, establish a foothold in Pleiku, and set the stage for a future assault on Saigon.[27] They were supported by heavy artillery and armor and utilized unprecedented amounts of force, including 400 armored vehicles, antitank missiles, heat-seeking SA-7 SAMs, and vast amounts of 122mm and 130mm artillery.

Nixon's first priority was to stop the offensive. Thailand-based fighters were sent on bombing sorties from South Vietnamese airfields. These aircraft would then return to Thailand. On April 15 and 16, the administration commenced B-52 attacks on fuel-storage depots in the Hanoi-Haiphong area and naval bombardments on the North Vietnamese shore. Supported by the tactical air forces, these attacks were instrumental in halting the offensive. For their part, the South Vietnamese held their own in the land battles, and the entire affair was touted by the administration as a showcase exhibition of Vietnamization in action.

On May 7, 1972, Nixon implemented operation Pocket Money, which included the mining of Haiphong harbor and other North Vietnamese coastal ports. The purpose of this operation was to cut off critical Soviet supplies coming into the North. Three days later the president gave full approval to the air force's 94-target list, comprised primarily of targets in the North. In a major speech to the nation, the president explained the objective of the attacks:

> All entrances to North Vietnamese ports will be mined to prevent access to these ports and North Vietnamese naval operations from these ports. United States forces have been directed to take appropriate measures within the internal and claimed territorial waters of North Vietnam to interdict the delivery of supplies. Rail and all other communications will be cut off to the maximum extent possible. Air and naval strikes against military targets in North Vietnam will continue.[28]

The May bombing campaign (Linebacker I) marked the fullest implementation yet of the JCS recommendations. The United States had by now fully abandoned the strategy of graduated reprisals and was employing air power in pursuit of traditional air power objectives, such as breaking the enemy's will to fight and destroying his economic and war-making industry (however limited the latter might have been in this instance). At the same time, Vietnamization of the ground war continued apace so that by the middle of 1972 about 100,000 men remained in Vietnam. This was less than a fifth of the commitment at its peak in 1968.

All the while, negotiations were proceeding in Paris between Nixon's national security adviser Henry Kissinger and a North Vietnamese delegation headed by Le Duc Tho, a central member of the North Vietnamese Politburo. By the end of 1972, a negotiated settlement appeared imminent, and as a goodwill gesture, the United States halted the bombing on October 23. However, this gesture increased the North's intransigence at the bargaining table and led to an increase of NVA activity in the South. Thus, on December 18, the United States reinstituted the bombing campaign with a vengeance.

Linebacker II marked the first time that bombing was permitted to proceed completely unrestricted. B-52 attacks were initiated in large numbers against the North Vietnamese heartland and against North Vietnamese sanctuaries on both sides of the 20th parallel. Essentially, the B-52s attacked the larger area targets, and tactical aircraft were employed against "point" targets. The Seventh Air Force, for example, suppressed SAM sites and went head-to-head with Soviet-supplied MiGs.[29] After eleven days of relentless attack, the North Vietnamese agreed to a cease-fire, and on January 23, 1973, Kissinger and Le Duc Tho initialed the Paris Agreement on Ending the War and Restoring Peace In Vietnam.[30]

THE SERVICES IN VIETNAM

THE NAVY

For the United States, the war in Vietnam was at first a ground war and, in its later stages, an air war. As in Korea, the navy's participation was considerable, but its role was largely supportive of its sister services. The U.S. naval presence in the South China Sea went largely unchallenged. Thus, as in Korea, the navy coast guard was involved in riverine operations but not in major sea wars. Admiral Elmo Zumwalt, who served as chief of naval operations under Nixon, summed up the navy's role in the war: "In the war in Southeast Asia, as in the Korean War, the enemy could not dispute U.S. control of the seas and so the Navy's main business became projection: amphibious landings, air strikes, and occasional episodes of naval shore bombardment."[31]

This is not entirely true, however, as the navy performed a number of tactical missions besides power projection throughout the war. The navy's Seventh Fleet operated from the Gulf of Tonkin, along North Vietnam's eastern shelf. Along with the embryonic South Vietnamese navy, U.S. destroyers and patrol aircraft of the Seventh Fleet established a coastal patrol of South Vietnamese waters on March 20, 1965. This operation, called Market Time, successfully choked off some enemy infiltration of supply lines at sea. Allied river-patrol operations, called Game Warden, further hindered the enemy's ability to use the inward waterways throughout the South.[32]

Nonetheless, the essential navy mission in Vietnam was indeed power projection. The marines established a short airfield for tactical support (SATS) at Chu Lai. From this airfield, marine aircraft were coordinated with carrier-based aircraft, and a carrier operations area was established off Saigon. Two to five carrier task forces, with cruisers and destroyers, operated from the Gulf of Tonkin. Carrier-based aircraft operating from the gulf participated in the air reprisals following the 1964 Tonkin Gulf incident and were coordinated with the Seventh Air Force throughout the war, until the end of the bombing campaigns in early 1973.

The construction of additional air bases in 1966 permitted the carriers to be moved northward to facilitate interdiction campaigns. The coastal-patrol forces pushed their operations up the Mekong Delta, forming Mobile Riverine Task Forces with one brigade of the Ninth Division of the U.S. Army. In this way, the river-based patrol forces could provide additional air support and firepower for the ground units.

At the peak of operations in 1968, 38,396 personnel were assigned to U.S. naval forces in Vietnam. As Nixon implemented Vietnamization, U.S. naval operations were phased downward, and the South Vietnamese navy assumed greater responsibilities. As U.S. ships were returned to reserve status, the size of the fleet declined from 960 active vessels in 1967 to 750 in 1970. While part of this decline can be attributed to the retirement of older ships, much of the decrease was attributable to the war. As Zumwalt explains, "Sea control forces—anti-submarine planes and their carriers and ships suitable for patrol and escort duty—were allowed to obsolesce and . . . retire without replacement. Work on future sea-control requirements . . . was postponed for many years."[33] Through the war years, therefore, most navy investment went into procurement of power-projection forces such as the carriers and the ships equipped for bombardment—quite the opposite of what McNamara had originally intended.

AN EVOLVING ARMY STRATEGY

While the navy's role in the war was peripheral, the army's was central from the start. At the onset of hostilities, the army's goal was *pacification:* to calm and stabilize the South Vietnamese countryside so that the people of the South could live free of military threat from the North and from the indigenous VC. This involved driving out the North Vietnamese Army and the Viet Cong guerrillas and establishing among the South Vietnamese a degree of confidence in the U.S. and South Vietnamese government forces.[34]

Counterinsurgency operations were initially the basis of the pacification campaigns. When the marines were first deployed at Da Nang, counterinsurgency tactics were employed with some success. The marines would comb the countryside near the beachheads to establish control in the hamlets and villages. Their plan was to gradually move up and down the coast and expand the beachhead.

From Westmoreland's perspective, however, this practice left the marines vulnerable to attacks from guerrillas operating from areas the marines had not yet taken:

> With the enemy free to recruit in regions the marines had yet to enter and to operate in nearby hills with impunity, every subsequent move of the marines to extend the peripheries of the beachheads would become progressively more difficult and would make the beachheads

more vulnerable . . . the main force VC battalions in the I Corps Zone during 1965 had more than doubled, reaching fifteen by the end of the year.[35]

Westmoreland's qualms were not with pacification per se but with the way it was originally proposed. Westmoreland has written that "the marines should have been trying to find the enemy's forces and bring them to battle, thereby putting them on the run and reducing the threat they posed to the battalion."[36] This philosophy was the basis of the "search and destroy" tactics Westmoreland employed as commander of the ground forces. The threat posed by the enemy's forces had to be eliminated. This meant aggressively taking the fight to the enemy.

As carried out by Westmoreland, pacification involved three basic operations. The first was search-and-destroy. Its purpose was to locate the enemy and evacuate him, without necessarily taking the territory on which the battle was waged. No fixed model existed for these operations. They could involve ambushes, direct attacks, "horseshoe" operations (whereby units would be placed in blocking positions and ground thrusts would drive into the center of the horseshoe), and "hammer and anvil" operations (whereby a blocking position would be occupied and an attacking force would move toward it).[37] The problem, however, was that in response to these tactics, the North Vietnamese would gravitate to the center of the peasant villages. As a consequence, the United States would some-times destroy entire villages in pursuit of the enemy.

Search-and-destroy operations tried either to chase an enemy from an area or destroy him. Clearing operations, the second stage of Westmoreland's strategy, were aimed at keeping the enemy off balance for extended periods of time, thereby not permitting him the opportunity to establish authority in the villages. In the broader sense, these operations sought to create an opportunity for the South Vietnamese government to extend its influence.

The final stage of pacification involved securing areas that had been taken. As Robert Doughty notes, these operations "protected pacification accomplishments, but concentrated on eliminating local guerilla units and the enemy's political infrastructure and support base. Although multi-battalion offensive sweeps could be used to secure an area, the norm was probably saturation patrolling and cordon and searches of hamlets."[38] While described sequentially, these operations were often conducted as necessary against a highly mobile enemy operating in terrain more familiar to him than to U.S. forces. As a result, search-and-destroy became an end unto itself. Simply finding the enemy and destroying him often took precedence over the long-term pacification aims at the heart of the army's operations.

Wearing down VC forces eventually replaced pacification as the main aim of counterinsurgency. In late 1966, Ambassador Robert Komer concluded that "few of our programs—civil or military— are very efficient, but we are grinding the enemy down by sheer weight and mass." In a statement dated April 14, 1967, Westmoreland told the press, "We'll just go on bleeding them until Hanoi wakes up to the fact that they have bled their country to the point of national disaster for generations. Then they will have to reassess their position."[39] Westmoreland pursued these operations relentlessly, as division or even multidivision-sized units were sometimes used for search-and-destroy missions. However, search-and-destroy campaigns were primarily conducted at the brigade, battalion, and company level.

Wearing down enemy forces proved an elusive goal. With few exceptions, Westmoreland's operations were limited to the South, making it impossible to cap the flow of infiltrating North Vietnamese forces. The VC operated in small units, such as a platoon or company. The Main Force VC units were organized into battalions and regiments, and the North Vietnamese Army was organized into regiments and divisions. Units could compensate for their relative lack of organic firepower by employing greater battlefield mobility. For example, the NVA could break down to brigades or carry out guerrilla actions if necessary (although this was rare). The VC units could break down into highly mobile task forces and platoons, as well. Their familiarity with the territory expedited their abilities to divide. For example, the North could simply elude U.S. troops by fleeing across the Vietnamese border into safe sanctuaries in the North, where U.S. and South Vietnamese troops were not permitted to follow.

Given the Viet Cong's ability to blend into the southern populace and the elaborate tunnel systems into which they would scurry out of sight, finding the North Vietnamese became a mission in itself. The helicopter had already proven indispensable in moving men and supplies across the rugged Vietnamese terrain. It proved equally valuable in this capacity. Helicopter-borne air assaults would strike enemy locations, and successive assaults would search out a number of potential areas where the enemy might be located.[40]

Even tanks were employed for these missions. Rapid and far-ranging sweeps by tanks and armored personnel carriers gave commanders considerable latitude in flushing out enemy camps. Tanks could also be used for "thunder runs": "small groups of tanks dashed down roads, often late at night, to surprise unsuspecting enemy troops or to preclude the enemy from mining important communications routes." U.S. commanders would also lure the enemy from his camps by fielding apparently vulnerable forces to attract an enemy attack. The enemy's subsequent attack would be met with resistance from mobile units quick to reinforce the besieged units. These "pile-on" tactics were designed to minimize U.S. casualties and exploit firepower: "The main idea remained to find the enemy, to fix him with small arms or immediate supporting forces, to encircle him with other units and to destroy him by an overwhelming mass of artillery and air support."[41]

Essentially, then, the army settled on strategies and tactics that combined maneuver and attritional elements. In many individual battles, these tactics were successful. Yet the seemingly endless supply of Viet Cong and North Vietnamese regulars crossing into the South, the limitations imposed by the civilian leadership on the conflict, and the inability of U.S. forces to cut off the North's supply lines made significant headway difficult to achieve.

THE SHIFT TO AIR POWER

As discussed, U.S. strategy in Vietnam gradually shifted after the 1968 Tet Offensive and Nixon's election. Under Nixon, the land war was deemphasized in favor of air power. General Creighton Abrams replaced Westmoreland as commander of the ground forces, and the army's role in the conflict fundamentally changed. The trend away from counterinsurgency that began under Westmoreland was accelerated, and Abrams abandoned most operations against the Communist ground forces. Protection of the South Vietnamese population against attacks by the North became the army's preeminent priority. American forces were deployed for defense in depth around major cities, and the South Vietnamese were given greater responsibility for fighting the ground war.[42]

By late 1966, sorties from bases in Thailand and carriers in the Gulf of Tonkin had reached 12,000 a month as Rolling Thunder escalated. Nonetheless, most attacks were conducted for interdiction missions, and the overall potential for air power was not realized. In 1967, perhaps the most significant air power–related event was the widespread use of laser-guided bombs, such as the Walleye, which improved naval and air force targeting capabilities. Even with such technologically capable systems in its arsenal, however, the air force ran into some fundamental problems in carrying out its missions. For example, the B-52s and other high-performance aircraft employed by the air force were not ideally suited for interdiction-type missions (as discussed below); air force (and carrier) targeting sets were still restricted; SAM sites and enemy fighters on the ground above the 20th parallel were off limits; and route and target assignments were inflexible.[43]

Air power was used to support tactical operations, and in this respect the air force was in fact able to develop a number of innovative uses for its air assets.[44] But the limits on its use combined with the relatively simple ground tactics employed by the North Vietnamese tended to reduce its effectiveness. The Communists would conduct troop and supply movements and attack primarily at night, while employing camouflage and dispersion tactics to protect themselves. In the South, the use of air power proved counterproductive to accomplishing at least one major U.S. objective: it proved difficult to win the hearts and minds of a people while simultaneously bombing their homeland.

Under Nixon, the B-52 took on increased importance in performing tactical missions. For example, it was used comprehensively in the Cambodian operation of 1969 and 1970. By then, B-52s were also participating in the bombing in the South and were being employed against supply lines in Laos and along the Cambodian border. While McNamara's systems analysts had found such tactical employments of the B-52 wasteful, the air force's position was that the B-52s could haul five times the load of a tactical fighter-bomber and had intrinsic capabilities lacking in tactical aircraft. For example, they were better equipped to perform day or night missions, as they were guided by precision ground-based radar.[45]

At the outset of Linebacker I, when Nixon directed the mining of Haiphong harbor and expanded the bombing offensive, the air force again employed laser- and television-guided munitions.[46] Using these weapons, the air force successfully demolished a number of North Vietnamese bridges and rail lines originating in Hanoi and China, as well as power plants and other targets that were earlier prohibited due to their proximity to civilian population centers.

As discussed, in December 1972, Nixon responded to the North's increased intransigence at the bargaining table and the increased NVA presence in the South by stepping up the bombing campaign (Linebacker II). As a general rule, tactical fighters equipped with guided bombs would attack by day, B-52s by night. Except for civilian areas, targeting was almost completely unrestricted and increasingly accessible. This was due to the depletion of enemy SAMs and increasingly sophisticated evasion tactics by U.S. air assets. By one estimation, the North fired 200 SAMs on the first night of Linebacker

II, 180 the second, and then only about 20 per night thereafter. This permitted B-52s and tactical aircraft relatively unimpeded access to targets, and by December 28 and 29, the final two nights of the operation, virtually no B-52s were damaged by enemy SAMs.[47]

CONCLUSION

Clearly, the North Vietnamese had many motives for signing the Paris accord, including the fact that Nixon dropped the demand that their troops evacuate the South as a prerequisite to an agreement. One also observes that the Linebacker campaigns seemed to increase the North's flexibility at the bargaining table and, without question, facilitated the war's conclusion. It is also significant that when Nixon (or Johnson) offered a respite to the bombing, the North's intransigence would return. The North Vietnamese leadership evidently viewed the bombing halts as signs of U.S. weakness and as opportunities to be exploited.

No doubt, some domestic factors also influenced Nixon's decision to step up the Linebacker campaign. Congress was to reconvene in January 1973, and Nixon was certain that Congress would cut off funding at that time. He no doubt wanted to reach an accord before this transpired. At this point, moreover, Nixon no longer needed a negotiated settlement to reassure his reelection.

There has been much debate as to whether a continuation of Linebacker could have won the war. This was the contention, for example, of British analyst Sir Robert Thompson.[48] The debate is conjectural, of course, but it does raise questions about U.S. strategy from the beginning of the U.S. involvement to the end. Could some of the bloodshed of Vietnam have been avoided had the civilian leadership fought to win the war decisively? Did it make sense for the United States to engage in a war against an enemy whose strengths were U.S. weaknesses and on the terms set by the enemy? Most importantly, perhaps, should the United States have fought a counterinsurgency war at all? Should the United States have resorted to full-scale air campaigns against North Vietnam from the outset?

Vietnam has been dissected as a failure of flexible response, the national strategy of which graduated response and counterinsurgency were components. In one analyst's view:

> Johnson followed the strategy of flexible response faithfully in Vietnam [and] . . . the American defeat there rather grew out of assumptions

derived quite logically from that strategy: that the defense of Southeast
Asia was crucial to the maintenance of world order; that force could
be applied in Vietnam with precision and discrimination; [and] . . .
that the effects would be to enhance American power and prestige,
and credibility in the world.[49]

There is merit to this point of view. But in the Cuban Missile
Crisis, the same author admits, the strategy was applied successfully.[50]
It thus cannot be said that flexible response as a strategy was
inherently flawed. Nonetheless, if the strategy was failing, perhaps
it should have been reassessed and discarded earlier than it actually
was.

Graduated response proved to be a no-win war-waging strategy.
If the president, having publicly disavowed going into the North,
switched gears and approved a more ambitious strategic goal, he
would have had to expand the war. This would have increased
domestic unrest at home and, in the short term at least, could have
increased U.S. casualties. Yet not expanding the war yielded the
initiative to the enemy, led to an essentially negative policy (i.e.,
convincing the North that it could not win rather than convincing
it that it would lose), and led to domestic and congressional dissatisfaction anyway.

Why the United States failed to achieve its goals in Vietnam
will long be debated. It is notable that the ground campaign as
carried out under McNamara has been criticized by some for inadequately emphasizing counterinsurgency and by still others for
emphasizing it too much. Colonel David Hackworth summed up the
first view as follows: "In Vietnam our country has tried to kill a fly
with a sledgehammer—a sledgehammer made of gimmicks and
gadgets. We have tried to wear down the enemy by a massive
outpouring of bombs, bullets, and materiel from the nation's great
assembly lines."[51] But to have put greater emphasis on counterinsurgency may have proven counterproductive, both in fighting the
war abroad and at home. The familiar and rugged terrain and the
maze of underground tunnels at the Viet Cong's disposal meant that
a guerrilla war would ultimately favor the North. There was also
the problem of adequate personnel to be devoted to stopping the
irregulars. General Bruce Palmer estimates that "the peak strength
of these territorial forces was 532,000 . . . reached in 1972, somewhat larger than the 1972 peak strength of the regular forces,
516,000."[52] The United States was simply outnumbered. The VC were
already experiencing greater manpower losses than the United States
and South Vietnam; the problem was that they were able to provide
new forces, while the United States was not. To counter the seemingly

endless numbers of irregular and regular North Vietnamese Army forces would have required an increased U.S. commitment in Southeast Asia, at the least necessitating a call-up of the reserves. This could have undermined domestic support for the war, which Johnson was unprepared to do.

In his powerful analysis of the Vietnam War, Colonel Harry Summers attributes the U.S. failure in Vietnam to an overemphasis on counterinsurgency. The North Vietnamese, he argues, were not primarily fighting a "people's war" of revolution and counterinsurgency but were engaged in a conventional war involving full-scale military operations. The counterinsurgency operations performed by the Viet Cong in the South were peripheral to the North's main efforts, even though they commanded most of the attention of U.S. planners.

> While a strategic offensive against North Vietnam may not have been politically feasible, we could have taken the tactical offensive to isolate the battlefield. But instead of orientating on North Vietnam—the source of war—we turned our attention to the symptom—the guerilla war in the South. Our new strategy of counterinsurgency blinded us to the fact that the guerilla war was tactical and not strategic. It was a kind of economy of force operation on the part of North Vietnam to buy time and wear down superior U.S. military forces.[53]

If pursued in conjunction with carefully coordinated and well-planned air campaigns, an army strategy that focused on defeating the North Vietnamese regular fighting forces may have been successful. If well coordinated with air power, such a strategy would not necessarily have required calling up the reserves or a massive commitment of U.S. ground forces in North Vietnam. General Bruce Palmer, for example, put forth a plan that he claimed would require *fewer* combat troops than were actually deployed in Vietnam. His plan utilized about seven U.S. divisions, as opposed to the ten and a half actually deployed. As Palmer sums up in his book,

> Most of the U.S. troops . . . would eventually be concentrated in the northern provinces to form an international force along the DMZ. . . . This defensive line would be extended into Laos across the narrow waist of the panhandle region . . . U.S. naval power would (threaten) possible invasion from the sea. . . . Additionally, U.S. air and naval power would be employed in a blockade of northern ports.[54]

In Palmer's schema, the U.S. role in the war effort would be principally supportive of the South Vietnamese Army, and efforts to cut off supplies going into the North would be made from the outset. The South Vietnamese would be responsible for confronting the

Viet Cong already in the South, who would be cut off from their northern suppliers by the massed U.S. forces at the DMZ. The United States would support the South's war efforts by providing artillery cover and close air support, as necessary. Whether this strategy would or would not have led to a better resolution of the war is of course debatable. But it is notable that there were other courses of action available to the United States besides full-scale escalation of the hostilities. This point seems to have been lost on U.S. officials in both the Johnson and Nixon administrations.[55]

In the seven and a half years that the army was involved in Vietnam, it won most of the battles in which it was engaged. In November 1965, for example, the 32nd, 33rd, and 66th regiments of the NVA clashed with the U.S. First Cavalry Division in the Ia Drang Valley in central Vietnam. After ten days of fighting, the North Vietnamese were in full retreat.[56] Yet this is evident in the later stages of the war, as well. As the North Vietnamese came to rely extensively on large-scale conventional operations, they were defeated by the sheer mass of U.S. firepower. This was the case in the first major North Vietnamese offensive at Tet in 1968 and again in 1972 when the North launched its Easter Offensive.

But the problem of preventing the South's eventual takeover by the North was one of strategy, not tactics. By rejecting strategies that would bring the war to the North, refusing to expand the war to include the concerted application of air power, and by not clearly defining the purposes for which the war was being waged, Johnson and McNamara followed a strategy that did not end hostilities but prolonged them. The respites built into graduated response allowed the North ample time to adjust to the campaigns. Pacification often resulted in the destruction of friendly territory and thus had an effect more detrimental than salutary. Indeed, when the South Vietnamese population provided covert aid to the VC guerrillas, it was probably due more to their desire to expedite the removal of the United States from their countryside rather than because of some heartfelt commitment to communism.

FORCE PLANNING AND PAROCHIALISM

Beyond raising questions of U.S. strategy and tactics, the war illustrated the illusory nature of two-and-a-half war planning. Vietnam was the half-war; yet the American people most certainly would not have supported a force buildup necessary to fight two larger wars in addition to Vietnam. Much of the total U.S. force structure was already concentrated in Vietnam. Between August 1964 and January 1973 a total of 8,744,000 men served on active duty; 3,403,000 served, at one time or another, in Southeast Asia. In 1968 at the height of the U.S. involvement, 550,000 active-duty personnel (of a total pool of 3,547,000) were in Indochina. The forces were comprised of seven of the army's active divisions, two of the marine corps's three divisions, and nine of the air force's 28 tactical fighter wings.[57] Most of the remaining divisions and wings were skeletonized and would have required considerable replenishment if called upon to serve.[58]

In addition, the war showed the imbeddedness of parochialism and service rivalry. The 1958 Defense Reorganization Act minimized the role of the JCS in the chain of command, which now ran from the secretary of defense directly to the unified commands. As a result, the JCS proved unable to resolve numerous disputes that arose between the various services. One of the more contentious disputes predictably involved army aviation. As discussed, the army successfully employed the UH-1 helicopter (officially designated the Iroquois but usually referred to as the "Huey") for a variety of combat missions in Vietnam. The army also operated a small two-engine, fixed-wing aircraft called the Mohawk, which was primarily employed for reconnaissance and surveillance missions. Given the army's success with the Huey, there was much support among army leaders for using the Mohawk in combat roles. The air force had enough problems with the Huey, which it felt was encroaching upon its own roles and missions; the use of the Mohawk in combat missions was completely unacceptable to General LeMay, who was now the air force chief of staff, and to the other air force leaders. This led to bitter and divisive debates within the JCS and eventually had to be decided by the secretary of defense, who relegated the Mohawk to reconnaissance missions. One commentator has looked at this incident and concluded that the JCS "should be able to sort out issues arising out of role and mission conflicts. . . . A good example occurred [over the helicopter]. The JCS should have settled this role and mission issue among themselves."[59]

Commensurate with the dictates of the 1958 Defense Reorganization Act, the U.S. Pacific Command served under the direct control of the secretary of defense and had much power in planning wartime operations. Yet the Pacific Command in many instances was unable to impose strict coordination over the services. For example, the

United States had five separate air forces devoted to the conflict, often only minimally coordinated. Besides the B-52s commanded by the air force,

> the Seventh Air Force was under the command of the senior military commander in Vietnam when it attacked targets in South Vietnam, but its control shifted to the Air Force's Pacific headquarters in Hawaii when it flew missions in North Vietnam. The Navy, Army, and Marine Corps controlled their own aircraft, reporting sorties to the Air Force, but refusing to relinquish operational command.[60]

Even within the air force there was considerable disagreement about control of the B-52s. The leaders of the Seventh Air Force (Tactical) argued that the strategic bombers should be under their command: they were responsible for coordinating the total air effort in South Vietnam and Laos and the coordination of air strikes in North Vietnam. The tactical command also sought to avoid duplicative targeting. Yet SAC worked vigorously to maintain control of the B-52s and only relinquished some control during the Linebacker II offensive in December 1972. Coordination never reached optimal levels, much mission duplication did occur, and procedures for targeting became increasingly and unnecessarily complex.[61]

EPILOGUE

On July 1, 1973, Congress approved the Fulbright-Aiken Amendment, forbidding the Nixon administration from resuming bombing or other combat activities in Indochina. The relevant section of that amendment stated:

> Notwithstanding any other provision of law, on or after August 15, 1973, no funds herein or heretofore appropriated may be obligated or expended to finance directly or indirectly combat activities by United States military forces in or over or from off the shores of North Vietnam, South Vietnam, Laos, or Cambodia.[62]

In January 1974, President Thieu of South Vietnam declared that the war had started anew. By June, the North had completed a massive buildup of men and supplies in the South. Soon afterward the final offensive began, and by January of 1975, the Communists had captured Phuoc Long province north of Saigon. The North quickly amassed a string of victories, and by March 25, it had overrun the key city of Hue. On April 25, Thieu left Saigon for Taiwan, and five days later the South's capital fell to the North Vietnamese Army. On April 29, the American evacuation of Saigon began.

President Gerald Ford, Nixon's successor, was prohibited by Congress from militarily reinforcing the South and declared the war was "finished." For the United States, it was; there would be no more active involvement in Southeast Asia.[63] However, the impact of the war on U.S. military planning began almost four years before the Paris Accords, with the announcement of the Nixon Doctrine in Guam on July 25, 1969, and did not end in 1975. By the time of the final pullout in 1973, the war had significantly impacted upon U.S. military planning and would continue to do so at least until the end of the decade. The United States, having so recently accepted its responsibilities as a great power, would turn inward once again.

NOTES

1. Army Field Manual 31-22, *U.S. Army Counterinsurgency Forces* (Washington, D.C.: Department of the Army, 1963), p. 4.

2. John F. Kennedy, quoted in Colonel Harry Summers, Jr., *On Strategy: A Critical Analysis of the Vietnam War* (New York: Dell, 1984), pp. 108–109. Summers details the notable extent of Kennedy's influence on the counterinsurgency evolution. Kennedy "took the lead himself in formulating the programs, pushing both his own staff and the government establishment to give the matter priority action" (p. 109).

3. Quoted in John Lewis Gaddis, *Strategies of Containment* (New York: Oxford University Press, 1982), p. 208.

4. William Momyer, *Air Power in Three Wars* (Washington, D.C.: GPO, 1978), p. 11.

5. Robert Doughty, *The Evolution of US Army Tactical Doctrine, 1945–1976* (Fort Leavenworth, Kansas: Combat Studies Institute, 1979), p. 29.

6. Army Field Manual (FM) 100-5, *Operations* (Washington, D.C.: Department of the Army, 1962).

7. FM 31-15, *Operations against Irregular Forces* (Washington, D.C.: Department of the Army, May 1961), p. 25.

8. Gaddis, *Strategies*, p. 246.

9. Document 167, "Joint Chiefs of Staff Memorandum, JCSM-46-64," January 22, 1964, in Gareth Porter, ed., *Vietnam: A History*

in Documents (New York: New American Library, 1981), pp. 260–263.

10. Porter, *History in Documents*, p. 262.

11. General David Palmer, *Summons of the Trumpet* (Novato, California: Presidio Press, 1978), p. 75.

12. General William Westmoreland, *A Soldier Reports* (New York: Doubleday, 1976), p. 142, quoted in Summers, *On Strategy*, p. 165.

13. Momyer, *Air Power in Three Wars*, p. 15.

14. Document 183, "The Tonkin Gulf Resolution," August 7, 1964, in Porter, *History in Documents*, p. 287.

15. Document 190, "Memorandum for the President from McGeorge Bundy," February 7, 1965, in Porter, *History in Documents*, p. 299.

16. In a telegram dated February 13, 1965, Secretary of State Dean Rusk told Army Chief of Staff Maxwell Taylor, "We will execute a program of measured and limited air action jointly with GVN [Government of Vietnam] against selected military targets in DRV [Democratic Republic of Vietnam], remaining south of 19th parallel until further notice." Document 192, "Telegram from Rusk to Taylor," February 13, 1965, in Porter, *History in Documents*, p. 301.

17. Civilian recommendations were often very specific and methodical. In a report by McNamara to Johnson following McNamara's visit to Vietnam, he recommended that "over a period of the next six months we gradually enlarge the target system in the northeast (Hanoi-Haiphong) quadrant until, at the end of the period, it includes 'controlled' reconnaissance of lines of communication throughout the area, bombing of petroleum storage facilities and power plants, and mining of the harbors. (Left unstruck would be population targets, industrial plants, locks and dams)." Document 204, "Report by McNamara On Visit to Vietnam," November 30, 1965, in Porter, *History in Documents*, p. 323.

18. General Bruce Palmer, *The 25-Year War: America's Military Role in Vietnam* (New York: Simon and Schuster, 1984), p. 37. Importantly, Palmer continues: "Ironically, the commander-in-chief eventually approved practically all of the targets on the JCS-CINCPAC [commander in chief, Pacific] list, but the overall impact was lessened by the piecemeal application of airpower which lacked the mass, consistency, and sustained nature espoused by the JCS" (page 37).

19. McNamara urged that the United States "expand promptly and substantially the U.S. military pressure against the Viet Cong in the South and maintain the military pressure against the North Vietnamese in the North." McNamara's specific recommendations were to raise the U.S. presence in Vietnam to 175,000 men. McNamara also recommended the call-up of 235,000 reservists and an increase in the total armed forces to 375,000 men. Document 202, "Memorandum for the President by McNamara," 20 July 1965, in Porter, *History in Documents*, pp. 319–320.

20. Quoted in Momyer, *Air Power in Three Wars*, p. 299.

21. Deleted from final draft of position paper of Johnson's civilian advisers, reprinted in Russell Weigley, *The American Way of War* (New York: Macmillan, 1973), p. 464. The JCS view, calling for increased level of activities, was supported by the intelligence community, which generally recommended a course of action paralleling the JCS recommendations. See, e.g., document 207, SNIE 10-1-66, "Possible Effects of a Proposed U.S. Course of Action on DRV Capability to Support the Insurgency in South Vietnam," 4 February 1966, in Porter, *History in Documents*, p. 326.

22. In 1962, the United States had set up Joint Task Force 116 in Thailand, composed mostly of air units, in response to activities of the North Vietnamese–supported Pathet Lao Communists in Laos. This potential conflict was temporarily settled when the North Vietnamese agreed to the terms of peace negotiations in Geneva. On this point see Momyer, *Air Power in Three Wars*, p. 12.

23. Quoted in Stanley Karnow, *Vietnam: A History* (New York: Viking, 1983), p. 17.

24. Quoted in Gaddis, *Strategies*, p. 263.

25. Herbert Y. Schandler, "JCS Strategic Planning and Vietnam: The Search for An Objective," in Harry Borowski, *Military Planning in the Twentieth Century*, Proceedings of the Eleventh Military History Symposium, USAF Academy, 1984 (Washington, D.C.: Office of Air Force History, 1986), p. 301.

26. Johnson seemed primarily driven by domestic opinion. For example, he was particularly concerned about losing any public support for the war effort. In his view, this was when the reserve forces would be mobilized. Thus, the reserves were never called up, even when Westmoreland and the JCS urged an increase in ground forces.

Johnson was as concerned about world opinion as he was about domestic perceptions. In a May 1965 message to General Maxwell Taylor, who was then serving as Johnson's ambassador to South Vietnam, Johnson wrote: "I have learned from Bob McNamara that nearly all ROLLING THUNDER operations for this week can be completed by Wednesday noon, Washington time. This fact and the days of Buddha's birthday seem to me to provide an excellent opportunity for a pause in air attacks which might go into next week and which I could use to good effect with world opinion." Document 198, "Message from Johnson to Taylor, May 10, 1965," in Porter, *History in Documents*, p. 311.

27. Momyer, *Air Power in Three Wars*, p. 32.

28. Richard Nixon, "Address to the Nation," May 8, 1972, in Porter, *History in Documents*, p. 405.

29. Momyer, *Air Power in Three Wars*, p. 32. The B-52s accomplished their missions, but they did not necessarily provide the best means to do the job. One analyst has noted that the USAF relied on B-52s to strike high priority targets in the South although studies indicated "that slower propeller-driven models would have been three times as accurate, from five to thirteen times less costly, but with roughly the same loss ratio." Gaddis, *Strategies*, p. 253. This argument misses the fundamental point: such planes were a limited part of the U.S. inventory at the time.

30. There is much speculation as to what brought about the war's conclusion. Possible factors include concessions by Kissinger to the North Vietnamese at the expense of South Vietnam's future security; North Vietnam's intimidation by Nixon's escalations; North Vietnam's concern that the Soviet Union and the People's Republic of China, cutting their own deals with the United States, could no longer be counted on as reliable allies; the attainment of an accord that the administration believed brought "peace with honor"; Nixon's belief that he could no longer milk the war for political benefit; and so on. Explanations tend to vary with the agenda of the explainer. For contrasting views, see Kissinger's *White House Years* (Boston: Little, Brown, 1970) and Seymour Hersh, *The Price of Power* (New York: Summit Books, 1983).

31. Elmo Zumwalt, *On Watch: A Memoir* (New York: Quadrangle/New York Times Books, 1976), pp. 62–63.

32. Palmer, *25-Year War*, p. 52.

33. Zumwalt, *On Watch*, pp. 62–63. Zumwalt points out that an exception was Rickover's nuclear-powered submarine fleet.

34. The forces fighting for the North Vietnamese were principally organized into three groups: local and provincial Viet Cong (VC) guerrillas, main force VC units, and the North Vietnamese Army (NVA).
35. William Westmoreland, *A Soldier Reports*, p. 165.
36. Westmoreland goes on to say that "Although . . . I was commander of all American military forces in Vietnam . . . I had no wish to deal so abruptly that I might precipitate an interservice imbroglio." Westmoreland also notes that the marines did have some success, so, "rather than start a controversy," he instead issued "orders for specific projects that as time passed would gradually get the marines out of their beachheads" (*A Soldier Reports*, p. 166).
37. Doughty, *Evolution*, p. 31.
38. Doughty, *Evolution*, p. 32.
39. Komer and Westmoreland quoted in Gaddis, *Strategies*, pp. 262–263.
40. The low-flying and slow-flying helicopters proved vulnerable, however, when flying over hostile terrain in Laos in 1971. See, e.g., Ray L. Bowers, "Air Operations in Southeast Asia: A Tentative Appraisal," in Alfred F. Hurley and Robert C. Ehrhart, eds., *Air Power and Warfare*, Proceedings of the Eighth Military History Symposium (Washington: Office of Air Force History, 1979), p. 316.
41. Doughty, *Evolution*, p. 36. Doughty details a "pile on" tactic: "Using the great mobility of heliborne or mechanized forces, units occupied peripheral blocking or ambush positions in order to destroy fleeing enemy forces. According to the size of the forces and area involved, such encircling methods were sometimes called 'rat hole' or 'bull's eye' tactics."
42. See, e.g., Kissinger, *White House Years*, p. 236.
43. Bowers, "Air Operations," pp. 311–312.
44. Two such initiatives, particularly employed in the Laos operations, were the use of gunships such as the AC-47, AC-119, and AC-130 in trail-interdiction operations, and the Igloo White sensor implant program, which increased overall air force fighter and bomber effectiveness in attacking enemy lines of communication. Igloo White was "an electronic anti-infiltration barrier across southern Laos, which would employ acoustic and seismic sensors capable of detecting enemy movements and transmitting them to relay aircraft overhead. By late 1967, sensors and various kinds of mines had been planted by air along enemy routes in Laos." Bowers, "Air Operations," p. 318.

45. Bowers, "Air Operations," p. 315.

46. Laser munitions are distinguishable from television-guided munitions in that the former require continuous laser illumination of a target during the bomb's fall, while the latter homes in on a point target just before release. See, e.g., Bowers, "Air Operations," p. 321, on this point.

47. Kenneth Werrell, "Linebacker II: The Decisive Use of Air Power?" *Air University Review* (January-March 1987): 56.

48. Sir Robert Thompson, remarks in W. Scott Thompson and D.D. Frizell, *The Lessons of Vietnam* (New York: Crane, Russak, 1977), pp. 104, 144. Quoted in Bowers, "Air Operations," p. 322.

49. Gaddis, *Strategies*, p. 238.

50. Gaddis, *Strategies*, p. 237.

51. Colonel David Hackworth, "Our Great Vietnam Goof," *Popular Mechanics* (June 1972): 72, quoted in Doughty, *Evolution*, p. 39.

52. Palmer, *The 25-Year War*, p. 9.

53. Summers, *On Strategy*, p. 127.

54. Palmer's strategy is quite comprehensive and is detailed in *The 25-Year War*, pp. 182–186.

55. Summers points out that the viability of Palmer's approach "was recently reinforced by statements of South Vietnamese leaders who believed that by providing a military shield behind which South Vietnam could work out its own political, economic, and social problems, the United States could have provided a reasonable chance for South Vietnamese freedom and independence." Summers, *On Strategy*, p. 172.

56. See, e.g., Summers, *On Strategy*, p. 126.

57. Jeffrey Record, *Revising U.S. Military Strategy: Tailoring Means to Ends* (McLean, Virginia: Pergamon-Brassey's, 1984), p. 26.

58. Record makes the important point: "To be sure, goals for expanded ground and tactical air forces were set and eventually fulfilled. Those goals, however, were themselves inadequate, certainly if measured against the drain on U.S. conventional military resources caused by the 1/2 war in Vietnam. They were moreover, predicated on the availability of a large, highly mobile strategic reserve, which proved politically impossible to create" (Record, *Revising*, p. 28).

59. Palmer, *The 25-Year War*, p. 199.

60. James Lacy, *Within Bounds: The Navy in Postwar American Security Policy* (Alexandria, Virginia: Center for Naval Analyses, 1983), p. 351.

61. These problems are detailed in Momyer, *Air Power*, pp. 99–107.
62. Document 269, "Fulbright-Aiken Amendment - Public Law 93-52, Section 108," 1 July, 1973, in Porter, *History in Documents*, p. 438.
63. Although two other aspects deserve note: one, controversy over remaining POWs and MIAs in the North remains to this day, and two, on January 21, 1977, one day after assuming the presidency, Jimmy Carter pardoned most of the 10,000 draft evaders.

9
Era V: Global Military Retrenchment

NIXON, FORD, AND REALISTIC DETERRENCE

The world Richard Nixon faced when he assumed the presidency in January 1969 had changed greatly since his days as Eisenhower's vice president. The United States was entrenched in an unpopular war. Congress, reflecting public sentiment toward the war, was increasingly involving itself in foreign and military policy decisions—traditionally the prerogative of the executive. The People's Republic of China and the Soviet Union were no longer allied, and by 1969, they were shooting at each other across their common borders. Perhaps most importantly, in the aftermath of the Cuban Missile Crisis, the Soviet Union had pursued a historically unprecedented peacetime military buildup.

Against this backdrop, the Nixon administration had to fashion policies that would entail the cutting back of U.S. forces. The domestic climate, in particular pressures from Congress to reduce the defense budget, made this a necessity; the Sino-Soviet split made this a possibility.

The administration's overall military and foreign policies proceeded under the rubric of detente, which sought to enmesh the Soviets in a complex web of interactions across the military, political, and economic spectrum. The underlying idea was to emphasize and link the mutual interests—such as arms control—that the superpowers shared and make these interests the basis of superpower relations. Detente's capstone achievement was the 1972 Antiballistic Missile (ABM) Treaty, which limited each side's antiballistic missile programs, and the Strategic Arms Limitation Talks (SALT) I agreement, which froze both sides' offensive launchers.

The administration's military policies were based on the Nixon Doctrine, the one-and-a-half-war strategy, and its nuclear weapons policies. Cumulatively these programs were referred to as the policy of "Realistic Deterrence." Here, the focus is primarily on the first two components.[1]

Speaking on the island of Guam on July 25, 1969, Nixon listed a number of conditions that would guide his administration's military planning. As later elaborated, the three pillars of the Nixon Doctrine, as they collectively came to be called, were,

> First, the United States will keep all of its treaty commitments.
>
> Second, we shall provide a shield if a nuclear power threatens the freedom of a nation allied with us or of a nation whose survival we consider vital to our security and the security of the region as a whole.
>
> Third, in cases involving other types of aggression, we shall furnish military and economic assistance when requested and as appropriate. But we shall look to the nation directly threatened to assume the primary responsibility of providing the manpower for its defense.[2]

The vital point was the third. Nixon was implicitly signaling that the United States would pull out of Vietnam, commensurate with improvements in the fighting capabilities of the South Vietnamese forces. As the last chapter discussed, Nixon did reduce American forces in Vietnam, beginning with 60,000 withdrawn by the end of 1969. But Nixon's words also signaled a major shift in policy. Henceforth, the United States would be reluctant to undertake a major commitment of manpower and materiel to a Vietnam-like conflict.

Nixon never specifically rejected flexible response as a guide for force planning and procurement. He did, however, reject one of its principal tenets, which called for the direct imposition of U.S. combat forces to resolve crises involving U.S. interests. This was at least in part due to the domestic political realities that confronted him. Nixon *expanded* the war into Cambodia and Laos, steps which in themselves proved highly contentious and divisive at home. But a combative Congress and an increasingly hostile public made it impossible for him to *escalate* the U.S. commitment in Southeast Asia or commit U.S. forces to Vietnam-like conflicts.

Nor would Congress support a two-and-a-half war policy. The budgets to support a force capable of fighting two-and-a-half wars would be impossible to generate in the prevailing antidefense climate. Along with the Sino-Soviet split, the antidefense climate in the United States led Nixon to consider a "one-and-a-half war" policy. The essence of this policy was that the U.S. would gear its force procurement toward thwarting a major Communist attack in Europe or Asia, but not both. The Soviets and the Chinese were no longer viewed as a monolithic entity, although both were still officially considered hostile. Therefore, planning would be based on conflict scenarios involving either, but not both, of the two great Communist powers. The United States also planned to meet a lesser contingency elsewhere, such as in the Middle East or South Korea. In 1969, two divisions remained there, and an attack from the North was considered a distinct possibility.

Toward the end of 1969, Nixon accepted the recommendation of National Security Adviser Henry Kissinger for the one-and-a-half-war strategy. In Kissinger's words, the strategy

> harmonized doctrine and capability. We had never generated the forces our two-and-a-half-war doctrine required; the gap between our declaratory and our actual policy was bound to create confusion in the minds of potential aggressors and to raise grave risks if we attempted to apply it . . . the political implications were even more decisive. We had to give up the obsession with a Communist monolith.
>
> Western Europe . . . was singled out as the theater in which the threat was most likely. We were, in short, concerned more with the danger of Soviet than of Chinese aggression.[3]

Consistent with the drawing down of resources implied by the one-and-a-half war strategy was the abolishment of conscription and the adoption of the "total force" concept. As Defense Secretary Melvin Laird explained to Congress, "Total force takes account of both active and reserve components of [the] U.S., those of our allies, and the additional military capabilities of our allies and friends through local efforts, or through provision of security assistance programs."[4] The fact was, U.S. strategic planning as embodied in the Joint Strategic Operations Plan (JSOP) had factored in allied and friendly forces since the mid-1950s. Once factored in, however, they were largely neglected. In that sense, Laird was doing no more than giving a priority to an aspect of U.S. planning that had been largely ignored for years.

But the total force concept did represent a major change in U.S. planning, at least since the Vietnam War. The aim of the total force concept was to compensate for the reductions anticipated in the active forces—due to Vietnamization and the abolishment of the draft—by enhancing the role of the reserves. The rationale was to interweave active duty and reserve personnel to the extent that any future U.S. participation in a conflict would necessitate calling up the reserves in the early phases of the conflict. This would force the United States to commit itself politically to the situation. Thus, in contrast to the days when Johnson refused to activate the reserves for the Vietnam War, the reserves were now given a preeminent role in U.S. planning. This was reflected in the increased funding now allocated to the reserves; throughout Nixon's tenure, total obligational authority for the reserve forces doubled, from almost

$2.2 billion in FY1968 to over $4.3 billion in FY1974.[5] By mid-decade, reservists provided half of the army's combat forces and maneuver battalions and were responsible for more than half of the air force's tactical aircraft and a quarter of the navy's surface combatants.

Even given the expansion of the reserves, however, it is clear that in this period the United States was undergoing a general protraction of its armed forces. The administration's rhetoric dealt with repelling a Soviet attack in Europe, but Vietnam continued to drain resources from the European theater. At the start of the decade, war expenditures were being drawn downward due to the troop withdrawals. From $21.5 billion in FY1969, expenditures for the war effort dipped to $11.5 billion in FY1971 and edged downward another $7 billion in FY1972. The North Vietnamese launched their spring offensive in March, however, and this downward trend was temporarily reversed. To support the U.S. response—which included the 1972 summer air campaigns, the Haiphong harbor mining, and the Christmas bombings—an additional $2.8 billion was allocated to the air force.[6] Due to these late reversals, Vietnam expenditures in 1972 actually rose as a percentage of the total U.S. defense budget.

In FY1985 dollars, the Vietnam War has been estimated to cost $333 billion overall.[7] As discussed in previous chapters, this spending made it difficult to invest in other areas, such as navy procurement. The problem was exacerbated by Congress, which sought to compensate for the Vietnam expenditures with cutbacks in the defense budget as a whole. Congress attempted to cut the administration's proposed FY1972 budget by 3.2 percent and the following year's request by 10.3 percent. This led the administration to propose its own cutbacks, to curtail these budget-cutting attempts.[8]

Two economic factors further hindered effective conventional force acquisition. One was the unanticipated high rates of inflation during the Nixon, Ford, and Carter administrations. Defense budgets are planned over a year before they are to take effect. If inflation rises steadily through that year, as was the case throughout the seventies, then (barring supplementals) the actual amount of buying power for the budget is reduced.

The second was the "cost-growth" of weapons systems. Cost-growth comes from either replacing old weapons, or upgrading existing capabilities with systems that promise (without necessarily delivering) greater performance. The further technology is stretched, however, the more costly will be its application. As the analyst Seymour Deitchman has observed,

All applications of technology reach performance limits imposed by strengths of materials, efficiency of energy conversion, or other physical phenomena. The essence of new applications of technology is the extension of such limits. But whatever the technology permits, the closer its technical limits are approached the more costly will be the achievement of the resulting performance.[9]

Throughout the 1970s, the actual level of weapons system cost-growth did not significantly increase from the 1960s; because of inflation, however, the impact of cost-growth was much greater in the latter decade. The cost-growth issue also became more salient in the seventies, as Congress took a much more critical look at defense policy and budgeting and as the defense budget began to decline. High cost-growth meant fewer total weapons systems would be produced.

In light of the above, one would expect to see a decline in the capabilities of the armed services, and this was indeed the case. It is not surprising that defense procurement declined after 1968, the height of Vietnam spending. A more meaningful comparison is seen in Table 9.1, which looks at FT1975 relative to FY1965 levels, the last budget not swollen by the Vietnam War.[10]

The final two budgets submitted by the Ford administration sought to curtail these downward trends. For each of the services, total active personnel end strength rose somewhat. Indeed, all of the above indices show a slight gain except naval combatants and

TABLE 9.1.
National Defense Allocations, Selected Years

Category	1965	1968	1975
Defense Outlays as a			
Percentage of Total Budget	42.8%	46.0%	26.2%
as Percentage of GNP	7.5%	9.6%	5.7%
Army Active-Duty Personnel*	969	1,570	784
Number of Army Divisions	16	19	14
Navy Active-Duty Personnel*	671	765	535
Navy Combatants	769	811	437
Fleet Carriers	25	23	15
Air Force Active-Duty Personnel*	825	905	612
Tactical Wings	23	28	22
Aircraft	3,761	4,169	1,984

* Figures are in thousands.

carriers, and army divisions. However, this was an era of high inflation, so total defense spending as a percentage of the total budget actually decreased to 24.2 percent by FY1977. In addition, tactical air wings and other systems were often fielded at less than full strength.

The U.S. military retrenchment left the Soviets little incentive to seek bilateral accommodation, and the high expectations of detente were never realized.[11] A key tenet of detente was that a multipolar world was in the U.S. interest; that the United States could flourish in a world of diverse power-centers operating interdependently with one another.[12] This should not have implied that worldwide developments that were deleterious to U.S. interests should proceed unchallenged. Yet, throughout the Nixon and Ford administrations, crises developed to which the United States proved hesitant to respond or reacted without appreciating the full implications of its actions.

Three such incidents occurred in 1975. The first was the fall of Saigon in April, after Congress refused Ford's request for military and economic aid to the South Vietnamese. The second occurred in May, when Cambodian gunboats seized the American freighter *Mayaguez* in the Gulf of Siam. Ford ordered air strikes against the port of Kompong Som and an amphibious assault on the island of Koh Tang. Yet the crew of the *Mayaguez* had already been released as the U.S. reprisal was commencing. Forty one American soldiers died unnecessarily in this irrelevant effort to free a crew of 39. The third incident was more of a long-term event, namely, the civil war taking place in Angola. Marxist guerrillas aided by over 5,000 Cuban soldiers and heavily supported by the Soviet Union were winning control of Angola in an intense three-way power struggle occurring there. Ford wanted to counter this by providing materiel support for the forces that leaned toward the West. As he put it in his memoirs, "We had no intention of sending any U.S. military personnel to Angola, but about $25 million worth of arms might give the pro-West forces there a chance."[13] But in 1975 Congress imposed strict limits on the levels of permitted military and economic aid (the Clark amendment), and the Communist involvement in Angola continued to deepen.

Such incidents continued under Ford's successor Jimmy Carter, and indeed the impression of U.S. haplessness and retrenchment would worsen before it would improve. In many ways, Carter's foreign policy seemed to be based on the acceptance and perpetuation of retrenchment, and military planning under Carter reflected this perspective.

THE CARTER ADMINISTRATION
AND NATO DEFENSE

To an extent unique among post-World War II presidents, Jimmy Carter's view of U.S. national security requirements was based less on the U.S.-Soviet competition than on emerging regional issues and conflicts. As for the Soviets, detente was simply accepted as the proper basis of superpower relations, so there was little need to reevaluate policy in that regard. Carter instead tended to focus on the problems involving the emerging nations of the Third World, particularly with respect to human rights. An early speech at the University of Notre Dame, where Carter proclaimed that the United States was now free of its "inordinate fear of communism," provided some clue to the new president's perspective:

> The unifying threat of conflict with the Soviet Union has become less intensive. . . . The world is still divided by ideological disputes, dominated by regional conflicts, and threatened by [the] danger that we will not resolve the differences of race and wealth without violence or without drawing into combat the major military powers. [But] we can no longer separate the traditional issues of war and peace from the new global questions of justice, equity, and human rights. . . . It is a new world that calls for a new American foreign policy—a policy based on constant decency in its values and on optimism in our historical vision.[14]

A number of steps were taken commensurate with this perspective. They included the negotiation of the Panama Canal treaties, an initiative to withdraw the American forces remaining in Korea, talk of recognizing the Communist government in Cuba, the establishment of full diplomatic relations with the People's Republic of China, and an emphasis on human rights improvements as a prerequisite to cooperation with Third World dictatorships.

Carter's national security policies clearly reflected his foreign policy orientation. Presidential Review Memorandum (PRM) 10 of 1977 envisioned five forms of potential wars: general strategic nuclear war; a protracted war between NATO and the Pact in Central Europe; an East-West war elsewhere; a conflict in East Asia; and a contingency war such as Vietnam. A future conflict did not necessarily have to involve the Chinese or the Soviets. The two-and-a-half and one-and-a-half war doctrines were predicated on Chinese and/or Soviet involvement, acting in accord or independently. The half-war aspect implicitly (and in the case of Vietnam, correctly) assumed that a smaller-scale contingency would be backed by one, if not both, of the two great Communist powers, in lieu of their direct participation. Now, the administration seemed to be saying that war could break out in a number of arenas, exclusive of Chinese or Soviet participation.

Given the Carter administration's Third World orientation and its recognition that war need not involve the major powers, it is notable (and perhaps curious) that the administration's early military planning focused excessively on central European war scenarios. In February 1977, Defense Secretary Harold Brown recommended a $2.8-billion net *decrease* in FY1978 total obligational authority (the last Ford budget). At the same time, Brown asked that $605 million of present budget authority be reprogrammed toward NATO for prepositioned army weapons and stocks, improvements in airfield readiness, and other programs.[15] Similar requests would appear in subsequent Brown budgets. The number of U.S. military personnel stationed in Europe rose from 303,000 in 1975 to about 330,000 by the end of the decade.[16] And at a spring 1977 NATO summit, Carter called on the allies to increase their countries' defense spending by 3 percent annually. (This was not approved by the allies until 1978, and to this day most have not fully upheld this commitment.)

No clear-cut military policy emerged from the Carter leadership, but there was a decided emphasis on reconstituting U.S. forces in Central Europe. One could argue that a maritime orientation would have been more commensurate with the administration's Third World rhetoric, but such an orientation would likely have required a larger and more expensive navy than the administration was prepared to finance. In 1977, military planning was still greatly influenced by the Vietnam War, and there was little domestic support (in Congress or within the population) for increased levels of military spending. On the other hand, a policy of continental defense—that is, a policy aimed at maintaining a robust deterrent in Europe—did not require the monetary resources associated with a maritime policy.

In the final analysis, a foreign policy aimed at managing Third World crises was pursued in conjunction with a military policy focused on Europe. Certainly, there were inherent tensions and contradictions in such a relationship. But the relationship was dictated by the president, who made no secret of his desire to deemphasize the military component of foreign policy, and by the era. The unpopularity of the Vietnam War made it virtually impossible to develop a military policy that risked U.S. intervention in Third World crises. Moreover, such a policy would likely have been costly, and at this time there was little congressional or popular support for defense spending. U.S. defense planners thus gave little consideration to the aggressive use of military power, and military planning proceeded within tight monetary parameters. As one commentator has said, in a statement about the army but applicable to all the services, "Planners emerged from the Vietnam experience with a crisis of confidence and an unsureness of purpose. Faced with dwindling personnel and equipment resources, they were hard pressed to bring resources into line with requirements. Budget allocations dictated strategy and doctrine ran counter to capabilities."[17]

As was the case under Nixon and Ford, all the services suffered under Carter's budget-based planning. In the FY1980 budget, defense outlays fell to 23.4 percent of the total budget. The navy was cut to 12 carriers, and its personnel end strength was reduced to 527,353. Active-duty air force personnel were cut to 557,969 and tactical air wings to 28. In fact, the latter were much skeletonized and only equaled about 22 full-strength wings. Total operational aircraft was reduced to 2,360.

The number of army divisions remained stable at 16, and active-duty end strength remained at just over 777,000. Rebuilding the army, however, proceeded under the parameters of lower overall outlays. Divisions were skeletonized, and army inventories were allowed to obsolesce. In the FY1977 authorization hearings, Secretary of the Army Martin Hoffman testified that

the Army currently has but one-half of the equipment necessary to equip fully the Active and Reserve forces and to provide for contingency replenishment. For example, only 39 percent of prime tanks, 32 percent of the TOW missile launchers, 71 percent of the attack helicopters and 51 percent of the armored personnel carriers that are presently required for the force are in the inventory.[18]

Under Carter, this situation improved in some areas but worsened in others. For example, the number of heavy- and medium-sized tanks in the inventory actually increased, from 8,704 in 1976 to 10,637 in 1979.[19]

The Carter era was particularly rough on the navy. The administration never seemed to know what it wanted the navy to do. The navy's role in the defense of Europe was reduced to defensive sea control, ASW, and convoy operations. In January 1978, the navy was told to "plan carriers, surface combatants, direct support submarines, underway replenishment groups and amphibious forces for localized contingencies outside Europe and [to promote] peacetime presence."[20] But accompanying all these assignments came some cuts from the navy's budget and overall reductions in the navy's capacity to carry them out.

The carrier once again came under fire. A long-planned nuclear-powered CVN was canceled altogether. The administration favored the smaller CVV, designed to launch helicopters and new aircraft with vertical takeoff and landing (VTOL) capability. The advantage of these systems, Defense Secretary Brown argued, was their cost:

> The CVV provides the capability that is needed, and is clearly the appropriate lower-cost carrier alternative at this time. The CV-67 and CVN would be more capable ships than the CVV but they would also be more expensive, particularly over the long term if the full cost of the additional aircraft is considered. The CVV gives us sufficient added capability in the carrier force to meet mission needs.[21]

Brown went on to argue that "the trend toward building fewer more expensive ships must be reversed, or the navy will have so few ships that U.S. superiority on the seas will be endangered." An examination of the acquisition process during the Carter administration makes clear, however, that quantity was not chosen in lieu of quality but that, in fact, both were sacrificed. In 1978 President Carter announced his intention to cut the administration's five-year shipbuilding program by over half, from 157 to 70.[22] In the FY1980 budget request, general purpose naval forces were accorded only 10 percent of the total defense budget and called for construction of only 67 new ships. By January 1979, the navy was reduced to 439 active combatants.

THE SOVIET UNION'S HISTORICALLY UNPRECEDENTED PEACETIME BUILDUP

Throughout this era of military retrenchment, the Soviet Union conducted a massive buildup of its general purpose forces. The origin of this buildup is generally attributed to decisions taken after the Cuban Missile Crisis. The Sovietologist Michael MccGwire has shown, however, that the pace of the buildup was accelerated after 1966, when the Soviets undertook a major reevaluation of their doctrine for war in Europe (see chapter 7). Table 9.2 presents key indices of Soviet forces for 1966 and 1980. The 1980 forces are also compared to U.S. forces at that time.[23]

These are necessarily rough indices. But in a number of key categories the table provides a revealing indication of the general trend of the Soviet buildup and how the military balance between the superpowers stood at the beginning of the decade. Although still rough, a more precise picture emerges in Table 9.3, which examines key indices of the 1980 NATO–Warsaw Pact European balance.[24]

TABLE 9.2.
The Soviet Force Buildup, 1966–1980
and Comparison to U.S. Forces, 1980

| Weapon System | USSR | | U.S. |
	1966	1980	1980
Land Forces			
Tanks (heavy and medium)	35,000	50,000	10,900
Divisions	140	173	16
Artillery/Rocket Launchers	11,000	40,800	16,000
Tactical Air Forces			
Combat Aircraft	4,000	5,000	3,700
Naval Forces			
Major Surface Combatants	260	314	173
Submarines	425	372	81
Carriers	0	2	14
Mil. Manpower (in thous.)	3,200	3,658	2,050

TABLE 9.3.
The NATO-Warsaw Pact Balance, 1980

Index	NATO	WPO	(of Which is Soviet)
Available divisions			
Armored	15 ⅔	29	15
Mechanized/Infantry/Other	50 ⅔	38	15
Total reinforcing formations available (division equivalent)	52 ⅓	113 ⅔	92
Main battle tanks in operational service	11,000	26,200	14,500
Tactical aircraft in operational service			
Fighter/Ground Attack	1,214	1,675	1,000
Interceptors	588	3,050	1,400
Reconnaissance	369	750	425

The story becomes more dire when one considers qualitative, technological changes in forces. A year-to-year examination of Soviet forces in the 1970s would show a gradual decrease in their growth rate. Nonetheless, the Soviets were still able to surpass the United States in most force indices and build a blue-water navy while significantly enhancing the technological quality of their forces. As such, the technological edge that NATO relied upon to offset the numerically superior Soviet forces in Europe had eroded throughout this period. The T-72 tank which entered the WPO arsenal in the late 1970s, for example, was probably the qualitative equivalent of some of NATO's tanks. Because of the cutbacks in investment that was experienced after the Vietnam War, moreover, the United States experienced some slowdown in the rate of new systems development. This further narrowed the gap between U.S. and Soviet forces.[25]

THE SERVICES IN AN ERA OF RETRENCHMENT

THE AIR FORCE AND THE HIGH-LOW MIX

The air force proved adept at reorienting itself to the budgetary and planning constraints ushered in by the new era. Reflecting its Vietnam experience and continuing a trend begun in its 1964 doctrinal manual, the air force's 1971 revision of manual 1-1 stated that "strategic force sufficiency may not be a credible deterrent against hostile acts by small powers alone or while serving as proxies for larger powers. Deterrence of these threats comes from the maintenance of sufficient general purpose forces capable of rapid deployment and sustained operations."[26]

But the most striking change came in the air force discussion of low-intensity conflict. In the 1964 manual, only two paragraphs were devoted to describing air force military responsibilities in low-intensity conflict, and little was envisaged beyond supporting indigenous forces and performing some interdiction. Now, however, the manual reflected the use of SAC's bombers in Vietnam when it noted that "all forces of the US Air Force are responsible for conducting and supporting special operations" and when it introduced a variety of "subelement" tasks, such as guerrilla warfare, evasion and escape, and subversion. While the manual stressed that indigenous forces are still principally responsible for carrying out such missions, it was also noted that "air power is used to infiltrate or exfiltrate unconventional warfare forces, to keep them supplied, and to strike targets located through unconventional warfare operations."[27]

The air force gradually accepted that strategic air power was insufficient to deter violence across the spectrum of violence. As a result, the procurement of tactical forces and consideration of the missions for which tactical forces were potentially responsible was taken more seriously by air force planners. This trend was to continue throughout the 1970s, but now the context would change: the budget for tactical force procurement would begin to go downward. As a result, procurement occurred primarily on the basis of an air force concept known as the "high-low" mix. The air force had always preferred expensive, high-performance aircraft, but now cheaper and less capable aircraft were also being procured at an approximate ratio of 1:2. As John Collins has described, the premise

> initially postulated that any war in Western Europe would be savage and short. Tactical combat aircraft would suffer astronomical attrition. U.S. leaders therefore chose to rely on large numbers of single-purpose, clear-sky interceptors with low price tags to win the counterair battle in "eyeball-to-eyeball" contact with Soviet Frontal Aviation, which featured quantity not quality. . . . We settled for fewer first-rate multipurpose types to fight at night and interdict targets in enemy territory during foul weather.[28]

Throughout the seventies, procurement pretty much proceeded on this basis. The versatile F-15, at "the top of the air superiority spectrum," was procured in fewer numbers than the less capable (although still quite sophisticated and maneuverable) but also less expensive F-16. The problem with this procurement strategy, however, was that since 1972, the Soviets had consistently modernized their own inventory of fighter aircraft. The United States was thus cutting back on its most sophisticated aircraft as the Soviets were increasing theirs. More than half of the Soviet 1980 fighter-aircraft inventory was introduced after 1972 (2,200 out of 3,850 assigned to squadrons). But in 1980 62 percent of the total U.S. fighter aircraft inventory consisted of F-4 Phantoms, which were first deployed as early as 1963.[29]

In the early 1970s, most new procurement was aimed at replacing the depleted aircraft inventory that, in the aftermath of Vietnam, the air force was experiencing worldwide. But planes were not replaced at a rate commensurate with their loss, and the overall size of the tactical air forces decreased. Nonetheless, one does not observe the same rate of decline in the air force inventory as one observes in the other services. For example, the number of USAF heavy bombers decreased throughout the decade from 465 in 1970 to 316 in 1979. However, in that period, the number of medium bombers designated for strategic missions rose from 4 to 60. Similarly, the number of active interceptors fell in this period from 321 to 108, but the number of medium bombers designated for tactical missions rose from 26 to 264. The number of fighter attack planes rose slightly in this period as well.[30]

THE ARMY AND ACTIVE DEFENSE

In 1976 the army virtually rewrote its doctrine in a manner that both refocused the army on Europe and reflected the lessons learned in the Vietnam War. As discussed in chapter 8, counterinsurgency operations were gradually deemphasized in Vietnam, and the 1976 revision reflected the army's discomfort with such operations. Army doctrine was revised to return the army to traditional war-fighting principles in an era not conducive to military planning.

A major impetus to the 1976 revision was the Middle East war of 1973. This war had an enormous impact upon army thinking. Numerous briefings on the war were conducted throughout the military, as the lessons of the war and their relevancy for the United States were contemplated. The modern weapons both Israel and Egypt employed were much more lethal than any that had ever previously been used in conflict. Moreover, the use of combined arms and the sophisticated use of terrain, suppression tactics, and camouflage provided a variety of tactical insights for future U.S. Army operations.

The Middle East war also reinforced the notion that grasping the initiative and winning the first battle was the key to success on the battlefield. This seemed especially salient in light of two factors that had long affected army planning in Europe. The first factor was the assumption, shared by most army planners, that war in Europe would begin with a Soviet blitzkrieg. The second was the traditionally reactive nature of NATO doctrine. The Soviets were expected to attack NATO, not vice versa. Therefore, war exercises tended to automatically accord the initiative to the Pact. NATO's flexible response policy, which posited a first and early resort to tactical nuclear weapons by the West, was predicated on just this assumption.

The Vietnam War and the inflation of the seventies may have slowed the rate of weapons development, but new, highly sophisticated weapons were still being produced on a regular basis. The 1976 manual detailed a number of new developments that would dramatically increase the tempo of wartime operations and make conflict more lethal than ever before. In particular, the manual pointed to new long-range tank and antitank weapons, long-range artillery, and improved air defense systems, as well as modernized and highly capable helicopters. The manual noted, for example, that in contrast to a World War II–vintage medium tank requiring 13 rounds to obtain a 50 percent hit probability on a standing tank at 1,500 meters, a mid-1970s tank needed only one round. Antitank weapons such as the TOW (Tube-launched, Optically tracked, Wire-guided) missile could theoretically attain a 50 percent hit-rate probability 3,500 meters away from its target. Automatic guidance, improved radar, and optical sights significantly enhanced the hit probabilities in the new air defense systems. The United States could now quickly scatter mines from helicopters and artillery-launchers, and the exploitation of the electromagnetic environment was now seen as essential to future combat success.[31]

Army planners closely monitored and studied the use of these weapon systems in the Arab-Israeli War and, as one commentator has noted, "If evidence was needed that future war might contrast sharply with the decade-long, painstaking experience of the U.S. Army in the rice paddies and jungles of Vietnam, here it was for all to see."[32] Examples that drove home this lesson were abundant since virtually all of the new systems mentioned above were actually used in the war. For example, in clashes of massed armor, the Arabs and Israelis sustained materiel losses of 50 percent in under two weeks. Surface-to-air missiles such as the Soviet SA-7 were effectively used against low-flying helicopters and airplanes. Other Soviet-supplied systems proved to be technologically equal, if not superior, to similar U.S. systems.

The concepts underlying the new doctrine, which became known as the active defense, reflected all the above considerations:

> We cannot know when or where the U.S. Army will again be ordered into battle, but we must assume the enemy we face will possess weapons generally as effective as our own. And we must calculate that he will have them in greater numbers than we will be able to deploy.
>
> Because the lethality of modern weapons continues to increase sharply, we can expect very high losses to occur in short periods of time. Entire forces could be destroyed quickly if they are improperly employed . . . the first battle of our next war could well be its last battle.[33]

The allusion to the lethality of modern weapons and the need to win the first battle reflected the lessons of the Arab-Israeli war. These were applied foremost to the European theater, where the battle in Central Europe was described as the "most demanding mission the U.S. Army could be assigned." The concern with an enemy possessing forces of greater quantity and generally as effective as those possessed by the United States was a direct reference to the Warsaw Pact.

The fundamental dilemma that the active defense had to resolve was how to attain the initiative in a conflict when the enemy was expected to attack first. In addressing this problem, the manual pointed to a number of factors that, it argued, permitted the defender to defeat an enemy up to three times as strong. These included, as put by John Romjue, the "full use of cover and concealment, selection of the ground on which to fight, weapons sited for maximum effectiveness, reinforcement of terrain with mines and obstacles, and the choice of firing first."[34] The manual also emphasized that, in contrast, the commander should have a force ratio of 6:1 before he committed his forces to offensive engagements.[35]

The manual discussed offensive and defensive operations, but its emphasis was clearly on the latter. According to the manual, the commander should attack "only if he expects the outcome to result in decisively greater enemy losses than his own, or result in the capture of objectives crucial to the outcome of the larger battle."[36] The commander's first priority was to defend his terrain and wear down the attacking enemy forces.

Most offensive operations were to be executed in a defensive context to make the total defense as effective as possible. Defensive operations involved three components. *Covering forces* would attack early and prematurely force the enemy to initiate his offensive, thus "getting in the first blow" and creating opportunities for U.S. forces to dictate the terms of the battle. *Main battle area* operations, aimed at preventing enemy penetration of the defense, were conducted by suppressing enemy advances with antitank weapons, air attacks, and any other means available. Finally, *rear area* operations were conducted to protect supply and maintenance support points and administrative and communications centers. According to the manual, "as enemy airmobile or airborne forces are detected, airmobile infantry or other available mobile forces can quickly concentrate to contain or destroy them."[37] As far as "counterattack in the defense" was concerned, it was to be conducted "only when the gains to be achieved are worth the risks involved in surrendering the innate advantages of the defender."[38]

ROAD's concept of a brigade held back in reserve for every two forward was abandoned, as the commander had to concentrate his main battle area forces against the Pact attack and would need all available forces. Reinforcement would now depend upon highly mobile armored and mechanized forces which would maneuver into position as needed.

The active defense was criticized for its preoccupation with Western Europe,[39] its overemphasis on the defense, and its assessment of likely Soviet tactics. Each of these is considered in turn.

NATO EMPHASIS The doctrine's European reorientation should be considered in the context in which it was promulgated. A similar reorientation was proceeding on the national level. While one-and-a-half war planning ostensibly provided capabilities to meet aggression in an Asian or European theater, the threat from China had obviously diminished, and military planning on the national level was subsequently oriented toward meeting the Soviet threat in Europe. In 1975 Defense Secretary James Schlesinger said as such: "We shall continue to maintain a small number of strongpoints in areas of the most critical interest to us. . . . Western Europe is the most obvious place for a strong point and a conspicuous display of collective security."[40] In this era, there was little public support for planning that addressed future Vietnam-like conflicts.

Naturally, this attitude permeated army planning. It was clear that there was no national support for counterinsurgency planning, but this was no problem for the army's doctrinal planners. The army could be fairly certain that a war in Europe would emphasize nuclear and conventional doctrine and forces. Counterinsurgency doctrine could prove useful against Soviet *Spetsnatz* forces but would probably not be a major factor in a European war. The active defense was thus a manifestation of the army's desire to return to the tactics and doctrine with which it was most at home. In any case, the Vietnam War led to an erosion of forces in Europe, and this problem had to be addressed.

DEFENSE EMPHASIS   The doctrine's supposed neglect of the offense came as a surprise to its authors. The essence of the critique was, how does one win the "first battle" when one sacrifices the advantages of the initiative? The side that initiates hostilities, critics of the new doctrine argued, benefits from choosing the time, terrain, and location that best suits his capabilities and planning.[41]

The doctrine stated that "the outcome of combat derives from the results of offensive operations." But the doctrine provided for offensive maneuver principally as a follow-on procedure to defensive actions. The first order of business was for the covering forces to slow the main attack and for the main battle forces to stop the attack early, as close to the inter-German border as possible. *Then* the United States and the NATO allies would take offensive measures. Certainly, this was a cautious approach to planning the battle, but it was not entirely defensive.

SOVIET TACTICS   In light of the anticipated tempo and lethality of the next war, however, could the U.S. "win the first battle" while maintaining a defensive orientation? Moreover, did such an orientation adequately account for likely Soviet tactics? William Lind, for example, argued that the organization of Soviet forces into echelons meant that even if the Soviets lost the first battle, they could still go on to win the second.[42]

There is some validity to this point. Indeed, addressing the threat of Soviet second-echelon forces was a major element of the 1982 revision of the manual (which, as chapter 10 discusses, was criticized for paying *inadequate* attention to defeating the Soviet first echelon). But to a large degree, the emphasis on winning the first battle was a product of necessity, not choice. A protracted engagement would favor the Pact, whose forces greatly outnumbered those of NATO. As Philip Karber has noted, "FM 100-5's emphasis on the first battle is not misplaced, it is mandatory. Unless the U.S. forces can win the first series of engagements they will have little opportunity to prevent being overrun or outflanked."[43] In other words, the existence of second echelons does not negate the importance of getting past the first.

The doctrine was also criticized for addressing only one form of Soviet attack—the massed armored breakthrough, or blitzkrieg. The manual envisaged a Pact attack of great depth, on very narrow fronts, with firepower massed in the breakthrough sector. This could mean as many as 600 Pact tanks could be thrown against NATO's forward deployed divisions. "This doctrine," the manual noted, "is deeply ingrained in the Soviet Army and those are exactly the tactics we would face."[44]

Yet analysts noted that the Soviets also drew lessons from the Arab-Israeli War. Karber wrote that by 1976, a major shift in Soviet tactical operational concepts had occurred. The Soviets, Karber argued, were increasingly concerned about the vulnerability of their fighting vehicles to the new antitank weapons being produced. Karber argued that the Soviets seemed to be moving toward multipronged attacks across a wide expanse of the battlefield, seeking and exploiting enemy weak spots as they were encountered. Another critic noted that "severe ramifications fall from FM 100-5 having built its edifice on but one of the possible Soviet operational maneuvers."[45]

This point—focusing on only one possible maneuver—was perhaps the least controversial; it was, after all, true. In subsequent doctrinal revisions that culminated in the AirLand Battle Doctrine of 1982, this point (along with many of the others) was addressed. This is discussed in the next chapter.

Other criticisms focused on the doctrine's discussion of concentration, which at times risked leaving critical sectors vastly outnumbered, and its inadequate attention to "when things go wrong," as, for example, when communications gear did not work as anticipated. Others questioned whether the systems to support the doctrine, such as the antitank weapons essential to the active defense, would be adequate against Soviet flat profile tanks, whether the rapid lateral movements needed to concentrate combat power could be accomplished on the European terrain, or whether concentrating forces might leave flanks overexposed.[46] Many of these points were addressed in subsequent revisions as well.

The essential point of the active defense was that it responded to the limits imposed by developments on the national level. Domestic constraints made it unrealistic to develop a doctrine that emphasized the offensive or planned for wars outside of Europe. At the same time, the Soviet buildup made it imperative to focus on fighting a war when badly outnumbered by technologically proficient forces. For all its flaws, the 1976 FM 100-5 can be credited for addressing these realities.

THE NAVY AND THE SWING STRATEGY

By 1970, the Soviets had developed a highly capable navy with a growing capacity for power projection. After the Cuban Missile Crisis, the Soviets built nuclear-powered submarines equipped with missiles, rockets, and torpedoes to replace their obsoleting diesel-powered ships. Numerous new cruisers and destroyers were deployed, and antisubmarine cruisers equipped to carry helicopters appeared. By 1968, Marshal Zakharov, the navy chief of staff, boasted: "The time when Russia could be kept out of the world's oceans has gone forever. The imperialists can no longer have them to themselves. We shall sail all the world's seas; no force on earth can prevent us."[47]

During the 1967 Arab-Israeli War 70 Soviet warships patrolled the waters of the Mediterranean Sea, and since that time, a Soviet Mediterranean squadron has been permanently stationed in that area. By 1970 the Soviet navy had overtaken the U.S. in total numbers of ocean-going ships, and by 1972 Soviet submarines equipped with nuclear-tipped missiles had been deployed in the North Atlantic. CNO Thomas Moorer told Congress: "There is a new and growing threat to the security of our sea lanes of communications, the Russian Navy. The Soviet Union has been embarked on a program which reveals a singular awareness of the importance of sea power and an unmistakable resolve to become the most powerful maritime force in the world."[48]

To some degree, the actual threat posed by the Soviet navy was exaggerated. Soviet ships tend to have longer maintenance cycles than U.S. ships and usually display considerably less endurance than their U.S. counterparts. Nonetheless, navy planners advocated an expansion of the carrier fleet to meet the growing Soviet naval threat. The Soviets, it was argued, could now impede U.S. access to critical sea lines of communications between the continental United States (CONUS) and Western Europe. Carrier-based aircraft were therefore essential, it was argued, to defeat Soviet challenges at sea.

By 1971 Admiral Elmo Zumwalt had replaced Moorer as CNO. Zumwalt, a product of the surface navy, came to the office convinced that the navy's carrier forces had been built up at the expense of the surface fleet. As a result, the Soviets had been able to build a powerful surface fleet at the same time the United States was neglecting its own. In light of his background and his conviction that the United States was now facing, for the first time since World War II, "a first rate Naval power as a potential enemy," Zumwalt assessed the navy's missions as follows:

> I. *Assured Second Strike Capability*. This capability will be provided by Polaris and Poseiden ballistic missile submarines.
> II. *Sea Control*. We must have the capability to use the world's oceans in furtherance of our policies in the face of the opposition. In the 1970's the Navy must seek to remedy the relative weakness and obsolescence which have accumulated in the past decade while Soviet power was increasing and while we were expending vast sums in the Southeast Asia war.
> III. *Projection of Force Ashore*. The U.S. must look to the oceans as a means to project our national power—to provide a demonstrated deterrent to conventional war and counter Soviet influence.[49]

Sea control has always been the essence of the navy. But in the postwar era, its preeminence has tended to vacillate, relative to power projection. Now, sea control was reemerging as the central navy mission, and the arguments for the carrier had to be made in this context. In Zumwalt's view,

> the sea control mission has now become paramount more than the projection mission of the carrier, because the power of the Soviet Navy had grown so dramatically . . . they have a very believable prospect of severing our sea lines of communication. Therefore the first mission and role of the carrier must be to try to keep open the sea lane to the United States and our allies.[50]

Throughout the 1970s, the navy sought to implement this charter under the political, domestic, and military constraints imposed by the one-and-a-half war doctrine and the antimilitary sentiment of the post-Vietnam era. This would prove to be difficult, given the navy's loss of forces due to the Vietnam War and its deemphasized role in Carter administration planning. Of all the services, the navy suffered the greatest losses in investment in this era of global retrenchment.

As early as 1969, Nixon announced that over 100 navy ships would be deactivated. By the end of 1973, the active fleet was nearly below its pre-Vietnam levels, and by 1974, the fleet had been reduced by 50 percent from its peak 1968 levels. Carriers were reduced from 23 in 1968 to 13 in 1973; amphibious assault ships from 157 to 65; other major surface combatants, 387 to 187; and support ships, 130 to 37. By 1973 the navy was reduced to 576 ships, and this would decline to 439 by the end of the decade. In 1976, the navy relied on its reserve forces to provide almost 37 percent of the total forces required in a major East-West war.[51]

The navy took a number of steps to compensate for this steady decline in force levels. To reduce costs and to maintain the five carriers which comprised the Sixth and Seventh fleets, two carriers (one from each theater) were homeported overseas. Also, the navy began a program of merging the capabilities of the ASW carriers (CVS) and the attack carriers (CVA). This program was somewhat, if not totally, successful.

Zumwalt devised a sea-based version of the air force's "high-low" concept. As Zumwalt explained in his memoirs,

"High" was short for high-performance ships and weapons systems that also were so high-cost that the country could afford to build only a few of them at a time; there are missions the Navy cannot perform without the great flexibility and versatility of such ships. "Low" was short for moderate-cost, moderate-performance ships and systems that could be turned out in relatively large numbers; they would ensure that the Navy could be in enough places at the same time to get its job done.[52]

Zumwalt was principally concerned with the vulnerability of the large carriers. In a conflict, he argued, the navy could first deploy the smaller ships. The larger carriers could deploy behind these ships and away from the front lines as they carried out their missions. Not surprisingly, Zumwalt's plan garnered little support among the navy's aviation-oriented hierarchy, who were unreceptive to a diminution of the role of the carrier. James Holloway III, Zumwalt's successor, had a long-held pro-carrier orientation, and Zumwalt's plans were abandoned altogether.[53]

A slightly different approach to the force restructuring problem emerged. If the navy could not build as many ships as it would like, it would retire its older ships and concentrate on building fewer ships, albeit at the high end of the technological spectrum. In his memoirs, Zumwalt makes clear that the decision to concentrate on modernization over procurement was essentially budgetary:

> Given the Nixon administration's determination to reduce military budgets, the only way I could see for the Navy to free funds for developing up-to-date ships and weapons systems that could cope with the new Soviet armaments was to retire immediately large numbers of old ships and aircraft. [However, this meant] seriously reduced naval capability during at least the early seventies, while the new systems were being designed, built, and deployed.[54]

However, even as the size of the fleet decreased, there was no commensurate drawdown in U.S. global commitments or in the navy's role in responding to threats to those interests. If "out of Europe" conflict broke out, the navy was still required to maneuver into position near the trouble and at least "show the flag," if not resort to force. At the same time, naval resources were to be devoted to protecting the SLOCs between North America and Europe as well as to protecting the convoy of men and materiel to the European conflict.

To accomplish these missions, the navy had to implement a "swing strategy," the essence of which was dual basing. In a NATO-Pact contingency, for example, Pacific-based naval forces would "swing" through the Panama Canal and into the Atlantic to position themselves for conflict on Europe's flanks. Harold Brown, who confirmed the viability of the swing strategy in the Consolidated Guidance Study no. 8 of May 14, 1979, later justified the strategy in strictly budgetary terms:

> In a conventional war in Europe . . . naval resupply would become important after about thirty days. A . . . question is whether to set in advance a geographical order or priority for such naval operations, or to try to deal simultaneously with the North Atlantic (perhaps even North of the Greenland-Iceland-United Kingdom gap), the Mediterranean, the Indian ocean and Southwest Asia, and Far Eastern waters. Ideally, the United States would want to sweep the seas all at once and push the Soviets back to their coasts, but this is clearly out of reach with reasonably available resources.[55]

Brown thus made clear that the swing strategy was derived from budgetary rather than geostrategic considerations. From the perspective of most navy planners, the answer to the dilemma Brown posed was to *increase* "reasonably available resources." But the administration's perspective was different; budgetary constraints were a reality around which planning had to proceed, not transcend.

From the navy's perspective, the problems with the swing strategy were numerous. According to one critic of the strategy, the 1979 Consolidated Guidance, which reaffirmed it, advocated that its existence be withheld from America's allies in Asia. Apparently, the administration came to doubt whether it could adequately defend these interests in a crisis. "There can be little doubt," notes Robert Hanks, that "Washington's public acknowledgment of [the strategy] would convince Japan, China, the Philippines, Indonesia and others that the United States had indeed decided to withdraw from the Western Pacific—militarily and politically as well."[56]

The problem was that in a conflict with the Soviet Union over half the U.S. Pacific forces, which are primarily naval, would head toward the Atlantic. This would leave the Pacific region vulnerable to a second front opened there. Navy leaders doubted that the remaining fleet would be adequate to meet fully the extensive U.S. commitments in that region; remaining forces would have to adopt "wholly defensive postures." In effect, it was argued, "this would mean drawing a defensive line from Alaska to Hawaii and then, from behind that line, striving to maintain essential communications between those two states and the rest of the nation. . . . The entire region [would be at] the mercy of the Soviet Navy and the sizable land forces Moscow has stationed in Siberia."[57] At its worst, then, the strategy could lead to a neutralized Japan, a rapprochement between the PRC and the Soviet Union, the loss of South Korea to the North, and the establishment of Soviet hegemony over the entire Asian region.

Another problem for the navy derived from the assumption held by many planners in both the Ford and Carter administrations that the next war would be a short war. In 1976, the Ford administration projected that a European war, the focus of its planning, would quickly escalate to the nuclear level. This view was also shared by many planners in the Carter administration.

If a war were to occur in Europe, the navy's Pacific Fleet was in part responsible for resupplying the war effort, both in terms of replenishing combat supplies and in reinforcing the air war. It was uncertain how the United States would fulfill these replenishment missions in a war of short duration, given that the ships in the Pacific would need time to make their way into the Atlantic region. JCS war plans emphasized airlift, because "sealift, while crucial, cannot contribute significantly to this early deployment before M+20 [days]."[58] The navy concluded that the administration was not really that concerned with logistical and supply replenishment or, therefore, with the navy's role in the European war. Some in the navy also suspected that Brown had little expectation of a nonnuclear war in Europe actually lasting thirty days. Therefore, the secretary was not genuinely concerned with whether the navy could swing into position to provide replenishment. From this perspective, it was easy to conclude that the swing strategy was created to placate naval leaders concerned about the diminishing role of their service in the European war. The administration's persistent focus on the ground war seemed to confirm these suspicions.

CONCLUSION

As discussed in the next chapter, a number of events in 1979, including the fall of the shah in Iran and the Soviet invasion of Afghanistan, led to fundamental changes in the world view of the Carter administration. These changes led to commensurate changes in military planning. One change was that greater importance was placed on protecting the vulnerable oil reserves in the Persian Gulf. The stress put on naval forces would therefore increase as Indian Ocean commitments grew. These commitments would stretch the credibility of the swing strategy still further, and Carter's creation of a rapid-deployment force to respond to Persian Gulf contingincies only began to address the problem. Under Reagan, the strategy was abandoned altogether.

By the end of 1979, Carter's regionalist foreign perspective gave way to a geostrategic focus on the U.S.-Soviet competition. The Vietnam-influenced era of global military retrenchment came to a close, and the United States reasserted itself as a major power with global interests and commitments. This era of military assertion is considered in the next chapter.

NOTES

1. The third component of realistic deterrence was nuclear policy. In its first term, the administration adhered to assured destruction and sufficiency, rather than superiority, as the basic cornerstones of nuclear policy. Assured destruction is discussed in chapter 7, sufficiency in chapter 6. By 1974 the administration adopted Schlesinger's Limited Nuclear Options, which was a counterforce doctrine, as the sanctioned basis of nuclear tar-

geting. This was an evolutionary development. The United States had always sought a counterforce regime. Now, however, technology was developing which apparently made counterforce targeting possible. The best discussion of the evolution of the Limited Nuclear Options policy and its implications remains Lynn Etheridge Davis's "Limited Nuclear Options: Deterrence and the New American Doctrine," *Adelphi Papers* no. 121 (London: International Institute for Strategic Studies, 1976).

2. Richard M. Nixon, *U.S. Foreign Policy for the 1970s: A New Strategy for Peace* (Washington, D.C.: GPO, 1970), pp. 55–56.

3. Henry Kissinger, *White House Years* (New York, Little, Brown, 1979), pp. 221–222.

4. Melvin Laird, *Annual Report of the Secretary of Defense, Fiscal Year 1972* (Washington, D.C.: Government Printing Office, 1971), p. 21.

5. Office of the Assistant Secretary of Defense (Comptroller), *National Defense Estimates for FY 1988/1989* (May, 1987), p. 76. See also James Lacy, *Within Bounds: The Navy in Postwar American Security Policy* (Alexandria, Virginia: Center for Naval Analyses, 1983), p. 414.

6. Colin S. Gray and Jeffrey Barlow, "Inexcusable Restraint: The Decline of American Military Power in the 1970s," *International Security* 10, no. 2 (Fall 1985): 55.

7. Robert Komer, "What Decade Of Neglect?" *International Security* 10, no. 2 (Fall 1985): 71. Komer points out that "(t)o this should be added the indirect cost of the cutbacks in U.S. defense spending as we expiated the war. Taking just the reduction in real spending FY1973–1976 below the level of the last pre-Vietnam defense budget (FY1965) adds another $150 billion or so, again in constant FY1985 dollars . . . thus the cost of the Vietnam war would be on the order of one-half trillion in today's dollars."

8. Gray and Barlow, "Inexcusable Restraint," p. 53. Barlow points out that "although ultimately [these] . . . did not prove sweeping, this activity necessitated a major expenditure of time and energy on the part of the Executive branch just in order to maintain the defense spending momentum that was present. . . . In fact, the administration avoided far more debilitating cuts by proposing defense cuts themselves." See also Kissinger, *White House Years*, p. 215.

9. Seymour J. Deitchman, *Military Power and the Advance of Technology* (Boulder, Colorado: Westview, 1983), p. 226.

10. This table is developed from figures in Jeffrey Record, *Revising U.S. Military Strategy: Tailoring Means to Ends* (McLean, Virginia: Pergamon-Brassey's, 1984), pp. 100–103; Gray and Barlow, "Inexcusable Restraint"; and Office of the Assistant Secretary of Defense (Comptroller), *National Defense Estimates for FY 1988/1989* (May 1987).

11. For example, in 1972, Nixon and Soviet Premier Leonid Brezhnev signed a "Statement of Basic Principles" to serve as a framework for international behavior. But the statement was ineffective without credible military forces and policies to back it up and proved ineffective in regulating international behavior between the superpowers.

12. Kissinger envisaged at least five such power centers: the United States, the Soviet Union, China, Japan, and Western Europe. See John Lewis Gaddis, *Strategies of Containment* (New York: Oxford University Press, 1982), p. 282.

13. Gerald Ford, *A Time to Heal* (New York: Harper & Row, 1979), p. 345.

14. Jimmy Carter, "Address at University of Notre Dame Commencement Exercises," May 22, 1977, *Public Papers of the President of the United States, 1977*, book one (Washington, D.C.: GPO, 1977), pp. 954–961.

15. Lacy, *Within Bounds*, p. 452, fn. 112.

16. Figures provided in Record, *Revising*, pp. 100–103.

17. Alexander Cochran, "The Impact of Vietnam on Military Planning, 1972–1982: Some Tentative Thoughts," in Harry Borowski, ed., *Military Planning in the Twentieth Century*, proceedings of the Eleventh Military History Symposium, 1984 (Washington, D.C.: USAF Office of History, 1986), p. 379.

18. In Gray and Barlow, "Inexcusable Restraint," p. 64.

19. Figures in John Collins, *U.S.–Soviet Military Balance, 1960–1980* (New York: McGraw Hill, 1980), pp. 474–475.

20. Brown, "Consolidated Defense Guidance," January 1978, quoted in Lacy, *Within Bounds*, p. 452.

21. Ibid., p. 456.

22. Orr Kelly, "U.S. Navy in Distress," *U.S. News and World Report* (March 6, 1978): 24–28.

23. All figures are approximations. Sources: International Institute for Strategic Studies (IISS), *The Military Balance, 1980–1981* (London: IISS, 1980); Laurence L. Ewings and Robert C. Sellers,

The Reference Handbook of the Armed Forces of the World, 1966 (Washington, D.C.: Robert Sellers, Assoc., 1966). U.S. manpower level reflects active-duty and reserve personnel. Active: 2,094,000. Soviet divisions are manned understrength. The number of actual divisions for the USSR in 1980, if manned full strength, would be closer to 80.

24. Source: International Institute for Strategic Studies, *The Military Balance 1980–1981* (London: IISS, 1980). Table combines forces for Northern and Central regions with Southern Region.

25. The Soviets oversee the production, standardization, and distribution of WPO armed forces. The Soviets thus enjoy greater interoperability and flexibility from their European-based forces than does NATO.

26. Air Force Manual 1-1, *United States Air Force Basic Doctrine* (Washington, D.C.: Department of the Air Force, 28 September, 1971), p. 1-3.

27. Air Force Manual 1-1 (1971), chapter 6. In 1975 the air force again revised its manual to take into account the developments under Nixon and Ford. This revision emphasized the Total Force policy and the importance of the air force in maintaining peacetime security. The 1975 version essentially codified the 1971 manual.

28. Figures are from John Collins, *U.S.–Soviet Balance 1960–1980*, p. 229.

29. Ibid, p. 229.

30. Ibid, pp. 566–567.

31. These and other capabilities are discussed in Field Manual (FM) 100-5, *Operations* (Washington, D.C.: Department of the Army, 1 July 1976), chapter two.

32. Major Paul Herbert, *Deciding What Has to Be Done: General William E. Dupuy and the 1976 Edition of FM 100-5, Operations.* Leavenworth Papers no. 16 (Fort Leavenworth, Kansas: Combat Studies Institute 1988), p. 30.

33. FM 100-5, *Operations* (1976), p. 1-1.

34. John Romjue, *From Active Defense to Airland Battle: The Development of Army Doctrine 1973–1982* (Fort Monroe, Virginia: United States Army Training and Doctrine Command, 1984), p. 8. See also, FM 100-5 (1976), op. cit., p. 5-7.

35. FM 100-5 (1976), op. cit., p. 3-5.

36. FM 100-5 (1976), op. cit., p. 4-3.

37. FM 100-5 (1976), op. cit., p. 5-14.

38. FM 100-5 (1976), ibid.

39. "Addressing NATO operations and military operations in built-up areas, the manual writers included such practical reminders and precise data as seasonal mean temperatures, rainfall, and frequency of morning fog in Central Europe, as well as data about cloud level ceilings (of interest to Cobra pilots) and . . . the nature of cover provided by the characteristic stone, concrete, and brick buildings of German towns and villages." Romjue, *From Active Defense to AirLand*, p. 10.

40. James Schlesinger, *Annual Report of the Secretary of Defense to the Congress, FY1976* (Washington, D.C.: Government Printing Office, 1975) pp. III-7-8.

41. See William S. Lind, "FM 100-5, Operations: Some Doctrinal Questions for the United States Army," *Military Review* (March 1977): 54–65.

42. Ibid. See also Romjue, *From Active Defense to AirLand*, p. 15. This argument was reiterated in the debates that followed the 1982 revision of FM 100-5, discussed in the next chapter.

43. Philip Karber, "Dynamic Doctrine for Dynamic Defense," *Armed Forces Journal* (October 1976): 29.

44. Quoted and described in Romjue, *From Active Defense to AirLand*, p. 16.

45. Philip Karber, "The Tactical Revolution in Soviet Military Doctrine," *Military Review* (November 1977) and Steven L. Canby, quoted in Romjue, *From Active Defense to AirLand*, p. 17.

46. These points are addressed in Romjue, *From Active Defense to AirLand*.

47. Quoted in James Mullen, *The Evolution of U.S. Naval Strategy 1945-1975* (Unpublished paper prepared for the Army War College, Carlisle Barracks, Pennsylvania, 1974), p. 29.

48. Thomas Moorer, *Joint Hearings before the Joint Senate House Armed Services Committee on CVAN 70, Aircraft Carrier*, 91st Cong., 1970, p. 5.

49. E.R. Zumwalt, *Chief of Naval Operations Posture Statement for FY1971*, reprinted in Mullen, *Evolution*, p. 31.

50. E.R. Zumwalt, *U.S. Military Posture*, testimony before the House Committee on Armed Services, 92nd Cong., 2nd sess., 1972, p. 11415.

51. Figures are provided in Lacy, *Within Bounds*, pp. 377–378, 399.

52. Elmo Zumwalt, *On Watch: A Memoir* (New York: Quadrangle/ New York Times, 1976), p. 72.

53. The smaller, cheaper carrier Zumwalt advocated was the "sea control ship" (SCS). It would hold only 14 helicopters and 3 Harrier VSTOL planes. The SCS would have no catapults, large landing platforms, or landing-arresting gear. See, e.g., Lacy, *Within Bounds*, pp. 436–437.

54. Zumwalt, *On Watch*, p. 59.

55. Harold Brown, *Thinking About National Security* (Boulder, Colorado: Westview, 1983), p. 174.

56. Robert Hanks, "The Swinging Debate," *Proceedings of the U.S. Naval Institute* (June 1980): 28.

57. Hanks, "Swinging Debate," pp. 29, 30.

58. *DOD Annual Report, FY1977*, p. 118.

10
Era VI: Global Military Assertion

CARTER'S NEW ORIENTATION

The year 1979 was a tumultuous one for the United States, as a number of events that occurred then led to a general evolution in the foreign and defense policies of the Carter administration. One such event was Washington's discovery, in September, of a brigade of 3,000 Soviet troops in Cuba. The United States launched formal protests with the Soviets over this issue but to no avail. This event was relatively unimportant in itself but was not without significance. The contrast between U.S. power during the time of the Cuban Missile Crisis, when Kennedy forced the Soviets down, and now, when Carter could not effect any Soviet concession on the issue, could not have been clearer. It was as if the parity (and in some ways, superiority) the Soviets had attained in military matters was now being visibly and embarrassingly exploited for political purposes.

On a practical level, the discovery of the Soviet brigade called into question the adequacy of U.S. verification and intelligence techniques, which emerged as issues in the congressional debates over a second SALT (Strategic Arms Limitation Treaty) accord. Critics of SALT II also pointed to the loss of a U.S. intelligence facility in Iran. Chances became increasingly slim that the treaty, for which Carter had lobbied intensely, would pass the Senate. Carter ultimately agreed to raise defense-spending levels in exchange for treaty ratification. Later events made Carter's concession superfluous.

More significant events occurred in Iran, where the regime of the shah of Iran, a close U.S. ally for over 35 years, fell to Islamic revolutionaries. Led by the Ayatollah Ruhollah Khomeini, the Islamic radicals came to power riding a wave of protest against the shah's generally pro-Western orientation. The shah was forced to flee, and the ayatollah was installed as the head of state. On November 4, the American embassy in Tehran was overrun by Iranian militants, and over 50 American personnel were captured (and not released until January 1981).

In December, the Soviet Union invaded Afghanistan. A civil war had been brewing there as Muslim insurrectionaries attempted to overthrow the Soviet-backed regime. On December 25, Soviet paratroops and armored columns entered the country. By spring 1980, nearly 100,000 Soviet troops were in Afghanistan, marking the first direct use of Soviet troops in a Third World conflict in the post-World War II era.

Cumulatively, the fall of the Iranian shah, the ascension to power of the virulently anti-Western Khomeini, and the Soviets' invasion of Afghanistan heavily impacted upon U.S. policy in the Persian Gulf. As described by Zbigniew Brzezinski, Carter's national security adviser, the administration grasped the fundamental relationship between the events in Iran and Afghanistan: "[T]he strategic context changed dramatically in the fourth week of December. The Soviet invasion of Afghanistan meant that henceforth any action taken by us toward Iran had to be guided, to a much larger extent than heretofore, by its likely consequences for regional containment of Soviet ambitions."[1]

Responding to the invasion of Afghanistan, the president announced that his perception of the Soviets had completely changed. He asked Congress to defer voting on SALT II, which was already unlikely to be ratified by the Senate; restricted the Soviets' access to U.S. fishing waters; limited their purchasing power of high-technology goods; and in February 1980 announced that U.S. athletes would not participate in the 1980 Moscow Olympics. In May, the president made a major foreign policy speech in Philadelphia. This speech was remarkable; in many ways, it consolidated Carter's embrace of containment—the foreign policy objective that had guided all of his predecessors in the post-World War II era. To be sure, Carter strongly reaffirmed his administration's commitment to human rights. But in striking contrast to his 1977 Notre Dame speech, where he assailed the nation's "inordinate fear of communism" and its overreliance on the military component of foreign policy, the president now described the world as a "dangerous place." And there was no doubt as to who was to blame:

The fact is that for 15 years the Soviet Union has been expanding its military capabilities far out of proportion to its needs for defense. . . . The Soviets must understand that they cannot recklessly threaten world peace. . . . The maintenance of peace must be predicated on adequate American strength and a recognition of that strength, not only by our own people and our allies but by our potential adversaries as well. . . .

The West must defend its strategic interests wherever they are threatened.[2]

The events in Afghanistan and Iran led the administration to elevate the oil-rich Persian Gulf region to paramount importance in its defense planning. In January 1980, just four months prior to delivering the Philadelphia speech, the president announced what quickly became known as the "Carter Doctrine." In his State of the Union address, Carter warned: "Let our position be absolutely clear: An attempt by any outside force to gain control of the Persian Gulf region will be regarded as an assault on the vital interests of the United States of America, and such an assault will be repelled by any means necessary including military force."[3]

The Carter Doctrine was intended as a message to the Soviet Union.[4] Defense Secretary Harold Brown compared a Soviet attack into northeastern Iran with an attack into Central Europe. He noted that if the Soviets mounted an attack into Iran, "the prize would be nearly as great, because control of Persian Gulf oil would make it possible to dominate Western Europe and Japan,"[5] due to their dependency on the Gulf oil reserves.

Carter recommended that by 1984 the United States spend $10 billion on outfitting ships, planes, and supplies as necessary to create a Rapid Deployment Joint Task Force (RDJTF or RDF) to operate in the Indian Ocean, mainly in the Persian Gulf and the Arabian Sea. The RDJTF, which in January 1983 was redesignated the U.S. Central Command, was organized around a unified command structure in order to facilitate rapid crisis mobilization. As described by Brown,

> The United States has deployed maritime prepositioning ships at Diego Garcia in the Indian Ocean. These ships contain the equipment and a month's supplies for a reinforced Marine brigade and several Air Force fighter and attack squadrons. They could combine with ground forces and aircraft—which could be flown into the region within a week or ten days—to make a total force of about 15,000 to 20,000. The United States is maintaining one or two battle carrier groups and other naval forces on station in the Arabian Sea. . . . U.S. airborne warning and control aircraft operate in Saudi Arabia. These would be able to monitor and control operations of U.S. F-15 aircraft that could be flown into the region within a matter of days.[6]

Few new forces were envisaged for the RDJTF. Fifteen new logistics ships, eight fast sealift ships, and a number of strategic transport aircraft were requested to enhance the RDJTF's capacity for quick mobilization and U.S. flexibility in conducting operations.

But actual fighting forces to fulfill the new commitments were not requested. This created a problem—forces would have to be requested from other commands, leading to potential shortfalls in some areas. NATO, for example, could conceivably have been left vulnerable in a crisis if forces had to be pulled from the European command.

The RDJTF was criticized on other grounds as well. These included the potential vulnerability in a crisis of prepositioned supplies and the insufficient size of the CONUS-based strategic reserve, upon which the force was heavily reliant.[7] By creating the RDJTF, however, Carter essentially conceded that the experiment in Third World military retrenchment had failed. The Carter Doctrine symbolized the administration's rhetorical embrace of traditional containment, and the RDJTF symbolized its willingness to prepare for conflicts outside of Europe.

Carter's new orientation was supported in his FY1981 defense budget. Carter requested an $11-billion defense increase from the previous year, representing 5 percent real growth in defense spending. Of that request, $10 billion was for the RDJTF. Congress actually increased appropriations above the amount Carter requested. The FY1981 funding bill Congress passed was for $159.7 billion and included an 18 percent increase for navy fighter planes and a 17 percent increase for warships.[8] Carter's proposed budget for FY1982 requested even greater increases over prior spending levels. But the really significant increases in defense spending would come after Ronald Reagan assumed the presidency in 1981.

RONALD REAGAN AND THE POLICY OF WORLDWIDE WAR

As a candidate for the 1980 presidency, Ronald Reagan argued that Jimmy Carter had neglected America's defenses in an era of worsening Soviet hostility. As president, Reagan committed his administration to reversing the "decade of neglect" that, he said, saw the United States "struggling not to regain the superiority we once enjoyed, but simply to restore the military equivalence we need to keep the peace."[9] In this vein, the administration initiated a massive buildup of the U.S. armed forces.

In a nutshell, the administration's approach to military planning and procurement was to build first and rationalize military policies later. Thus, early Reagan pronouncements with respect to the buildup tended to stress the Soviet threat but offered little of interest conceptually.[10] The importance of flexible response, balanced forces, the allies, and strategic nuclear deterrence was stressed, but this hardly added up to a conceptual breakthrough.

Not only was the Reagan buildup without strategic underpinnings, but it was also expensive—the administration estimated that close to $1.5 trillion was required to assure the continuation of deterrence. Between FY1981 and FY1985, budget authority for defense increased by approximately 30 percent, after adjusting for inflation.[11] This marked an unprecedented growth in the defense establishment during peacetime. But to Reagan administration officials, the issue was not one of strategy or resources but of rebuilding U.S. might to turn back the Soviet threat. As Weinberger repeatedly stressed, "American defense budgets should be based on defense needs, not on political expediency or short-term fiscal goals."[12] Soon after assuming office, the administration requested an $8.1-billion defense supplemental to Carter's FY1981 budget, and an additional $18.1 billion for Carter's proposed FY1982 budget. These outlays were directed primarily to force procurement, research and development into new weapons systems, and to strategic nuclear force modernization.

In 1981, congressional support for Reagan's Long-Term Defense Program was unquestionably strong. The Republicans controlled the Senate, and the national mood was clearly supportive of increasing expenditures for the armed forces. But over time, that support declined. In 1982, the United States endured a difficult recession and was running a huge deficit, two factors which began to undermine congressional and public support for the buildup. Democratic opposition to the Reagan program grew more unified and stronger (and would be further galvanized in 1986, when the Democrats regained the Senate). The administration was increasingly pressured to provide some sort of rationale for its buildup.

The notional basis of the policy that emerged was National Security Decision Document (NSDD)-32, dated May 20, 1982. According to NSDD-32, war with the Soviets was likely to occur in multiple theaters, and the United States had to prepare to conduct simultaneous operations wherever challenged.[13] In contrast to the one-and-a-half war planning that guided its predecessor, the Reagan administration's military planning was much more ambitious. As Weinberger stated in an early report to Congress:

> [U.S. forces must] be able to meet the demands of a worldwide war, including concurrent reinforcement of Europe, deployments to southwest Asia and the Pacific, and support for other areas . . . given the

Soviets' ability to launch simultaneous attacks in [Southwest Asia], NATO, and the Pacific, our long-range goal is to be [able to defend] all theaters simultaneously.[14]

Indeed, the administration categorically rejected tallying up an arbitrary number of potential theaters of conflict. Weinberger argued that the U.S. must reject the "mistaken argument as to whether we should prepare to fight 'two wars,' 'one and a half' wars, or some other such tally of wars. Such mechanistic assumptions neglect both the risks and the opportunities that we might confront. We may be forced to cope with Soviet aggression or Soviet backed aggression on several fronts."[15]

Thus, not only was one-and-a-half war planning discarded, but the Carter administration's assumption that the next war would have a short conventional stage was also rejected. Weinberger noted that "the two wars in which the United States has fought since the beginning of the nuclear era . . . were both of long duration. Unless we are so strong or our enemy so weak that we could quickly achieve victory, we cannot count on a war ending within a few months."[16] The administration was saying that the United States had to prepare for protracted war, which required greater numbers of forces and enhanced readiness from forces in being. The administration thus rejected just about all the planning assumptions of its predecessor.

Weinberger also endorsed a strategic concept which later came to be called (although mainly by the administration's critics) "horizontal escalation." In his FY1984 Annual Report, Weinberger argued that in a protracted, multi-front war, the United States

> might choose not to restrict ourselves to meeting aggression on its own immediate front. We might decide to stretch our capabilities, to engage the enemy in many places, or to concentrate our forces and military assets in a few of the most critical arenas.
>
> Our counteroffensives should be directed at places where we can affect the outcome of the war. If it is to offset the enemy's attack, it should be launched against territory or assets that are of an importance to him comparable to the ones he is attacking.[17]

The administration's policy and the strategies that supported it were aggressive and assertive. They aimed to take the fight directly to the enemy and, in the event of hostilities, force terms of conflict that were consonant with U.S. war aims. As these policies solidified, therefore, they were subject to much criticism by outside observers. These criticisms included

1. *A lack of priorities.* The argument was that a policy aimed at fighting wars in a virtually unlimited number of theaters redis-

tributed resources so broadly that no theater was adequately protected. In particular, Europe was singled out as the area where superpower conflict remained most dangerous but was potentially the most neglected in the administration's worldwide strategic conception.

2. *Insufficient funding of the operations and maintenance (O&M) account.* One of the most troubling aspects of the Reagan buildup was the attention directed toward force procurement and research and development (R&D) at the expense of maintaining existing forces in a high state of readiness and preparedness. According to one estimate, the rate of growth for force procurement was approximately 75 percent between FY1981 and FY1986 and for R&D, approximately 86 percent. Yet in the same period, the rate of growth for the O&M account was only 17 percent.[18] The problem with such an agenda was twofold. First, the United States risked fielding what has been called a "hollow force"—one incapable of sustained combat. Second, the United States risked fielding highly sophisticated forces without the equipment or manpower required to maintain them.

3. *Inadequate account of the opponent's strengths and weaknesses.* As Jeffrey Record has argued,

> It is one thing to argue the likelihood or even the inevitability of horizontal escalation of a war with the Soviet Union; it is quite another to assume that horizontal escalation would somehow work to the advantage of a defender compelled, as would be the United States with respect to hostilities on the Eurasian land mass, to operate along exterior lines of communication.

Record's argument is that "historically, successful operations along exterior lines of communication have in almost every case required a substantial preponderance of force over that of an opponent enjoying interior lines of communication."[19] This argument, however, may overestimate the Soviet capacity to quickly move men and materiel across great distances within the USSR. The main transloading points of the Soviet railroad would be vulnerable to attack by NATO's long-range weapons (discussed below); another problem is that winter could seriously hamper the rate of railroad movement. Closer to the front, the Soviets rely on trucks to a much greater extent than in the theater rear. However, the points where materiel is transferred from trains to trucks are well-known and would also be subject to attack by NATO. Such attacks could seriously hamper Soviet reinforcement capabilities. It is therefore difficult to assume that the Soviets' internal lines of communications would necessarily be advantageous.

4. *Overconfidence in the U.S. ability to keep the war conventional.* This may have been the case, although the important question was whether the policy and attendant strategy made nuclear escalation more or less likely. If anything, the possibility of escalating to the nuclear level underscored the importance of thorough planning to avoid such a contingency. It seems logical that by planning for protracted conventional conflict, one is better prepared to carry out such a contingency without resorting to nuclear weapons than if one has no such plans.

5. *An illusory plan to seize the initiative.* As the army realized in the aftermath of the *active defense,* seizing the initiative from a defensive orientation was a difficult, if not impossible, goal. The Reagan administration tried to develop a policy that originated (at least on the declaratory level) from the defensive but immediately progressed to the offensive. To deter war or to prevent a Soviet victory was no longer enough; to prevail in the event of hostilities was now given just as much priority. The administration argued that such an approach to military planning would enhance deterrence, and the Reagan administration's policies were generally consistent with this point of view.

Overall, however, the critics of the Reagan administration buildup raised some legitimate arguments.[20] It is not certain that the policy and the strategies associated with it were ever anything more than post-hoc rationalizations for the buildup. Similarly, one can question whether the extent of the buildup was necessary and whether it was pursued in a particularly farsighted manner. In 1986, actual outlays for defense began to decline and continue to do so as of this writing. Defense planning is thus in the midst of yet another vacillation, this time turning downward (see chapter 11). A more measured buildup, requiring less growth in defense spending levels at the outset but perhaps sustainable over a greater period of time, may have better institutionalized the buildup and allowed for more rational planning.

The administration never really developed a strategic rationale for its buildup; post-hoc rationalizations satisfied few of the administration's congressional critics. It is not surprising, then, that over time, the administration's rhetoric focused on other questions raised, at least in part, by the massive influx of dollars into the defense establishment. One constant criticism of the Reagan defense program was that, in consonance with the administration's often inflammatory and rabidly anti-Soviet rhetoric, the buildup made the world less, not more, safe. The existence of such a powerful military would make the administration less cautious about using force in a crisis.

The administration was also criticized as potentially leading the United States into "another Vietnam," particularly in Nicaragua, where the Marxist Sandinista government was at odds with the administration throughout the Reagan years.

To address these criticisms, Weinberger developed six principles, or tests, which would govern any decision to use force. In the spring of 1986, Weinberger enunciated those principles as follows:

- The United States should not commit forces to combat unless our vital interests are at stake.
- [If the decision to commit forces is made, the United States] must commit them in sufficient numbers and with sufficient support to win.
- We must have clearly defined political and military objectives.
- The relationship between our objectives and the size, composition and disposition of our forces must be continually reassessed and adjusted as necessary.
- Before the United States commits combat forces abroad the U.S. government should have some reasonable assurance of the support of the American people and their elected representatives in the Congress.
- Finally, the commitment of U.S. forces to combat should be a last resort—only after diplomatic, political, economic and other efforts have been made to protect our interests.[21]

Whether these tests were ever actually applied in any subsequent administration decision is not known. And in many ways, they raise more questions than they answer. How is a vital interest defined? To some, the Grenada rescue mission was conducted to support a "vital interest"; to many others, no vital interest was at stake. Other questions that the six tenets raise are, for example, how can the U.S. government be assured that it has the support of the American people? What if, as was the case in Vietnam, initial support rapidly declines over the course of the commitment? When are diplomatic, political, and economic efforts exhausted?

Clearly, the answers to these questions are a matter of judgement. In enunciating these questions, however, the administration was probably less concerned with providing real tests to govern the application of force than with quieting its critics and showing that it had assimilated the "lessons of Vietnam" and was not about to apply U.S. force at whim. As Weinberger explained,

The caution sounded by these six tests for the use of military force is intentional. The world consists of an endless succession of hot spots in which some U.S. forces could play, or could at least be imagined to play, a useful role. . . . The belief that the mere presence of U.S. troops in Lebanon, or Central America or Africa or elsewhere could be useful in some way is not sufficient for our government to ask our troops to risk their lives.[22]

But even given these considerations, it can be said that the Reagan administration did come to office with a general conception of what it wanted to do—rebuild U.S. military forces—and in general did it. There is also no question that under Reagan, U.S. force was used to a much greater extent than in any period since Vietnam. Under Reagan, the United States ordered the marines and U.S. warships into Lebanon (at a cost of 231 lives); deployed combat troops into Central America for maneuvers and shows of force; ordered the invasion of Grenada, in the Caribbean; and in April 1986, ordered a bombing raid against Libya's Colonel Khadaffi in reprisal against Khadaffi's state-sponsored terrorism. Under Reagan, the United States called out the Sixth and Seventh fleets to show the flag to an unprecedented degree. Carriers were deployed in 1981 in the Gulf of Sidra, where they participated in the downing of two Libyan fighter planes. They were also used in the Libyan bombing raid and attacks on a Libyan radar site in March 1986. In 1987, U.S. naval forces were used to conduct Persian Gulf escort missions and at that time skirmished with Iranian Revolutionary Guard mine-layers and destroyers.

THE 1986 DEFENSE REORGANIZATION ACT

As discussed, one effect of the Reagan administration's "buy now, strategize later" approach to force procurement was that as the requested expenditures continued to rise, many of the administration's critics in Congress and elsewhere increasingly demanded some rationale for the requests. The lack of strategic rationale at the heart of the procurement process exposed a number of other problems with the process as well. There was a public perception that the defense industry was "feeding at the trough." This perception was fed by the widely publicized stories of $700 toilet seats and $500 bolts. But if these had proven to be the biggest problems with the buildup, the buildup would have to be judged an unqualified success. The fact was these problems were insignificant, compared to the bigger problems that emerged, such as the weapons systems that did not perform as well as anticipated (such as the air force's B-1 bomber) and those that did not work at all (such as the army's DIVAD).

It also became clear that the Pentagon's problems riddled most every aspect of the planning process. A lack of coordinated planning seemed to permeate the entire defense establishment, from the OSD to the JCS, to the service planners, and to the commanders of the unified and specified commands. It appeared that these actors were giving little thought to how the new procurement could most effectively be put to use.

In 1958, President Eisenhower took the lead in attempting to reform the process. In 1986, however, it was the executive that was under fire, and it was up to Congress to undertake a major examination of the flaws in defense planning, procurement, and policy making. To be sure, President Reagan responded to congressional pressures and created a high-level commission to examine these issues and recommend steps for reform. Headed by the industrialist David Packard, the Packard Commission submitted to the president a comprehensive agenda for reforming the procurement and planning processes.[23] But the Reagan administration never embraced the Packard Commission reforms wholeheartedly, and little was done to actually implement the recommendations. It remains to be seen whether the Bush administration will pursue the Packard Commission recommendations with more vigor.

A broader and more wide-ranging examination of the defense establishment was commissioned by Senator Barry Goldwater (R-Arizona) and Senator Sam Nunn (D-Georgia), respectively the chairman and ranking minority member of the Senate Armed Services Committee at the time, and by Representative William Nichols (D-Alabama). A year of hearings and study culminated in the Defense Reorganization Act of 1986, a major piece of legislation which has already been partially implemented.

The act addressed virtually the same issues as had been addressed in 1958. Once again, an effort was made to strengthen the role of the JCS and the unified commanders in the planning process. Specifically, the act

- strengthened the role of the chairman of the Joint Chiefs of Staff. The chairman was designated the principal military adviser to the president, the National Security Council, and the secretary of defense. "The clear purpose here," explain Frederick Hartmann and Robert Wendzel, "was to ensure that the civilian leadership receives independent and integrated military advice cutting across service boundaries, the chairman being the only chief not tied directly to one of the services."[24]

- decreed that henceforth, the Joint Staff would be directly answerable to the chairman, rather than the entire JCS, and created a position of vice chairman, to be held by an officer of four-star rank.

- increased the power and influence of the commanders in chief of the Unified and Specified Commands. This was a particularly important aspect of the Act, as it attempted to garner greater input with respect to weapons requirements from those who would be charged with using them. Specifically, reforms will be aimed at enhancing the authority of the CINCs over the service component commanders in operational matters. How this will be done is not entirely clear as of 1989.

- altered the service promotion and personnel system to encourage "jointness." The JCS system has been inherently flawed because the officers assigned to the Joint Staff tend to be foremost loyal to their own service. A new occupational category called "joint specialty" was established to encourage the services to reward joint-duty assignment. Guidelines were also established to ensure that serving in a joint-duty capacity could not be harmful to an officer's career.[25]

What is most clear from the above is that the general thrust of the 1986 reorganization was aimed at increasing service cooperation and coordination by putting greater emphasis on joint planning at the procurement and operational levels. As will be seen, this is consonant with a trend already under way between the army and the air force. Since it is too early to conclude that the trend toward jointness will survive future eras, when the military budget is once again constrained, it is not yet feasible to judge the 1986 Reorganization Act a success or a failure. It is worth noting, however, that the act did not increase the chairman's authority in determining service budgets. The service components are still responsible for equipping and training their forces and for determining their annual requirements. The tendency for planners to define their defense requirements in terms of their individual service may therefore remain basically unchanged. Until there is some adjustment to this fundamental reality, the potential effectiveness of the 1986 Reorganization Act will probably not be realized.

THE SERVICES IN THE EIGHTIES

Service planning has reflected the administration's assertive orientation. The two major service developments—the navy's maritime strategy and the army's AirLand Battle Doctrine (which has been fully endorsed by the air force)—seek to instill an offensive, victory-oriented spirit into U.S. Navy and Army plans for war. They both explicitly reject concepts from the 1970s, such as the swing strategy and the active defense, which so reflected the retrenchment of the era.

Most of the Reagan administration's conventional force reconstitution was devoted to much-needed capital reinvestment in weapons, base upkeep, production facilities, and equipment, all of which had depreciated through the Seventies. In FY1986 dollars, defense spending rose from $224.4 billion in FY1981 (prior to Reagan's supplemental) to $313.7 billion in FY1986, which was still a considerable increase even after factoring for inflation. General purpose force allocations rose from $87 billion to $132.1 billion, a 52 percent increase, and in airlift and sealift (particularly for CENTCOM), from $3.7 billion to $8 billion, a 116 percent increase.[26]

Most of Reagan's investment was dedicated to modernization and new procurement, and all the services experienced some growth in the 1980s. In 1988, the army had 18 divisions, only two more than it had at the beginning of the decade. However, there has been some change in the army's division structure, as two divisions were reorganized into light divisions. The light divisions consist of approximately 10,000 soldiers, are infantry intensive, and stress flexibility and mobility. In part, their creation reflects a growing national concern with future combat in Third World environments, where only a limited role for heavily armored forces is projected. Army active-duty personnel end strength has remained stable at approximately 780,000 through FY1987. As for the air force, its tactical air remained at 38 wings until 1988, when budgetary pressures forced the elimination of two wings. During the 1980s, air force personnel levels have risen only marginally, by 6 percent, with only a fraction of that increase coming from the tactical forces.

The navy, on the other hand, saw steady and impressive growth. The number of carriers increased from its postwar low of 12 in 1979 to 15 in 1988. Two battleships were taken out of mothballs and were reactivated. Although the total number of destroyers and cruisers declined from 107 in 1980 to 99 in 1985, this was compensated for by a rise in the number of frigates from 71 to 110. Nuclear-powered attack submarines rose from 74 in 1980 to 96 in 1985. Deployable battle forces—which include missile boats, mine warfare, logistic, and support ships—rose from 95 in 1980 to 117 in 1985. Finally, naval aviation increased significantly from 60 squadrons with 894 aircraft in 1980 to 65 squadrons with 967 aircraft in

1985. Levels of navy active-duty personnel rose from 527,000 in 1980 to 587,000 in FY1987.[27] All told, budget authority for the Department of the Navy increased in real terms by 49 percent between FY1980 and FY1986.[28]

The heart of the Reagan global strategy was power projection: to carry the fight to any corner of the world, including the shores of the USSR, in a conflict. Not surprisingly, this led to an emphasis on naval force procurement and the adaptation of a vigorous and aggressive maritime strategy. Versions of the maritime strategy had been conceived and developed in 1978 by Admiral Thomas Hayward, who at that time was commander in chief, Pacific Command, and many of the ideas essential to the maritime strategy appeared in the navy's 1979 *Sea Plan 2000*.[29] It remains questionable whether the Carter administration would have procured the forces the strategy required, even though some increases for the navy were programmed in the final Carter budget. But the pro-defense atmosphere experienced during the Reagan administration and the effective and unflappable advocacy of Navy Secretary John Lehman created an accommodating environment for the assertive and controversial maritime strategy and for the ascendency of the navy in the national security planning process.

THE NAVY AND THE MARITIME STRATEGY

In the Kennedy administration, as discussed, the army assumed a somewhat elevated role in administration planning. In the Reagan administration, such a status was accorded to the navy. Publicly, officials from both the navy and the administration vigorously objected to the view that the Reagan policy was oriented toward maritime operations. In the 1986 elaboration of the maritime strategy, for example, Admiral James Watkins stated:

> The maritime strategy is firmly set in the context of national strategy, emphasizing coalition warfare and the criticality of allies, and demanding cooperation with our sister services. . . . As the naval component of the National Military Strategy, the maritime strategy is designed to support campaigns in ground theaters of operations both directly and indirectly. Its success depends on the contributions of our sister services and allies. Accordingly, we place great emphasis on joint operations.[30]

Watkins, at that time CNO, discussed a number of joint cooperative agreements between the three services. In an era of $300-billion defense budgets, when few hard choices among weapons systems were required, cooperation among the services in planning and procurement was more civil than in the past. Nevertheless, the global orientation of the Reagan strategy and the extensive buildup of the navy that occurred in the 1980s undercut Watkins's claim; the Reagan buildup did have a maritime emphasis. At the heart of the navy agenda was the attainment of a 600-ship navy, based on the procurement of forces described in Table 10.1.[31]

The fundamental aim of the maritime strategy was to force the Soviets to fight on terms favorable to the United States. In practical terms, this meant preventing the Soviets from opening multiple fronts on terms favorable to them (for example, in Europe and in the Middle East), while forcing them to expend military resources on additional fronts favorable to the United States (for example, at sea). In other words, the United States would try to force the Soviets to concentrate resources on the sea war and, in the process, hinder their capacity to concentrate their efforts on the land war. Watkins stated the objectives of the maritime strategy as follows:

> Deny the Soviets their kind of war by exerting global pressure, indicating that the conflict will be neither short nor localized;
> Destroy the Soviet Navy;
> Influence the land battle by limiting redeployment of forces, by ensuring reinforcement and resupply, and by direct application of carrier air and amphibious power;
> Terminate the war on terms acceptable to [the U.S.] and to our allies through measures such as threatening direct attack against the [Soviet] homeland or changing the nuclear correlation of forces.[32]

TABLE 10.1.
The Navy's Force Structure Goals
for the 600$^+$-ship Navy

Type Ship	Number Sought
Ballistic Missile Submarines	20 to 40
Deployable Aircraft Carriers	15
Reactivated Battleships	4
Principal Surface Combatants	238
Nuclear-Powered Attack Submarines	100
Mine Countermeasures Ships	14
Amphibious Ships	75
Patrol Combatants	6
Underway Replenishment Ships	65
Support Ships and Other	60 to 65
TOTAL	597 to 622

There were three phases involved in implementing the maritime strategy: *Phase I*—deterrence, or the transition to war; *Phase II*—seizing the initiative; and *Phase III*—bringing the fight to the enemy. Each of these is discussed.

PHASE I: DETERRENCE, OR THE TRANSITION TO WAR The initial phase of the maritime strategy, argued Watkins, "would be triggered by recognition that a specific international situation has the potential to grow to a global superpower confrontation. Such a confrontation may come because of an extra-European crisis or because of problems in Europe."[33] The maritime strategy would be implemented to deny the Soviets the option of concentrating their forces in a single, massive attack and force them into war on the flanks or in a peripheral theater. The purpose of this phase, Watkins explained, was to deter an escalation of the crisis. If deterrence failed, however, the United States had to be prepared to engage the Soviets in a war involving the early and decisive application of sea power.

Deterrence was realized through the rapid movement of forward deployed forces into crisis areas. The purpose of such operations was to force the Soviet fleet as far back toward the Soviet coast as possible.

> Aggressive forward movement of anti-submarine warfare forces, both submarines and maritime patrol aircraft, will force Soviet submarines to retreat into defensive bastions to protect their ballistic missile submarines. This both denies the Soviets the option of a massive, early attempt to interdict our sea lines of communication and counters such operations against them that the Soviets undertake.[34]

PHASE II: SEIZING THE INITIATIVE In language that mirrored the rhetoric emanating from the Pentagon, Watkins stressed the importance of seizing the initiative. Watkins explained that

> Naval forces will destroy Soviet forces in the Mediterranean, Indian Ocean, and other forward areas, neutralize Soviet clients if required, and fight our way toward Soviet home waters.
>
> Seizing the initiative . . . demonstrates to our allies this country's determination to prevail. . . . The history of war tells us that gaining the initiative is the key to destroying an opponent's forces. Finally, [it] opens the way to apply direct pressure on the Soviets to end the war on our terms—the new goal of our strategy once deterrence has failed.[35]

This phase involved the *horizontal escalation* of the conflict. In carrying out this phase, maritime forces must "counter a first salvo, wear down the enemy forces, protect sea lines of communication, continue reinforcement and resupply, and improve positioning."

These tasks can involve the entire range of naval missions, including antisubmarine warfare, antisurface warfare, amphibious operations, anti-air warfare, mine warfare, and special operations. Enhanced sealift capabilities were stressed, simply because the forces must be supported to fight effectively.

PHASE III: CARRYING THE FIGHT TO THE ENEMY   In this phase, the United States and the allies aggressively seek to terminate the war on terms favorable to the West. The objective of Phase III operations is to complete the destruction of all remaining Soviet naval assets, including nuclear submarines:

> During this final phase the United States and its allies would press home the initiative worldwide, while continuing to support air and land campaigns, maintaining sealift, and keeping sea lines of communication open. Amphibious forces, up to the size of a full Marine amphibious force, would be used to regain territory. In addition, the full weight of the carrier battle forces could continue to "roll up" the Soviets on the flanks, contribute to the battle on the Central Front, or carry the war to the Soviets.
>
> At the same time, antisubmarine warfare forces would continue to destroy Soviet submarines, including ballistic missile submarines, thus reducing the attractiveness of nuclear escalation by changing the nuclear balance in our favor.[36]

The last two phases of the strategy were the most controversial, and even some of the admirals who would be charged with carrying them out raised some objections. Many of the objections centered around the strategy's task of attacking Soviet forces at the Kola Peninsula. Concerns were also raised over the strategy's task of changing the nuclear equation through direct attacks against Soviet submarines carrying nuclear weapons, known as SSBNs.

Both of these propositions, involving attacks on the Northern Fleet at the Kola Peninsula, entailed great risk. Admiral Watkins stated that the strategy should not imply "some immediate 'Charge of the Light Brigade' attack on the Kola Peninsula or any other specific target." Yet he just as clearly stated that allied naval forces will "fight our way toward Soviet home waters" to "defeat Soviet maritime strength in all its dimensions, including base support."[37] Such operations may carry with them an undue risk of nuclear escalation.

Moreover, the carrier forces that form the nucleus of the 600-ship fleet would be put at great risk. The carriers would be required to carry out the phased operations described above. But the closer the carriers are brought to the Soviet bases, the more detectable they would be to Soviet reconnaissance capabilities and the more vulnerable they become. As Admiral Stansfield Turner and George Thibault have argued,

> The Soviets would have time to minimize their forces left in port or on airfields and to put the rest on full alert. By the time the carriers were within 1,600 miles of Soviet air bases, they would be within range of over 90 percent of the U.S.S.R.'s land-based bombers. Yet the Soviet bases would still be over 1,000 miles beyond the range of carrier aircraft.
>
> Traveling at 25 knots for those last 1,000 miles, the carrier force would be subject to Soviet air bombardment for nearly two days before it was close enough to strike Soviet bases . . . in short we would be fighting the Soviets on their turf at the times and places of their choosing, well before we could assume the offensive.[38]

In short, there is some doubt as to whether the strategy adequately accounts for likely Soviet behavior in the midst of a national crisis. A number of the assumptions in the maritime strategy may be overoptimistic. The possibility that U.S. attacks on Soviet SSBNs would lead to a Soviet response involving nuclear weapons is not given enough consideration. Nor does it seem likely that the close-in operations described in the maritime strategy could be executed without considerable loss of the carriers and their support ships.[39]

It is also unclear that Phase I operations would really push the Soviets back to their defensive bastions or that the United States could attain the initiative without striking first. In testimony, Admiral Watkins made clear his dissatisfaction with this particular tenet of U.S. policy:

> Senator Cohen: You are saying that it may not be possible to absorb that first shot and maybe we ought to take some action first.
>
> Admiral Watkins: Not just that it may or may not be possible to absorb it, but it may be wrong for the nation to do that. . . .[40]

Put into perspective, the maritime strategy clearly reflects the national strategy of which it is the handmaiden. It is aggressive, and in the event that deterrence breaks down, uncompromising in its determination to prevail in a superpower war. In addition, it represents a concerted navy effort to break with the retrenchment of the post-Vietnam era. For the navy, who denounced the seventies as that era when its role in a European war was reduced to "convoy escort for the reinforcement flow,"[41] an era of assertion was welcome and perhaps inevitable.

THE ARMY'S AIRLAND BATTLE DOCTRINE

In 1982, the army unveiled a new doctrine, discarding the active defense of the 1970s for an aggressive and offensively oriented doctrine known as AirLand. No doubt, a number of factors led to the promulgation of the AirLand Battle Doctrine, such as the development of long-range, precision-guided technology and battlefield experience with said technology as far back as Vietnam. But the widespread acceptance and institutionalization of AirLand within the army was in large part due to, and reflected, the new assertive thinking that was occurring at the national level.

The new doctrine was formally articulated in the army's 1982 revision of its capstone doctrinal manual, FM 100-5, *Operations*. Consistent with the emerging national policy of worldwide war, the doctrine stressed that war could occur in a number of theaters. Nonetheless, the emphasis of the 1982 manual was the war in Europe. AirLand reflected the army's newfound emphasis on the operational level of war,[42] and the battlefield was now perceived to be extended, perhaps tens to hundreds of kilometers in depth. The importance of engaging the Soviets from positions throughout the extended battlefield (in close, rear, or deep theaters) was emphasized throughout the document.

Maneuver as a complement to firepower was stressed, and the active defense was rejected in favor of a variety of defensive maneuvers, appropriate for the fluid nature of the envisaged battlefield. The emphasis once placed on getting in the first blow was replaced with an emphasis on extended battles and engagements. The new doctrine emphasized the importance of combined service operations, and a number of joint procedures with the air force were worked out by the doctrine's planners.[43] AirLand also sought to depart from its predecessor's somewhat mechanistic view of warfare and refocused on the human element of war.

In its statement of purpose, AirLand echoed the national emphasis on seizing the initiative:

> AirLand Battle Doctrine . . . is based on securing or retaining the initiative and exercising it aggressively to defeat the enemy. . . . The AirLand Battle will be dominated by the force that retains the initiative and, with deep attack and decisive maneuver, destroys its opponent's abilities to fight and to organize in depth.
>
> Initiative, the ability to set the terms of battle by action, is the greatest advantage in war. Whether US forces are attacking or defending, they must seize and preserve the initiative to hasten the enemy's defeat and to prevent his recovery.[44]

Gaining the initiative was a key ingredient of the manual's highly assertive approach to the land war. Also indicative of this new approach was the emphasis now put on offensive operations as the key to victory. This was a marked change from the active defense, which was so cautious in planning for offensive operations. In describing offensive actions, the 1982 manual stressed that the commander employ a tactical combination of maneuver and firepower. The aim of maneuver was to facilitate the indirect approach to defeating overwhelming forces or to "focus maximum strength against the enemy's weakest point, thereby gaining strategic advantage." Firepower provided the necessary force to support maneuver, through the "skillful coordination of fire in depth with the movement of large units."[45]

Defensive operations were envisaged to be fluid and encompassing the entire battlefield. Unlike the active defense, which relied heavily on carefully coordinated lateral movements by the defending force, defensive maneuvers under AirLand encompassed a number of techniques ranging from static positional defenses to deeper and more dynamic configurations. Altogether, defensive operations had five complementary elements: deep battle operations in the area forward of the contact line, covering force operations in support of the main battle, the main effort in the main battle area, rear-area protection operations, and reserve operations supporting the main effort.[46]

Ultimately, the army wants to be able to perform deep operations while relying strictly upon its own organic assets. A number of long-range weapon systems, such as the multiple launch rocket system (MLRS), are being developed and procured precisely for that purpose. But such systems are only beginning to be deployed, and there is some question as to whether sufficient quantities for extensive long-range operations will be attainable over the next decade or so. The army, therefore, has had to rely on the air force for long-range operations. Thus, army–air force cooperation is an essential element of the AirLand concept.

The air force has signed on to AirLand, as discussed below, and officials from both the army and the air force have worked closely to resolve a number of potentially contentious issues. These involve the command of theater assets and delegation of theater missions. A 1981 agreement worked out by the two services detailed theater responsibilities and command authority, thus breaking this potential logjam.[47] The air force agreed to apportion tactical aircraft for various roles and missions as determined by the guidance of the joint force commander. "The key feature of the agreement," writes Romjue, "was Army recognition of Air Force management and selection of its deep attack capabilities, and Air Force recognition of the corps function of locating and prioritizing targets for battlefield air interdiction."[48]

Numerous other agreements were reached between the army and the air force, culminating in the Joint Attack of the Second

Echelon Joint Service Agreement (J-SAK) of November 1984,[49] and the December 1984 publication of the J-SAK Procedures Manual. The J-SAK, which was signed by both the air force and army chiefs of staff, attempted to further institutionalize army and air force cooperation in operations and procurement procedures.

In 1986, FM 100-5 was again revised. The new manual provided few substantive doctrinal changes from the 1982 version. Essentially, the new manual

- maintained the offensive orientation of the 1982 manual but provided a better balance with the defense. As one commentator has noted, "Within the expanded discussion of the operational level of war, the new manual also explains how offensive actions fit into major defensive operations and campaigns."[50]

- emphasized that deep operations must be closely synchronized with close and rear operations. This was to address the criticism that the 1982 version's emphasis on deep strikes drew down air support assets from the close and rear theaters.

- attempted to make AirLand compatible with NATO's Allied Tactical Publication (ATP) 35(A), *Land Force Tactical Doctrine*.[51] The doctrine remained distinctive from NATO doctrine, however; it was a general guide for U.S. Army operations worldwide and was not to be restrictive to operations in the European theater. (Changes in NATO doctrine are discussed, below).

- emphasized further that the future battle could involve nuclear and chemical operations and that the army had to be prepared to fight in all such environments.

- reemphasized the essential importance of effective joint operations: "All ground actions above the level of the smallest engagements will be strongly affected by the supporting air operations of one or both combatants."[52] The manual apparently "clears up root concerns" the air force had over AF theater-wide vs. army corps-level perspectives, especially concerning theater-wide flexibility of air power vs. corps-level needs for guaranteed air interdiction.[53]

Most newly planned or actual army and air force procurements are at least consistent with, if not determined by, AirLand doctrine. The F-15, F-16, and F-111 are all capable of performing interdiction missions. To enhance their ability to perform missions against echelon forces operating in the dark or in bad weather, the air force plans to provide those planes with the highly sophisticated Low Altitude Navigation and Targeting Infrared System for Night (LAN-

TIRN).[54] The air force is also seeking to enhance its reconnaissance capabilities—an essential on the extended battlefield. Some army units use attack helicopter scouts to radio reconnaissance updates, but the army hopes that modern electronics will provide a more reliable means of accomplishing this mission. As such, a number of radio and reconnaissance electronics programs are being developed. They include the All Source Analysis System (ASAS) to collect and correlate data with other targeting information, and two new radios, the Single Channel Ground and Airborne Radio System (SINCGARS) and the Mobile Subscriber Equipment (MSE). Jointly the services are developing the Joint Surveillance and Targeting Attack Radar (JSTARS) to serve as a long-term surveillance system.

Criticisms of the AirLand doctrine have focused on its dependence on the air force to carry out critical support missions, its assumption that Soviet-Pact forces will attack in a two-echelon deployment, and its neglect of Soviet–Warsaw Pact doctrine in effecting the outcome of the battle.[55] As discussed, AirLand does rely on the air force, but until the army procures the long-range capabilities it envisages, the situation is unavoidable. The other arguments, however, require some elaboration.

The successful prosecution of AirLand depends on the United States finding and destroying the Soviet second echelon. Yet, there is no certainty that the Soviets would attack in such a manner. In the face of forward deployments, such as planned by NATO, the Soviets may group into single echelons and employ mobile groups to break through enemy defenses, opening the way for major attacking forces.[56] Major Jon Powell has summarized this view: "If our forces seek and attempt to strike enemy second echelons [supposedly forming deep to the rear], they will attack phantoms while the real and most immediate threat confronts them face to face."[57]

However, the 1986 manual states that the U.S. Army must be prepared to fight at the forward line of troops (FLOT) while *simultaneously* attacking the enemy in depth. The necessity of coordination between close, rear, and deep operations is stressed. The United States may presently lack the capability to engage in a number of arenas, but the necessity of attaining such a capability is not neglected in the doctrine.

Another criticism of AirLand was that it did not adequately account for Soviet doctrine, which calls for the employment of Operational Maneuver Groups (OMGs) as a preemptive component of WPO/Pact follow-on attacks. The mission of the OMG is to conduct "pre-emptive raiding of the enemy's rear area. . . . Unlike first- or second-echelon forces, OMGs will penetrate ahead and create conditions for rapid advances by main body forces. Constituted with a strength of 20% of the main force . . . OMGs will operate on multiple axes of advance."[58]

OMGs are designed to quickly penetrate NATO defenses and counteract deep-striking U.S. and NATO ground forces as they are encountered. OMG attacks could therefore negate AirLand operations by depleting U.S. forces that would otherwise be dedicated to defeating the second echelon forces.

But the capabilities of the OMG may in some cases be overestimated. The OMG will be highly dependent on surprise and speed. To fully exploit such factors, the OMGs must meet and penetrate into NATO defenses within 48 hours or so. After that, NATO command will have an opportunity to at least begin mobilization. In attacking, the OMGs will have to bypass NATO defensive strongholds. As Guy Swan notes, "The risk then becomes one of whether operational/strategic objectives can be seized before NATO can redirect its strength at the rear or open flanks of penetrating forces."[59] Soviet OMGs attempting such attacks would have to maneuver through terrain scattered with NATO land mines, which could greatly hinder their movement. There is also some question as to whether the OMGs would have adequate air support and air cover, and they could be cut off from critical reinforcement. Such factors could seriously diminish OMG effectiveness.[60]

THE AIR FORCE: INITIATIVE, INTEGRATION, AIRLAND

Unlike the army and the navy, the air force did not announce any sweeping doctrinal or strategic planning breakthroughs in this era. The air force's 1983 version of its doctrinal manual, AFM 1-1, reaffirmed its commitment to support the national strategy and emphasized the importance of attaining the initiative in the offensive. The primary objectives for the employment of air assets remained controlling the enemy's air space, wearing down his will to fight, and destroying his war-waging capabilities. But two concepts that began to emerge in the post–massive retaliation years continued to be prominently discussed. One had to do with the tactical air campaign. Where tactical missions were once considered no more than a planning inconvenience, the manual now emphasized that "strategic and tactical actions are not mutually exclusive and to consider one in isolation of the other disregards their interdependence and their synergistic influence in warfare."[61]

The second concept had to do with integrated operations. In older manuals, the air force repeatedly asserted the decisiveness of air forces in battle. In the 1975 manual, the role of balanced force operations was introduced. Now, it was emphasized:

> Military operations are coordinated actions. . . . To accomplish national military objectives, our military forces train to fight as an integrated and interdependent team of land, naval, and aerospace forces. . . . The doctrine of unified action describes how US military forces are integrated and employed with unity of effort.[62]

In particular, the manual endorsed the army's new focus on deep operations in the enemy rear. AirLand was not named directly, probably indicating that many disagreements over specifics remained to be resolved. Nonetheless, the importance of rear area operations was featured:

> Neutralizing or destroying rear echelon targets will generate stresses and strains on the enemy by disrupting his scheme of operation and depleting his resources. . . . While the urgency of enemy actions may require direct attacks against forces in contact, efficient use of air forces should emphasize attack in depth upon those targets that deny the enemy the time and space to employ forces effectively.[63]

Finally, the new manual introduced a new term, Battlefield Air Interdiction (BAI), defined as "attacks against hostile surface targets which are in a position to directly affect friendly forces, but are not in close proximity to friendly forces."[64] While the distinction between BAI and "the remainder of the interdiction effort" is not entirely clear, the apparent inference is that BAI corresponds to shorter range attacks and is therefore relevant to close battle operations.

FOFA: NATO'S NEW STRATEGIC CONCEPT

Of course, Soviet second echelons and OMGs are NATO problems as much as, if not more than, U.S. Army AirLand problems. General Bernard Rogers, until recently Supreme Allied Commander, Europe (SACEUR), developed a concept to counter Soviet second echelon attacks. As Rogers explained, the objective of "Follow-On Forces Attacks" (FOFA) is "to attack with conventional weapons those enemy forces which stretch from just behind the troops in contact to as far into the enemy's rear as our target acquisition and conventional weapons systems will permit." Rogers explained that "in recent years, some promising improvements in acquiring targets and in the lethality, range, and accuracy of conventional weapons have made FOFA a much more realistic subconcept."[65]

FOFA shares conceptual similarities to the AirLand doctrine. Both stress the importance of attacking Soviet troops in the second echelon. As such, FOFA has been subjected to many of the same criticisms as AirLand. For example, critics have maintained that the doctrine does not adequately account for Soviet behavior, which may not involve echeloning. The Soviets may instead mass their forces for full-scale attacks against NATO General Defensive Positions (GDP). FOFA has been called to task for inadequately addressing the OMG threat. Finally, FOFA has been criticized as no more than AirLand doctrine applied to NATO operations.

However, in a December 1984 discussion of FOFA, General Rogers emphasized that the key to successful NATO operations is the defense against the Soviet lead-attacking echelons. Rogers listed three priorities that NATO has pursued for the purpose of strengthening the GDP. The first was to improve the forces already committed to thwarting the lead attacks at the GDP. In so doing, NATO would reduce its reliance on reinforcements and therefore defeat a primary goal of Soviet doctrine. The second priority was to improve and modernize the weapons systems these forces would operate. The third was to augment NATO's force structure with mobilizable and highly trained reserves.[66] If realized, Rogers argued, these objectives could strengthen NATO's capabilities against Pact forces attacking at the GDP *and* against the follow-on forces.

Rogers emphasized that OMGs were accounted for: "We consider the OMG to be a high priority target for FOFA, and for early counterattack should it penetrate our General Defensive Position. Much of the new target detection and sensing capability we seek to acquire is necessary for us to identify which follow-on forces are organized as OMGs so they can be attacked early on." He addressed the possibility that the Soviets could compress part of their second-echelon forces into their first echelon to form a massive attacking force: "Not only are we aware of this possibility, we also take account of the fact that terrain can only accommodate a finite number of Warsaw Pact battalions abreast, thus causing the rest to be out of contact, i.e., to be follow-on forces."[67]

Rogers also addressed the similarities and differences between AirLand and FOFA, and he detailed the independent development of FOFA within NATO, to show that its development was rooted in NATO efforts to strengthen conventional capabilities going as far back as 1979. He noted a number of specific differences: for example, FOFA does not focus on the integrated use of conventional, nuclear, and chemical weapons to the extent that AirLand does; FOFA specifically rejects preemptive attacks. "We are a defensive alliance and as such will never fire the first shot." Finally, FOFA has no qualms with relying on air assets for the successful prosecution of deep strikes and does not plan for attacks into the enemy's rear with ground forces. "We will, however, use the counterattack—the essence of a viable defence—to restore our borders."

It remains unclear, however, how AirLand and FOFA would be reconciled in the event of hostilities. Rogers states emphatically that

> although some of NATO's national forces operate under tactical and operational doctrines and procedures which exhibit varying approaches to land combat, all forces which would come under SACEUR's command in the event of war would operate under an ACE [Allied Command Europe] Chain of Command and ACE policies, doctrine and concepts—not those of any single Alliance nation.[68]

It is difficult to imagine U.S. troops aggressively attacking behind enemy lines if the remainder of NATO forces are staying back. In the European theater, NATO doctrine would take precedence over U.S. operational doctrine. One notes, however, that in general FOFA and AirLand are consonant, and this consonance provides a basis for accommodation.

CONCLUSION

It does not appear that the Reagan administration assumed office with a clear vision of future military strategy. Yet the Reagan years saw a renaissance in military thought. The basic assertiveness at the root of the Reagan administration's military policies and strategies permeated all the services. It led to an aggressive naval strategy intent on regaining maritime superiority and to a joint army–air force doctrine intent on fighting and winning not just the first salvo but the protracted campaign. For all its makeshift, build-as-you-go qualities, the Reagan defense program can be seen as fairly consistent and organized.

As a collection of global policies, strategies, and doctrines, the Reagan administration's initiatives serve as conclusive evidence that the United States had broken from the self-imposed shackles of Vietnam. Along with the Reagan Doctrine, which posits the right of the United States to aid Third World guerrilla movements struggling against communist dictatorships, the new strategies and doctrines that emerged in this era reflected the administration's efforts to reverse the inward turn of the seventies. If nothing else, they were successful on that level. Whether the 1986 reorganization will effectively reform the procurement process remains to be seen.

NOTES

1. Zbigniew Brzezinski, *Power and Principle* (New York: Farrar, Straus, Giroux, 1983), p. 485.
2. Jimmy Carter, "Address Before the World Affairs Council of Philadelphia," May 9, 1980, in Public Papers of the Presidents, *Administration of Jimmy Carter, 1980,* book 1 (Washington: GPO, 1981), pp. 867–874.
3. Jimmy Carter, "State of the Union Address," January 1980.
4. In his memoirs, Carter specifically notes that the warning was addressed to the Soviets and adds, "I had already discussed my concerns about the Persian Gulf area with the Soviet leaders during the Vienna summit conference in June 1979, but their subsequent invasion of Afghanistan made it necessary to repeat the warning in clearer terms."

   Carter elaborates on the doctrine by noting that the statement "would have been backed by concerted action, not necessarily confined to any small invaded area or to tactics or terrain of the Soviets' choosing. We simply could not afford to let them extend their domination to adjacent areas around the Persian Gulf which were so important to us and to other nations of the world." Jimmy Carter, *Keeping Faith* (New York: Bantam, 1982), p. 483.
5. Harold Brown, *Thinking About National Security* (Boulder, Colorado: Westview, 1983), p. 147.
6. Brown, *Thinking,* p. 155. Brown also points out that the United States has conducted numerous joint exercises with friends and allies in the region.
7. For a detailed critique of the RDJTF, see William Kaufmann, *Planning Conventional Forces 1950–1980* (Washington, D.C.: The Brookings Institution, 1982).
8. See Congressional Quarterly, *U.S. Defense Policy,* 3d ed., (Washington, D.C.: Congressional Quarterly, Inc, 1983), p. 120.

9. Ronald Reagan, statement of March 3, 1984, *Current News* (Washington, D.C.: U.S. Department of Defense, January–June, 1984), p. 33.

10. Reagan's second National Security Adviser William Clark made the point: "At that time our strategy was a collection of departmental policies which had been developed during the Administration's first year in office." White House News Release, "Remarks of Judge William Clark," at the Center for Strategic and International Affairs, Georgetown University, May 21, 1982, p. 2, quoted in James Lacy, *Within Bounds: The Navy in Postwar American Security Policy* (Alexandria, Virginia: Center for Defense Analyses, 1983), p. 505.

11. See Dennis S. Ippolito, "Defense Budgets and Spending Control," in William P. Snyder and James Brown, eds., *Defense Policy in the Reagan Administration* (Washington, D.C.: National Defense University Press, September, 1988), p. 170.

12. See, for example, Casper Weinberger, *Annual Report to the Congress, FY88*, executive summary, p. 8.

13. NSDD-32 is classified; its elements are discussed in Hearings, *Department of Defense Authorization for Appropriations, Fiscal Year 1985*, Committee on Armed Services, U.S. Senate, 98th Cong., 2nd sess., March–May 1984, part 8: *Sea Power and Force Projection*, p. 3854.

14. Weinberger, *Annual Report FY1983*, p. I-91.

15. Weinberger, *Annual Report FY1983*, p. I-15.

16. Weinberger, *Annual Report FY1984*, p. I-16.

17. Weinberger, *Annual Report FY1984*, ibid.

18. Michael M. Boll, *National Security Planning: Roosevelt through Reagan* (Lexington: University Press of Kentucky, 1988), p. 228.

19. Jeffrey Record, "Jousting With Unreality: Reagan's Military Strategy," in Steven Miller, ed., *Conventional Forces and American Defense Policy* (Princeton: Princeton University Press, 1986), p. 71.

20. These criticisms and many others are elaborated in Record, "Jousting With Unreality," pp. 70–78.

21. Casper Weinberger, "U.S. Defense Strategy," *Foreign Affairs* 64, no. 4 (Spring 1986): 686.

22. Weinberger, "U.S. Defense Strategy," p. 689.

23. The President's Blue Ribbon Commission on Defense Management (The Packard Commission), *A Quest For Excellence, Final Report to the President*, June 1986 (Washington, D.C.: GPO, 1986).

24. Frederick H. Hartmann and Robert L. Wendzel, *Defending America's Security* (McLean, Virginia: Pergamon-Brassey's, 1988), p. 181.

25. Hartmann and Wendzel, *Defending America's Security*, p. 182.

26. Figures are from Leonard Sullivan, "The Defense Budget," in George Hudson and Joseph Kruzel, eds., *American Defense Annual, 1985–1986* (Lexington, Massachusetts: Lexington Books, 1985), p. 56.

27. Manpower figures provided by Office of the Assistant Secretary of Defense (Comptroller), *National Defense Estimates for FY1988/1989* (May 1987). Other figures from various tables in Edward Luttwak, *The Pentagon and the Art of War* (New York: Simon and Schuster, 1984), pp. 257–258.

28. William Kaufmann, *A Thoroughly Efficient Navy* (Washington, D.C.: The Brookings Institution, 1987), p. 9.

29. Sea Plan 2000 is discussed in James K. Oliver and James K. Nathan, "The Reagan Defense Program: Concepts, Continuity, and Change," in Stephen J. Cimbala, ed., *The Reagan Defense Program: An Interim Assessment* (Wilmington, Delaware: Scholarly Resources, Inc: 1986), pp. 13–14.

30. Admiral James D. Watkins, "The Maritime Strategy," in *The Maritime Strategy* (Annapolis, Maryland: Naval Institute *Proceedings*), January 1986 supplement.

31. Casper Weinberger, *Department of Defense Annual Report, FY1987*, p. 1979.

32. Watkins, "Maritime Strategy," p. 14.

33. Watkins, "Maritime Strategy," p. 9.

34. Watkins, "Maritime Strategy," p. 9.

35. Watkins, "Maritime Strategy," p. 11. Wakins goes on to say, "Indeed, it is possible that, faced with our determination, the Soviets can be induced to accept war termination while still in this phase." This seems overly optimistic, to say the least.

36. Watkins, "Maritime Strategy," p. 13.

37. Watkins, "Maritime Strategy," p. 10–11.

38. Stansfield Turner and George Thibault, "Preparing For the Unexpected: The Need for a New Military Strategy," *Foreign Affairs* 61, no. 1 (Fall 1982).

39. Questions can also be raised over the logic of counterforce-coercion as the basis of strategy; the ability of the navy to actually implement the strategy in a crisis; the extent to which

the maritime strategy enhances or detracts from deterrence; and whether counterforce-coercion would have a significant effect on the NATO conflict.

40. In U.S. Congress. Senate. *Hearings on Department of Defense Authorization for Appropriations for Fiscal Year 1985*, Committee on Armed Services. 98th Cong., 2nd sess., part 8, *Sea Power and Force Projection*, p. 3865.

41. See P.X. Kelley and Hugh K. O'Donnell, "The Amphibious Warfare Strategy," in Watkins, "The Maritime Strategy," op. cit., p. 23.

42. The "operational level of war" has been defined as that level of hostilities "applicable to the operations of army and corps below the level of military strategy and above the tactics of battles and engagements—in practice the planning and conduct of campaigns." John Romjue, *From Active Defense to AirLand Battle: The Development of Army Doctrine 1973–1982* (Fort Belvoir, Virginia: TRADOC Historical Monograph Series, September 1985), p. 68.

43. These are detailed in Richard Davis, *The 31 Initiatives: A Study in Air Force–Army Cooperation* (Washington, D.C.: Office of Air Force History, United States Air Force, 1987).

44. Army Field Manual 100-5, *Operations* (1982), pp. 1-5, 4-1, 2-1, 7-2.

45. FM 100-5, *op. cit.*, p. 2-4.

46. FM 100-5, *op. cit.*, p. 11-2.

47. U.S. Army and U.S. Air Force, *USA and USAF Agreement on Apportionment and Allocation of Offensive Air Support* (OAS), (May 23, 1981), reprinted in Romjue, p. 100.

48. Ibid., p. 63.

49. U.S. Army and U.S. Air Force, *Joint Service Agreement for the Joint Attack of the Second Echelon* (Washington, D.C.: Departments of the Army and the Air Force, November 1984).

50. General William R. Richardson, "FM 100-5: The AirLand Battle in 1986," *Military Review* 66, no. 3 (March 1986): 6.

51. As discussed below, however, there remain important distinctions between AirLand and NATO doctrine.

52. FM 100-5, *Operations* (1986), quoted in Millard Barger, "What USAF Has to Do to Put the 'Air' in AirLand Battle," *Armed Forces Journal International* (June 1986): 58.

53. Ibid., p. 64.

54. Ibid., p. 60. Much of this discussion of AirLand related systems comes from Barger, "What USAF Has to Do," and Romjue, *From Active Defense to AirLand Battle*.

55. See, e.g., Major Jon Powell, "AirLand Battle: The Wrong Doctrine for the Wrong Reason," *Air University Review* 36, no. 4 (May–June 1985).

56. Col. William Hanne, "AirLand Battle: Doctrine, Not Dogma," *Military Review* (June 1983): 17.

57. Powell, *Wrong Doctrine*, p. 17.

58. Captain Guy Swan, "Countering the Daring Thrust," *Military Review* (September 1986): 46.

59. Swan, "Countering," p. 48.

60. These problems and others are discussed in General Donn A. Starry, "The Evolution of US Army Operational Doctrine—Active Defense, AirLand, and Future Trends," in Lars Wallin, ed., *Military Doctrines For Central Europe* (Stockholm: Swedish National Defense Research Institute, 1986), p. 47, and Swan, "Countering."

61. Air Force Manual (AFM) 1-1, *Basic Aerospace Doctrine of the United States Air Force* (Department of the Air Force, 10 May 1983), p. 2-9.

62. AFM 1-1 (1983), p. 1-2, 1-3.

63. AFM 1-1 (1983), p. 2-12.

64. AFM 1-1 (1983), p. 3-4.

65. General Bernard Rogers, "Follow-On Forces Attack: Myths and Realities," *NATO Review* 32, no. 6 (December 1984): 2–3.

66. Rogers, "Follow-On Forces Attack," p. 1.

67. Rogers, "Follow-On Forces Attack," p. 4.

68. Rogers, "Follow-On Forces Attack," p. 7.

69. A good discussion of the Reagan doctrine is in Raymond Copson and Richard Cronin, "The Reagan Doctrine and Its Prospects," *Survival* 29, no. 1 (January/February 1987).

11

U.S. Conventional Force Planning Since World War II

This chapter has two parts. Part one considers the broad lessons of this book in terms of U.S. military planning. It is seen that while there has been much vacillation in the methods chosen to achieve U.S. foreign and defense policy goals, there has also been much continuity. This is particularly the case with respect to the overarching goal of U.S. policy—containment. General conclusions relevant to service planning, force procurement, and the NATO alliance are offered.

Part two is subdivided into two sections. The first looks at the implications of the past for the "seventh era"—the present and the short-term future. The United States is now in the midst of a seventh era of defense planning, and U.S. defense spending will not, at least in the short term, reach the levels of the peak Reagan years. But in terms of U.S.-Soviet relations, the Reagan buildup did seem to have some salutary effects, and many in the Democrat-controlled Congress now appear to agree that the United States should not allow an overerosion of U.S. forces. Defense spending will probably not be cut back dramatically. Part two also considers the long-term implications of this history.

PART ONE

VACILLATION AND CONTINUITY IN AMERICAN DEFENSE PLANNING

Despite the vacillations in postwar U.S. military planning, there has been remarkable continuity in U.S. decision making for defense, particularly with respect to containment. In this light, then, it can be said that varying administrations have had different ideas of how that objective should be reached. Each has tried to tailor its strategies for meeting that objective to its own view of the seriousness of the threat, its assessment of the challenges and opportunities available, and its conception of what the country could afford to expend on defense.

Certain factors have consistently influenced U.S. officials in planning new strategies of containment, in effect creating the parameters within which planning has proceeded. The generally shared perception these officials have held about the nature of the postwar system and certain geographic realities that influence U.S. defense planning and procurement profoundly affect the manner by which the services conceptualize their own roles, missions, and strategies and the forces the United States procures.

THE POSTWAR SYSTEM In the aftermath of World War II, two European alliances—NATO and the Warsaw Pact—soon emerged. Each was dominated by one of the superpowers, and the nature of the postwar system was soon consolidated: two opposing alliances with sharply different political systems and beliefs emerged in Europe to battle for the allegiance of other nation states elsewhere.

As leaders of the Atlantic alliance, U.S. decision makers have all perceived themselves as reacting to Communist threats to Europe and the Third World. This defensive orientation and the emphasis U.S. decision makers have placed on the preservation of Western democratic freedoms have been the most essential components of continuity throughout the postwar era. They reflect the idea U.S. decision makers have of the world and the U.S. role in that world.

An important implication of this bilateralism is observed in the basic European thrust of U.S. planning. Postwar planning has largely been based on the proposition that if the Soviet threat to Europe is contained, Third World threats will be as well. This has not always been the case, but planning has proceeded in this manner nonetheless.

GEOGRAPHIC REALITIES Whereas the Soviet Union is adjacent to its East European allies, the United States is separated from its European allies by the Atlantic Ocean. Indeed, the United States is essentially an "island" nation. Not only must it procure forces to fight a war, it must devote considerable resources to procuring the means for sending men and materiel to a conflict. This affects U.S. planning for Europe as well as conflicts in other areas. For example, both the United States and the USSR have interests in the Persian Gulf. The Soviet Union shares a common border with Iran and can both station troops near the border and rely on quick mobilization from the central USSR-based strategic reserve. The United States, however, must rely primarily on the navy to protect its interests in this theater, and to get its forces to this distant theater in a time of crisis. The United States can also count on rapid redeployment of forces stationed in Europe, but this would obviously deplete the forces there. Whether or not such redeployment would be realistic would depend upon the nature of the conflict and the parties involved.

The problem of transporting forces raises significant questions about force procurement. Planners calculating service requirements tend to give priority to force acquisition first, and airlift and sea-lift procurement after that. Yet in a crisis, such transport capabilities would be essential for effective U.S. operations. Problems related to airlift and sea-lift will continue as long as the services are responsible for providing their own forces and determining their own requirements.

Geographic realities dictate that the United States procure a vastly different mix of forces than the Soviet Union. The USSR is essentially a landlocked country, and its pattern of force procurement, with a strong army component, reflects this. While a navy benefits the Soviet Union in the Persian Gulf, for example, the Soviet Union has (at least until recently) concentrated on massing its armies along its common border with Iran. Similarly, the USSR consistently devotes a significant amount of its defense budget to maintaining a large standing army on its common border with the People's Republic of China. In Europe and at home, the Soviet Union has deployed a massive standing army with divisions throughout Eastern Europe.

In contrast, the United States has tended to deemphasize the army in the overall strategic planning process. This is not to say that the army has not played an important role, for example, in maintaining deterrence in the European and Korean theaters. Indeed, before the Korean and Vietnam wars, U.S. planning emphasized the land service. But in the postwar era, the army has generally not been the dominant force in U.S. defense planning. The fact that the threat is an ocean away has dictated that the United States concentrate its force procurement on long-range, mobile forces. This has generally led to an emphasis on the navy and the air force in the planning process. These services also supply the aforementioned transport capabilities upon which the army is dependent.

As discussed, however, there has been much vacillation with respect to how the United States has sought to implement containment. There has been a tendency for new administrations to base their defense programs on either the budget (how much they think the nation can afford or will support) or the threat (their perception of the nature and extent of the threat to U.S. national security). This is a matter of emphasis. At no time in history were considerations of either the budget or the threat ignored by decision makers. Nor can it be said that planning based on budgetary conservatism has necessarily been strategically unsound. In the context of his times, Eisenhower's policies were clearly well rooted in a strategic context, however wise or unwise that context may have been. Nonetheless, there has been a persistent vacillation in emphasis.

Alternate eras have seen different services emphasized as the basis of planning. Thus the post-NSC–68 Truman administration, the Kennedy administration, and the Reagan administration all supervised buildups of the U.S. armed services. But Truman and Kennedy emphasized the army, while Reagan emphasized the navy. Similarly, immediately following World War II, throughout the entire Eisenhower administration, and throughout the 1970s, the budget was emphasized in determining defense priorities. In the first two periods, the air force was the favored service but not in the 1970s. In the era of retrenchment, no service did particularly well.

THE SERVICES

The vacillation in emphasis described above has numerous implications for the services charged with implementing national strategy. Perhaps most important is that, given the likelihood of potentially radical changes in the distribution of the defense budget every few years, long-range service planning becomes extremely difficult. A service that in one era is emphasized cannot count on maintaining that lofty position indefinitely. Its share of the budget may be cut back when a new administration with new strategic priorities takes office. This was certainly the army's experience when Eisenhower assumed the presidency. Conversely, a service that has been largely ignored by one administration may find itself suddenly thrust into a prominent position by the next president. This happened to the army in the Kennedy administration and to the navy in the Reagan administration.

Along with numerous other factors, these uncertainties make it difficult for service planners to think in terms longer than five years—the traditional service-planning horizon. Developing long-term procurement plans, therefore, may appear to be an exercise in futility. As such, it becomes all too easy for short-term considerations to dominate the planning process. This short-term focus has two deleterious results. First, procurement costs are driven up; second, factors not related to the geostrategic threat—including the budgetary process and service parochialism—take on roles of elevated importance in the planning process.

The problem is that budget-related factors can sometimes lead to strategies and doctrines that are not necessarily the most effective for promoting U.S. national security. For example, the Pentomic Divisions stand as an army reorganization that was not determined by sensible military considerations or by an appreciation of what the service was best suited to do. Creating the Pentomic Divisions was not wise policy, yet their formation seemed to be the most effective means of ensuring a steady flow of budgetary resources to the army. Similarly, the swing strategy of the mid-1970s clearly stretched the navy's operational capabilities beyond reason. To have implemented the strategy may very well have exhausted naval resources and led to the abdication of U.S. responsibilities in the Pacific Far East. The strategy was based on a perception, shared by Carter's military decision makers, of what the nation could not afford—more ships. The result was a gross mismatch of resources and potential commitments and of interests and capabilities to meet those interests.

As for parochialism, it would no doubt emerge even if service planners could be assured of their respective service's place in the planning process over the long term. Service parochialism is to be expected from individuals who have dedicated significant parts of their lives to an institution and who have given their allegiance to its traditions and mores. It may also be somewhat unrealistic to expect that strategies of containment could, or for that matter should, be long term. As the geostrategic environment changes, so will the threat. As the threat evolves, so must the strategies for containing it, if the strategies are to be effective. In turn, evolving strategies will emphasize different services.

Of course, military planners should not allow the interests of their own service to distort their view of what is best for the nation. But parochialism can have some beneficial effect. In determining the services' role in national military policy or in actual combat situations, service representatives should be expected to put the best case forward for their respective service. Then an effective authority, particularly the secretary of defense, must sort through the service arguments, filter out the obviously infeasible aspects, and make the hard decisions about the role of the services in both policy and in wartime operations. This may be the most enduring lesson of the Reagan administration, where such an authority was generally missing.[1]

Parochialism often stems from long-held conceptions of roles and missions, sheer obstinacy among service decision makers, or organizational inertia. Such impediments to cooperation emerged as early as March 1948 immediately following the Key West meeting of the Joint Chiefs of Staff, when the navy reinterpreted the Key West agreements days after they were reached. They are also evident in the early battles between the army and the fledgling air force over tactical aviation.

Unbridled parochialism hinders effective service planning and can also translate into actual deficiencies in operations. This occurs whether the nation is experiencing generous or parsimonious defense budgets. Army and air force disputes over theater control of aircraft arose in the Korean War and, to a lesser extent, in the Vietnam War. In the Grenada invasion of 1983, the services proved particularly unable to subordinate their own interests to those of the national command. Each successfully vied for a role in the invasion, with the army and navy competing for roles and missions that were clearly better suited to one or the other service. Again, stricter authority should have been imposed upon the services from the OSD and JCS levels but was not. As a result, coordinating efforts between the services was remarkably poor throughout the operation.[2]

The sixth era of global military assertion saw much less overt parochialism among the services in the area of force procurement. But the sixth era was an era of budgetary plenty, when few hard procurement choices were required. Along with the navy, the army and the air force prospered in the 1980s, and this increased cooperation between these two services. Concrete steps have been taken to cement the cooperative relationships, including the signing of numerous memoranda and agreements between army and air force leaders. These agreements are generally intended to cut duplication in weapons procurement and to improve cooperation in combat. But the trend toward cutting into the defense budget, which has already begun under President Bush, could lead to the reemergence of blatant parochialism.

FORCE PROCUREMENT

This history shows that forces procured for deterring a war may be less than optimal for fighting one. Conventional forces are expensive; nuclear weapons, relatively speaking, are not. About 40 percent of the defense budget is dedicated to the procurement and modernization of nonnuclear forces, while only about 10 percent of the overall defense budget is dedicated to nuclear force procurement. Given the disparity in cost, it is not surprising that both Truman and Eisenhower sought to rely heavily on atomic weapons when they were unwilling to devote budgetary resources to conventional weapons. But both presidents discovered that nuclear weapons were ineffective in preventing conflicts in the Third World, and subsequent presidents discovered that if the military establishment is to be used in sustained conflict, robust nonnuclear forces are essential.

Indeed, a fundamental conclusion of this book is that, however well-intentioned and budget-conscious the administration, relying heavily on nuclear weapons does not diminish the importance of maintaining robust conventional forces. When the United States attempted to rely too heavily on nuclear weapons in its overall deterrence posture, as it did under Eisenhower, it was not able to exploit this superiority to political advantage. In an era of relative nuclear parity, a heavy reliance on nuclear weapons is simply not an option. The army leaders that argued repeatedly of the dangers of such a reliance were essentially correct. Bilateral nuclear stockpiles may have successfully deterred the superpowers from strategic war and from war in Europe, but they have not effectively prevented the United States or the Soviet Union from pursuing other military activities "in the national interest."

Too often the United States has not developed a sufficiently flexible and versatile force structure. Because of decisions made at the national level, the army was not prepared for the Korean War. Its doctrine was geared toward a World War II-like conflict, and its forces lacked the sustainability and mobility the Korean War required. Many of its forces were skeletonized. Ironically, in July 1949, George Kennan had urged a buildup of the ground forces, including two mechanized and mobile army divisions prepared to fight "brush" wars when needed. But such divisions were not developed until the army was on a mobilization footing.

Finally, in looking at the forces the services have procured, it is instructive to consider the relationship between planning and technology. While we have focused on the budgetary and other internal factors that influenced these organizations, the technological factors must be noted as well. In general, the possibility of a weapons system functioning at a more sophisticated level than the system it will replace has often driven force procurement and doctrinal innovation. This is seen in the nuclear realm—such as in era three—but it is also quite evident in the conventional realm as well. The army's current AirLand Battle Doctrine is a particularly appropriate example, given its extensive reliance on a whole battery of long-range attack and reconnaissance systems that are only now being fielded. Yet the army has adhered to the AirLand Battle Doctrine since 1982. Technology's influence on force procurement and planning was also a factor, for example, in the army's Pentomic reorganization of the 1950s and the navy's nuclear reorganization of the same period.

As technology becomes increasingly more sophisticated, it will continue to exert a major influence on procurement and planning. Indeed, the Pentagon is now considering a new approach to planning called Competitive Strategies, which is based precisely on the exploitation of technology as the basis of U.S. national security strategy. Competitive Strategies aims to leverage U.S. technological strengths against Soviet weaknesses, that is to make the Soviets respond to U.S. technological initiatives. The Pentagon often points to the radar-evasive Stealth bomber as such an innovation. In one dramatic gesture, the United States plans to render an entire generation of Soviet air defense systems obsolete. It is argued that the Soviets will have to devote considerable resources to the modernization of their air defense network if they are to thwart the new U.S. ability to penetrate its airspace.

However, the Stealth bomber has inadvertently illustrated the problems with a technological orientation. It is no longer certain that it will even be procured. It is exorbitantly expensive, costing as much as $600 million per unit, and the program has reportedly been riddled with management problems and technological difficulties. Arms control initiatives could limit its procurement altogether. Technological innovation is important to the defense planning process. Definite risks exist, however, with viewing technology as a panacea, and future planners must be particularly cognizant of those risks.

THE NATO ALLIANCE

It is remarkable that the NATO alliance has endured throughout the entire postwar era, given that peacetime alliances are usually short lived, that there has been no war to galvanize and strengthen it, and that there have often been formidable divergences in the interests of the parties involved. Instead, the simple threat of war, as embodied by the Warsaw Pact, has provided the common interest around which the alliance has been galvanized. Indeed, the most serious disruptions to alliance cohesion have come when U.S. and European perceptions of the immediacy of the Soviet threat have diverged. Such divergences have at times led to sharp differences over strategy and force procurement. Emerging as early as 1949 during the NATO treaty-ratification debates, these differences reemerged over the Lisbon goals; in the debates, particularly in the late 1960s, over the credibility of the nuclear umbrella; and have reappeared many times since. Indeed, differences in U.S. and European perceptions regarding the immediacy of the Soviet menace are threatening the cohesion of the alliance today.

As the history indicates, the United States has often perceived the Soviet Union as a much more imminent threat to European security than the Europeans. The United States has consistently urged the Europeans to assume a greater share of the defense burden, but in general, they have backed away from such a commitment. Even when the United States withdrew troops from the European theater to fight the Vietnam War, the Europeans did not act to fill this gap. For their part, the Europeans have generally preferred to rely on the U.S.-provided nuclear umbrella than commit themselves to an extensive conventional force buildup.

Generally the United States has perceived its own security as highly interwoven with that of the Europeans and has provided much of the forces, including the nuclear forces required for the nuclear umbrella, required for European security. There has therefore been little incentive for the Europeans to pick up their share of the defense burden. This situation momentarily appeared to change in the late 1970s, when the NATO members agreed to 3 percent annual increases in their defense budgets, but in fact, most of the alliance members did not meet this obligation.

Now, the terms of the military relationship appear to be changing dramatically. To many in Europe, the Soviet threat appears to have diminished. In large part, this is due to the rhetoric and activities of Soviet General Secretary Mikhail Gorbachev, who has pursued a relentless "peace offensive" aimed at reducing tensions in the European theater. Gorbachev has painted a picture of a "common European home," where all the inhabitants of the continent may not always agree on political matters but nonetheless share numerous interests (such as avoiding war) that override these differences. Gorbachev has also committed the Soviet Union to a more defensive-oriented posture, although what this means precisely remains unclear. He has also proposed numerous disarmament proposals for European-based nuclear and conventional forces. Along with President Ronald Reagan, the general secretary has signed the Intermediate-range Nuclear Forces (INF) Treaty eliminating these forces from Europe and announced unilateral cutbacks in Soviet short-range nuclear weapons and conventional forces.

In terms of the European military balance, these unilateral cuts in forces would be insignificant. But in terms of political capital, they have served Gorbachev well. No doubt, Gorbachev is interested in reducing his country's military burden to better allocate resources into the domestic economy. But Gorbachev is just as clearly seeking to divide the Atlantic alliance, and in some ways, he may be achieving his objective. The 1989 dispute between Bonn and Washington over the timing of negotiations on short-range nuclear missiles well illustrates this. Anxious to see more reductions in German-based nuclear weapons systems, the Kohl government argued for immediate negotiations. The Bush administration was much more cautious, arguing that short-range nuclear weapons are necessary to offset the Soviet Union's conventional superiority in Europe and that such negotiations should only occur after significant progress has been made in conventional arms reductions. In short, Bonn was much more willing to accept Gorbachev as representing a reduced threat, but Washington, on the other hand, wanted more concrete signs of change in the Soviets' European policies before rushing into negotiations.

The terms of the debate are changing significantly. Most European governments were once content to rely on U.S. nuclear weapons to compensate for their unwillingness to build robust conventional arsenals. But the very prospect of arms control appears to offer the possibility of eliminating the need to rely upon either. The sense of threat is changing; consequently, the force that galvanized the alliance is also changing. Conventional arms control now seems a distinct possibility, and if close to equal levels of nonnuclear arms can be achieved, the West's concern over Warsaw Pact superiority in that realm declines. As that occurs, the utility of both the U.S. strategic nuclear umbrella and short-range nuclear missiles also appears to diminish.

The quandaries facing the European alliance are but one element of a changing world order. Clearly, Gorbachev is but one challenge facing the United States in the seventh era. That era, and its implications for U.S. defense planning in light of the above discussion, is considered in part two.

PART TWO

IMPLICATIONS FOR THE SEVENTH ERA

The United States is now in the early stages of a seventh era. As stated at the outset of this chapter, the next few years should see some scaling back of the defense budget, although not drastically.

Moreover, diplomacy will play a greater role in U.S. foreign policy, but the military component will not be excessively downplayed. Indeed, while the prospects for significant arms control in conventional forces now appear promising, the administration will undoubtedly argue the importance of maintaining robust, highly ready forces until a formal agreement is reached. Defense spending will probably not decline too deeply.

As of this writing, the Bush administration is beginning to provide a clue to its national security and defense policies. It has completed a major review of extant policy, but early indications are that these reviews have essentially codified Reagan's policies. Whether or not this remains the case in terms of the Bush administration's program is still to be seen. What can be discerned, however, are certain characteristics of the present era that distinguish it from era six and will have to be accounted for in any future policy formation.

MODERATION A recession in the near future could lead to dramatic cutbacks in defense spending, and an abruptly more aggressive Soviet Union could lead to increases in defense procurement. Either, or both, is possible. Most likely, however, defense spending and procurement will not reach the heights of the Reagan years but will not be scaled back so dramatically as to represent a fifth-era retrenchment.

George Bush represents the moderate wing of his party. He is not likely to push defense spending beyond sixth-era levels and will probably have to settle for less in any case. Nonetheless, Bush has made clear his commitment to follow through on much of the Reagan defense agenda, including strategic force modernization, the Strategic Defense Initiative (SDI), and new nuclear and nonnuclear force procurement. Bush also backs the Pentagon's Competitive Strategies program, discussed above. However, the seventh era should be one of declining budgets, and following through on the considerable procurement Bush's commitments would entail will be increasingly difficult.

In contrast to all of these potentially expensive propositions, however, is Bush's enthusiastic support for a conventional arms control agreement, particularly one cutting forces in Europe. In May 1989, the Soviets announced their willingness to make drastic cuts in their European-based conventional forces, and this was greeted with enthusiasm from Bush administration officials, including the president himself. At a NATO summit in late May, Bush made a dramatic proposal responding to the Soviet initiatives, calling for truly significant cuts in U.S. forces in Europe.[3] Thus, an agreement cutting conventional armaments may be realizable in the short term. Bush has also endorsed the work of the Reagan-appointed Packard Commission, which was charged with recommending reforms of the Pentagon's procurement process. The Packard Commission's recommendations were largely disregarded by Caspar Weinberger but may be given greater accord by Bush's Defense Secretary Cheney, particularly in light of the 1988 Pentagon procurement scandal.

A NEW NATIONAL SECURITY FRAMEWORK? While the administration's overall planning priorities are not yet discernable, it may be feasible to assume that some effort to rethink U.S. national security requirements will emerge from the administration. Early clues to this new framework are already emerging. In a series of speeches delivered in May of 1989, Bush introduced the notion of "moving beyond containment, to seek to integrate the Soviets into the community of nations, to help them share the rewards of international cooperation." A senior member of the National Security Staff described the concept as "a positive reaction to reform in the Soviet Union and a radical conceptual departure for American policy in the postwar period toward the U.S.S.R."[4] Whether this description proves correct remains to be seen. But one can speculate as to what U.S. policy would be, if containment was truly deemphasized in U.S. policy.

As shown, U.S. policy toward Europe has been the most representative manifestation of U.S. national security policy as a whole. Thus, it is not surprising that Bush would use the occasion of a NATO summit to announce his dramatic arms control proposals for conventional forces based in Europe. As mentioned, the Soviet threat, particularly to Europe, has tended to dictate U.S. military policies, and as that threat appears to be diminishing, such proposals appear increasingly viable. But a diminution of the threat to Europe could lead to an emphasis on potential threats elsewhere. Thus, a new national security framework could emphasize U.S. economic interests in the Pacific region, where Japan, Taiwan, the Republic of Korea, and, to a lesser extent, Malaysia and Singapore are becoming increasingly strong economic powers.

A new framework that attempts to account for new economic powers would also seek to account for new military powers. Such a framework may anticipate future U.S. requirements for low-intensity conflict (LIC). In particular, many observers anticipate that over the next few years, numerous Third World powers will acquire highly sophisticated weapons, including ballistic missiles and advanced conventional munitions, and that the United States could become more involved in regional and local conflicts. That was the conclusion of a 1988 government-sponsored report on the future security environment. In that report, it was noted that

> technology has already produced weapons systems that could be effective against major United States and Soviet weapons systems. The use of antiship cruise missiles by Argentina, Iraq, and Iran has made this clear, as has the use of short-range ballistic missiles by Iraq and Iran. . . . [Such systems] could proliferate to give countries the ability to deny sea or air space to American or Soviet patrols in crisis, and to raise the military "cost of entry" if either superpower wished to intervene against the state possessing them.[5]

The process of procuring such forces could be facilitated by a conventional arms accord in Europe. Cuts in European forces could require some of the heavy forces stationed there to be repositioned in the United States. This could provide a surplus of such forces and create incentives to develop the lighter, more mobile and flexible forces required for the conduct of LIC.

There should be greater emphasis on basing forces in the continental U.S. (CONUS). A number of recent developments indicate that the trend toward centralization has already begun. They include the creation of two CONUS-based unified commands—the Special Operations Command formed in April 1987 and the U.S. Forces Command established in July of that year. The former is commissioned to enhance the U.S. capability for rapid access to trouble spots requiring the application of special operations forces. The latter is configured to ensure the timely deployment of U.S. ground forces and is primarily an army command. Other possible indicators are the army's reorganization of two of its divisions into "light" divisions, as discussed in chapter 10; the navy's new emphasis on Strategic Home Porting; and the development of forces with multimission capability, such as the air force's new Advanced Tactical Fighter (ATF).

National strategy and service planning efforts will no doubt reflect the concepts at the heart of the new emerging framework. The navy, for example, may develop a new version of the maritime strategy that will include a contraction of overall objectives in Europe and greater emphasis on meeting threats elsewhere. Elements of parochialism can be expected to reemerge. In the last few years, numerous mechanisms to control parochialism and encourage service cooperation in all aspects of the defense acquisition and procurement process have been institutionalized. These include measures agreed upon by the services themselves, such as the joint army–air force 31 initiatives intended to enhance their force procurement and doctrinal coordination[6] and measures imposed by Congress, such as the Goldwater-Nichols DOD Reorganization Act of 1986. The coming era will severely test the effectiveness of these reforms.

The perception of an imposing threat to U.S. security, which the Reagan administration deftly exploited to justify its military buildup, has diminished. In Reagan's second term, a new superpower detente was established; Reagan embraced arms control and signed the first superpower accord (the INF Treaty) requiring actual reductions in nuclear arms. Negotiations for a strategic arms reduction treaty (START) made significant progress, and the basis for talks on reducing European-based conventional forces was established. The Bush administration has pursued these initiatives, in particular the latter.

The sense of a reduced threat was also facilitated by the diplomatic skills of the Soviet General Secretary Mikhail Gorbachev. Under Gorbachev, the Soviets withdrew their forces from Afghanistan and ended their involvement in the Angolan civil war. In an unprecedented summit held in the People's Republic of China in May 1989, Gorbachev and Chinese leaders negotiated an end to their long-standing feud, and Gorbachev has even proposed removing significant numbers of Soviet and Chinese forces massed along their common border. All of these activities—Gorbachev's overtures to the Europeans and the Chinese and his numerous initiatives at home aimed at revitalizing the Soviet economy (*perestroika*) and permitting greater political freedom (*glasnost*) for the Soviet people—have combined to create the impression of a reasonable, sophisticated Soviet leader not shackled to the ideological baggage of the past. Of course, few assume that Gorbachev's motives are entirely altruistic; obviously, his initiatives are all in the Soviet political and military interest and, in some instances, at the potential expense of the West. Nonetheless, the fact remains that while most Americans and Europeans continue to see Gorbachev as a potential threat to Western security, he is also seen as a man whom the West (in Margaret Thatcher's words) "can do business with."

Commensurate with this sense of a reduced threat has been a rise in the public's concern about the budget deficit. Most analysts agree that the budget deficit simply must be brought down, that the "excesses" of the Reagan years must be reined in, and that the Pentagon procurement process is out of control. No doubt, the Defense Department budget will be a prime target for congressional budget cutters. In this vein, the seventh era can be said to have begun with the FY1986 defense budget, when outlays for defense began to decline.

In a bipartisan budget agreement with the Democrat-controlled Congress reached in April 1989, the Bush administration agreed to a defense-budget ceiling of $299.2 billion in outlays (and $305.5 billion in overall authority) for FY1990. Secretary of Defense Richard Cheney then took on the ardous task of slicing approximately $22 billion from the administration's initial five-year defense plan. As discussed below, the Pentagon plan took these reductions primarily from the procurement account.

TOUGHER AND LEANER FORCES   In his FY1989 report to Congress, former Secretary of Defense Frank Carlucci wrote that

> Over the last few years, domestic economic considerations once again have dictated the level of defense spending, as reducing the federal deficit became the primary objective in setting the level and allocation of federal resources. . . .
>   Just as in the 1970s, we are being forced to delay important programs, reduce training, defer maintenance, and curtail plans to complete stockpiles of ammunition, spare parts, and other essential equipment.[7]

Cheney indicated that these problems will be addressed by cutting back new force procurement and devoting resources to improving the operability and maintainability (O&M) of the existing force structure. Many of the cuts Cheney proposed were quite dramatic, including recommendations to cut one navy aircraft carrier, to cancel a new marine corps transport aircraft, and to reduce the size of existing army divisions.

POSSIBLE EUROPEAN WITHDRAWAL?   The dual trends of increased CONUS basing and force procurement for LIC would be encouraged by a decision to cut U.S. forces in the European theater. A number of factors could lead to this cut. The two most likely are an arms control agreement cutting conventional forces in Europe, or a congressional decision that, given the deficiencies in alliance burden-sharing, the United States had no choice but to cut its commitment there. Cutting U.S. forces in Europe would likely (although not necessarily) be a cost-cutting measure, although the wisdom of such a course can certainly be debated. Nonetheless, it would significantly impact upon how the United States would procure its forces.

LONG-TERM HISTORICAL IMPLICATIONS

If history is a guide, the present drawdown of defense resources will last a few years, after which the pendulum will once again swing back toward a greater U.S. commitment to defense spending and procurement. But the lessons of history should not be overstated. The parameters of the containment framework, which have endured for over 40 years, may be changing so fundamentally that our old notions of what is required for U.S. security may finally be replaced with new conceptions and visions. Thus, there may be relative increases in defense spending, but spending (as a percentage of gross national product) will probably not come close to Reagan-era levels. Even that assessment may be optimistic.

The most significant questions for the long-term are, appropriately, posed by the Soviet challenge that we have discussed throughout this conclusion, as embodied in the person of Mikhail Gorbachev. How serious is the Soviet leader about reducing tensions, and what military tradeoffs might he be willing to make in pursuit of his objectives both at home and abroad? What will be the long-term effects of *perestroika* and *glasnost* on Soviet foreign policy? Can Gorbachev's reforms endure changes in the Soviet political leadership, and to the extent that they are institutionalized, what will be the ramifications of the new Soviet policies on the European alliances and on the global security system as a whole? The last question is perhaps the most important. It goes to the essence of the Gorbachev reform effort and the extent to which the Soviet political and economic system can be so fundamentally restructured that it can withstand changes in the Soviet leadership hierarchy.

These difficult questions beget another challenging question: How will the United States respond to these developments in terms of future national security policy and force procurement? The answer depends upon the future direction of Soviet policy and the boldness and imagination of U.S. leaders in dealing with new challenges. To some extent, U.S. planners are beginning to prepare for a world of diverse threats. But preparations for tomorrow's environment will have to be accomplished in a climate of constrained resources. Force centralization and increased CONUS basing is the beginning of the answer, but how complete an answer that will be depends, of course, upon future developments in the U.S.-Soviet strategic relationship. That relationship will in many ways continue to be the basis of U.S. planning and will therefore demand the most resources and attention for a long time to come.

The answers to the questions posed, as well as the effectiveness of the institutionalized service procurement and acquisition reforms discussed above, will ultimately make evident the contours of the eighth era and beyond. These answers, of course, may be disconcerting to planners comfortable with the familiar postwar framework. The future threat will be increasingly diverse, and the proper role for the United States in meeting tomorrow's threat may grow increasingly ambiguous. A security framework that raises Third World, localized, and regionalized instabilities to an increasingly greater level of threat to U.S. interests could prove less manageable and therefore more dangerous than the bipolar, containment-based framework. But this may be the reality confronting future planners.

NOTES

1. This is shown effectively in two recent books: Richard Stubbing, *The Defense Game* (New York: Harper & Row, 1986) and Mark Perry, *Four Stars* (Boston: Houghton Mifflin, 1989).
2. A good discussion of the mishaps in planning and execution in the Grenada invasion is in Edward Luttwak, *The Pentagon and the Art of War* (New York: Simon and Schuster, 1984), in particular pp. 51–58.
3. See, e.g., R. Jeffrey Smith, "Soviets offer Large Reduction in Arms, Troops in Europe," *Washington Post*, May 24, 1989, p. A1.
4. Dan Oberdorfer, "Bush Finds Theme of Foreign Policy: 'Beyond Containment,' " *Washington Post*, May 28, 1989, p. A30.
5. The Report of the Future Security Environment Working Group, *The Future Security Environment*, submitted to the Commission on Integrated Long-Term Strategy, October 1988, p. 50.
6. The most thorough discussion of which is Richard G. Davis, *The 31 Initiatives* (Washington, D.C.: Office of Air Force History, 1987).
7. Frank Carlucci, *Annual Report to the Congress, Fiscal Year 1989*, February 1988 (Washington, D.C.: GPO, 1988), p. 123.

APPENDIX

National Defense Spending, 1945–1968

Year	Total Federal Outlays ($ Billion)	National Defense Outlays ($ Billion)	Percentage of Federal Budget (%)	Percentage of GNP (%)	Percentage of DOD TOA, G.P. Forces* (%)
1945	92,7	83	89.5	38.2	51.6
1946	55	42,6	77.3	21.1	44.6
1947	35	12,8	37.1	5.8	42.8
1948	29,7	9	30.6	3.7	39.4
1949	38,8	13	33.9	5.0	37.8
1950	42,5	13,7	32.2	5.1	35.2
1951	45,5	23,5	51.8	7.5	46.5
1952	67,6	46	68.1	13.5	45.1
1953	76	52,8	69.4	14.5	40.4
1954	70,8	49	69.5	13.3	38.7
1955	68,4	42,7	62.4	11.1	39.2
1956	70,6	42,5	60.2	10.2	35.8
1957	76,5	45,4	59.3	10.3	33.6
1958	82,4	46,8	56.8	10.4	35.3
1959	92	49	53.2	10.2	32.5
1960	92	48	52.2	9.5	32.7
1961	97,7	49,6	50.7	9.6	32.9
1962	107	52,3	49.0	9.4	34.9
1963	111	53,4	48.0	9.1	34.4
1964	118,5	54,7	46.2	8.7	33.4
1965	118	50,6	42.8	7.5	36.5
1966	134,5	58	43.2	7.8	42.1
1967	157	71,4	45.4	9.0	41.8
1968	178	82	46.0	9.6	40.2

* DOD TOA, G.P. Forces stands for the Department of Defense's Total Obligational Authority dedicated to General Purpose Forces.

Source: Figures are from the Office of the Assistant Secretary of Defense (Comptroller), National Defense Budget Estimates for FY1989–1989, April 1988. The percentages of DOD Total Obligational Authority dedicated to General Purpose Forces are from Richard Cohen, National Defense Spending Patterns: Implications for Future Nuclear Weapons R&D Funding (Washington, D.C.: Washington Defense Research Group, 1987).

National Defense Spending,
1969–1989[1]

Year	Total Federal Outlays ($ Billion)	National Defense Outlays ($ Billion)	Percentage of Federal Budget (%)	Percentage of GNP (%)	Percentage of DOD TOA, G.P. Forces[2] (%)
1969	183	82,4	44.9	8.9	37.7
1970	195,6	81,6	41.8	8.3	36.8
1971	210	78,8	37.5	7.5	33.9
1972	230,6	79,1	34.3	6.9	33.4
1973	245,7	76,6	31.2	6.0	32.2
1974	269	79,3	29.5	5.6	34.6
1975	332	86,5	26.0	5.7	33.5
1976	371,7	89,6	24.1	5.3	35.6
1977	409	97,2	23.8	5.0	36.3
1978	458,7	104,4	22.8	4.8	37.0
1979	503,4	116	23.1	4.7	38.5
1980	591	134	22.7	5.0	37.9
1981	678	157,5	23.2	5.3	39.1
1982	745,7	185,3	24.9	5.9	42.1
1983	809,4	210	26.0	6.3	41.6
1984	851,7	227,4	26.7	6.2	39.1
1985	946,3	252,7	26.7	6.4	41.9
1986	990	273,3	27.6	6.6	41.6
1987	1,015	282	27.8	6.4	N/A
1988	1,064	281,9	26.5	5.9	N/A
1989	1,149	289,8	25.5	5.7	N/A

1. Figures for 1989 are DOD approximations.
2. DOD TOA, G.P. Forces stands for the Department of Defense's Total Obligational Authority dedicated to General Purpose Forces.

Source: Figures are from the Office of the Assistant Secretary of Defense (Comptroller), National Defense Budget Estimates for FY1989–1989, April 1988. The percentages of DOD Total Obligational Authority dedicated to General Purpose Forces are from Richard Cohen, *National Defense Spending Patterns: Implications for Future Nuclear Weapons R&D Funding* (Washington, D.C.: Washington Defense Research Group, 1987).

INDEX

About the Author

Maurice A. Mallin is a national security and defense consultant in the Washington, D.C., area. He holds a B.A. from Oberlin College and a master's in international affairs from the Graduate School for Public and International Affairs at the University of Pittsburgh. He works extensively with Orion Research, Inc., in Vienna, Virginia, and with Leon Sloss and Associates in Washington. He has written or contributed to numerous studies of U.S. strategy and force planning for both nuclear and nonnuclear forces.